Congratulations on
Graduation Gabby and may
the years ahead bring you
good health, and much happiness.
         Best Wishes Val

NEVER
TELL ME
NEVER

NEVER TELL ME NEVER

JANINE SHEPHERD

Sun
Pan Macmillan Australia

First published 1994 in Macmillan hardback by Pan Macmillan Publishers Australia
First published 1995 in Sun by Pan Macmillan Australia Pty Limited
St Martins Tower, 31 Market Street, Sydney

Reprinted 1995 (3 times), 1996 (twice), 1997 (3 times), 1998 (3 times)

National Library of Australia
cataloguing-in-publication data:
Shepherd, Janine.
Never tell me never.
ISBN 0 7251 0747 2 (pbk.).
1. Shepherd, Janine. 2. Crash injuries - Patients -
Rehabilitation - Australia. 3. Skiers - Australia -
Biography. I. Title.
362.43092

Typeset in 11/15 pt Sabon by Midland Typesetters
Printed in Australia by Australian Print Group

Lovingly dedicated to

Mum and Dad, *for showing me that through
the power of love, anything is possible.*

Tim, *a one in a million husband, whose love, patience
and understanding never fails to astound me.*

My two precious 'miracles', Annabel and Charlotte, *who
have taught me so much about love and life.
I am truly blessed.*

Acknowledgements

IN WRITING THESE acknowledgements, I am reminded of the enormous amount of love and support that has sustained me over the past eight years. To all who helped me, I am forever grateful.

In particular, special thanks must go to my wonderful husband, Tim—a man of extraordinary talents. Without his support it would have been difficult to juggle the demands of writing and being a mother. I love you.

And to the loving members of my family. To Mum and Dad, who devoted their lives to my rehabilitation. I couldn't have done it without you both. Kim, Kelley and Lenny, who have been there for me at every turn. Thank you all.

Warm thanks to my dear friend and 'adopted' brother Brian 'Hap' Hannan, godfather to Annabel and Charlotte. Your friendship is greatly treasured.

To my soulmate Elizabeth Etherington. Without her timely arrival at the scene of the accident, I certainly wouldn't be walking around today. Many thanks.

To my friend, Dr Adrian Cohen, for his help in

proofreading the book and for so much more. You're invaluable. Thank you, Ado.

To all my wonderful and amazing friends. For all the visits to hospital, the letters, the phone calls, the neverending support—there is so much to be thankful for. I love you all.

To all the medical personnel from Prince Henry Hospital, the Westpac helicopter and everyone involved in my transfer from Katoomba Hospital, in particular Doctor John Stephen and Doctor Peter Blum, for doing such a great job of putting me back together again. Thank you.

To my friend and social worker at the hospital, Donna Percy, for getting us through the rough patches. For your compassion and understanding, especially to Mum. Thank you.

To Bob Lawton, many thanks for writing the Foreword for this book, and to my good friend Tony Peters for getting the shot we were looking for. Thank you.

To my solicitor and friend, Kim Rickards, for always acting in my best interests. Thank you.

And of course I am deeply grateful to my publishers, Pan Macmillan, for their enthusiasm for the book. To everyone who worked on the team, thank you. With that special thanks must go to my trusty and more than capable editor, Jane Palfreyman, who was the first to hear my story and believed that it should be told. Many thanks.

Be patient toward all that is unsolved
 in your heart ...
Try to love the questions themselves ...

Do not now seek the answers,
  which cannot be given
  because you would not be able
  to live them.
And the point is,
  to live everything.

Live the questions now.
Perhaps you will then
  gradually,
  without noticing it,
Live along some distant day
  into the answers.

RAINER MARIA RILKE

*F*oreword

THE STORY OF Janine Shepherd reads like a Hollywood movie
plot. Top endurance athlete critically injured in a motor
accident, not expected to live, then not expected to walk, and
certainly not expected to be able to have children. The
difference is that this story is factual. Janine was a potential
Olympic team member in the arduous sport of cross-country
skiing. Winner of a university Blue in cross-country skiing,
she was so highly regarded that she was invited to train with
the Canadian team by the head coach, Marty Hall, the doyen
of North American cross-country coaches.

A near-fatal accident brought an end to her plans for the
Olympics, but made her focus her life on rehabilitating herself.
Slowly with the determination that made her the best at her
sport, she fought the odds, survived, learnt to walk, met her
future husband, learnt to fly and capped it all by having a family.

Janine's story should be an inspiration to all who need
motivation, to all who feel that life offers very little. This is
the story of a gutsy young lady who defied the odds and won.
The title, *Never Tell Me Never*, says it all.

Janine has often asked me if I felt she would have succeeded in her ambitions in sport. My response has been and always will be, 'No doubts—what you have achieved is living proof that you would have succeeded.' Janine is a gold medallist in the race of life. I salute her and her courage and determination.

In the words of Rudyard Kipling, 'If you can meet with Triumph and Disaster/And treat those two impostors just the same,' you have proved yourself.

May her story give inspiration to those who read it. She is my special hero.

Bob Lawton
Manager, Australian Winter Olympic Team,
Albertville, France, 1992

Preface

IT WAS NOT long after my accident that I decided to write
about my experience. However, when I left hospital I realised
that I would have to postpone the task, as I had only really
begun the journey—a journey that would take me to places I
had never dreamed of, doing things I had never imagined.

I wanted to write because I felt I had something to say, not
only to those people who have themselves been victims of a
serious accident, but for others who have never really thought
about the possibility of it happening to them. Most people are
so terrified of such a prospect that they simply try to ignore
it. I once felt the same way and never imagined it could
happen to me—but it did.

To be going about doing all the things you normally do and
then suddenly find yourself waking up in a hospital, as if you
have been in some sort of a time warp, unable to connect the
places or events that led up to it is nothing short of a
nightmare. You are at the mercy of something incomp-
rehensible, and there is nothing you can do about it.

It only takes a split second and your life can assume an
entirely new and unforeseen dimension. You will be forced to

reassess everything, look at the world in an utterly different light and face the most difficult and challenging time of your life. It will change you forever.

But despite the harrowing experiences that follow, there is still hope. The fact is that there *is* life after an accident. I don't mean that you will go on to live a semi-fulfilled existence, merely making the best of a bad situation. You can make a self-fulfilling and satisfying life, which can lead you to the realisation of your true potential, allow you to do things that you never dreamt of before and above all you can be happy. I know this is true because I have been there.

There is no denying that it will be the most challenging and, at times, the most soul-crushing journey that you will ever take but the rewards can be great. It's all yours for the taking. It will lead you to new horizons, it will open your eyes to things that you were once blinded to, and it will truly enrich your life.

Confronting my accident and my injuries has given me hope and reaffirmed my faith in the strength of the human spirit. This is what enables us to achieve our goals and gives us the strength and courage to keep going, even in the face of apparently insurmountable obstacles. It is our greatest natural asset, and we all have it inside us. Find it, nurture it, and it will never leave you.

I also wanted to write this book to help the friends and families of the victims, to help them understand what it is like for their loved ones and what they are going through. Perhaps it will help them to understand why they are sometimes difficult to be with and why they react the way they do. But we are all individuals and we all react differently to pain and suffering. I am not saying that how I have done it is the right way. It is just one way—my way—and this is my story.

So, I hope that this book will ease the burden of all who read it, because you are not alone.

'What have we got here?'

'Twenty-four-year-old female, transferred from Katoomba hospital.'

'What are her vital signs?'

'Multiple trauma, internal bleeding, fractured L1 and T10 paraparesis, frank haematuria ... query pelvic damage. Heart rate 90, blood pressure 96 over 65 and falling ... Still shocked, may need more fluid. She's had two units of blood, one unit Hartmann's and pethidine 25 mg. Looks like you'll be with this one for a while.'

'Thanks, we'll take it from here.'

'Good luck. I wouldn't plan on getting any sleep tonight!'

'Nurse, let's get moving. What's her current status?'

'I can't find a pulse ... Hang on. I'll see what her blood pressure is ... No luck, I still can't find it!'

'Come on, let me try. It's dropped, it's 40 over nothing! Let's get moving. We've got to get her out of here. Phone Intensive Care and tell them we've got a hot one!'

$P_{rologue}$

GASPING FOR BREATH, I reached for the oxygen mask that was covering my face. Something, or someone, stopped my attempt to free myself from it. I couldn't see anything even though my eyes were open, but I could feel the pressure of the grip that now had my wrist in a tight lock.

A tube in my mouth reached down to my stomach and made me feel nauseous. Slowly, I lifted my hands and blinked to clear my vision. I could see that they were attached to a series of tubes that prevented me from moving them any distance. There was something cold attached to my chest. I tried to raise my head to see what it was. The pain shot through me like a bullet and my head crashed back. *What was it?* There was something around my neck holding it in place. I could hear a strange noise above my head. I strained to see clearly and made out a large screen that was giving out a series of beeping sounds.

I looked around the room and found myself in unfamiliar surroundings. The glowing white light above me struck my face with such intensity that I was forced to close my eyes.

Where am I? How did I get here? Am I dreaming? I felt drowsy. My head started to spin. I felt as if I was spiralling down a deep funnel and I was out of control. *What's happening to me?* Fragments of memories started to appear in front of me, visions of faces, my parents, my friends. This is all so crazy, I'm losing control. *Someone help me ... please help ... me ...*

I became aware of an electrifying and all-consuming pain in my back. I tried to move but the pain was too great. It was as if I was pinned to the bed. I couldn't feel my legs. I tried to lift my arms but they were held down by a great weight. The pain enveloped my body. I began to retch.

Please somebody help me, my mind screamed, *my back is so sore I can't stand this pain.* I tried to move. It was hopeless. The frustration was overwhelming. I felt alone, helpless.

Somebody must be able to hear me. *Where am I? Mum, Dad, where are you? I need you ...* I couldn't breathe, I felt as if I was suffocating. *What is covering my face?* I reached up again to pull this thing off my face. Again I was stopped.

'Janine, it's all right. You need this to breathe.'

At last, a voice! Someone was with me. The voice was unfamiliar.

'Pl-please ... off ...' I strained to be heard. A feeling of nausea overcame me and everything started to fade.

'Janine, Janine can you hear me?'

That voice again! *Who is talking to me?*

'Can you tell me your name?'

I opened my eyes to see a figure standing above me. The mask had been partially removed. I gulped for air, relieved to be able to breathe again. I inhaled frantically, trying to take in as much air as possible. I opened my mouth to speak, but no words came out.

'Can you tell me your name?'

'Y-Yes,' I stammered. 'J-nine ...' The words were hardly audible.

'Do you know where you are?'

My mind raced with confusion. *What did she mean? Where am I? How did I get here?*

'Janine, you have to answer me. Can you tell me what has happened to you?'

What is happening?

'Janine, you have had an accident. You were hit by a car while you were riding your pushbike.'

No, no, this can't be true! Please God, let this all be a bad dream.

Why was she persisting? *If I close my eyes all this will go away. I will wake up at home in my bed. Surely this will all go away?* I felt a terrible ache in my head. *Someone help ... the pain ...* Everything seemed utterly hopeless. *Why can't anybody help me?* I'm losing control ...

C*hapter 1*

'JANINE, JANINE, WAKE UP,' the voice persisted again. 'Janine, you can't go to sleep, please try to stay awake.'

Why won't they let me sleep? I must try to answer them. Then maybe they will leave me alone. I am so tired, if only I could close my eyes ...

'Chris, are you almost ready?' I asked impatiently as Chris stuffed a few last things into the backpack he would need once we arrived at our destination.

James had dropped over the night before to collect the bags we had packed with a change of clothes and other items. These would be taken up with one of the support vehicles, so that we could ride without the extra weight.

I grabbed my bag and kissed Mum goodbye.

'When will you be home?' she asked.

'About 10 o'clock tonight,' I answered as I rushed out the door and grabbed my bike. We were already running late and the others would be waiting for us.

I was dressed in bike pants and bright yellow shirt. I made a point of wearing brightly coloured clothes as I had already had a minor accident on my pushbike. As I was riding home from the pool one day I was passed by a truck whose driver didn't see me. I was forced off the road into a ditch and suffered some nasty cuts and bruises. This was enough to make me aware of the dangers of the road and I wanted to stand out as much as possible in the heavy traffic.

I put my helmet on, filled my water bottle and mounted my bike, with Chris close behind me.

We waved goodbye to Mum and set off. I was feeling very tired and wondered whether I was pushing myself too hard. The ride would take about five hours, most of it was uphill. Normally I wouldn't have given it a second thought, but my training schedule had been quite demanding lately and my energy levels were very low. I had visited the doctor a few days before to have a blood test, thinking I might be anaemic. But all my friends would be going on the ride, so I decided that I would go along and just make sure to take it easy.

We were the first to arrive at the meeting place. It was starting to get hot. I took off my training jacket and packed it in my bag.

It was midday before we finally got going and the sun was beating down fiercely on our backs. By the time we reached the base of the mountains the group had already begun to spread out.

There were about twenty of us on the ride this day and, as usual, I was the only female. We used to call it the 'Rooster ride', as our destination was a restaurant at the top of the mountains called the Red Rooster.

There was always a group of friends who preferred to drive up to the mountain rendezvous, so many of the bikes ended up in the backs of cars for the return trip.

The first hour was flat riding and then we hit the hills. This was the part of the ride that I enjoyed most. I loved to push myself to the limit, to feel at one with my body, as I had all my life. I had held national records in athletics, played State-level softball and netball and been NSW triathlon champion, as well as being a current member of the national cross-country ski team. My entire life had been devoted to sport. That was what I did best and what I lived for. I was fortunate that whatever sport I tried my hand at, it all came very easily. I couldn't imagine a life without sport. It was my passion.

I was drawn to cross-country skiing because it was the ultimate endurance sport. I thrived on the demanding training it required and after jumping from sport to sport all my life felt I had finally found one that I truly loved, that I could really get my teeth into. I was born for this sport. It obsessed me in a way that no other had.

I always pushed myself hard in my training sessions and as a result my team-mates nicknamed me 'Janine the machine'. I guess it said a lot about the sort of person I was. I was a dedicated athlete and my dream was to represent my country at the 1988 Winter Olympics in Calgary. For me this was the ultimate goal.

We stopped a few times before reaching the hills to regroup and replenish our water supplies. I was already feeling very tired and decided to slow down a bit.

As we started our assault on the hills the mood became serious. We put our heads down and concentrated on making it to the top. The steep incline made for challenging riding and as you came up to other riders you could hear their laboured breathing as they pushed themselves and their bikes to the utmost. Once you hit the mountains the temperature dropped significantly and the crispness of the air produced a burning sensation in your lungs.

As I approached one of the final hills I saw another rider ahead of me. It was John. I caught up to him and saw that he was looking very tired.

'John, how are you going?' I asked as I drew alongside.

'I am starting to bonk,' he replied. 'I think I might stop and get the train back to the city.'

'Bonk' is a term used by athletes to describe the feeling of sheer exhaustion when the body's energy stores begin to deplete. Runners call it 'hitting the wall'—a common phenomenon for the long-distance athlete.

We exchanged a few more words and then I continued up the hill. I could see the next rider ahead but couldn't make out who it was. There wasn't far to go, perhaps only a few kilometres, and then we would all be enjoying an afternoon of fine cuisine at the Rooster. This was all the incentive I needed to push my weary legs up these final hills.

I looked up to see the hot autumn sun shining in my face and then everything went black.

I was awakened by the pungent smell of anaesthetic and the loud crash of something dropping on the floor. I opened my eyes to find myself surrounded by faces and in the background I recognised the beeping sound that I had heard earlier. The mask was back over my face. I tried to lift my hands again to get it off, but I didn't have the strength.

I remembered the woman's voice I had heard before. She said I had been in an accident. Maybe this was true. I couldn't be sure, but how else could I be here? My mind raced with confusion. Nothing made sense. *Where are my friends? Where has everybody gone?*

The pain gripped my body like a vice. *What is wrong with me? Am I hurt badly? Please, someone tell me what's happening.*

I could hear voices around me, but I could barely make out what they were saying. Amid the clatter and clutter of bottles and trays I sensed they were talking about me.

'Janine, I want you to tell me if you can feel this,' I heard someone who must have been a doctor say in a matter-of-fact way. 'Can you feel that? Or this?'

He went through a sort of ritual as he methodically pricked me with a pin to test each part of my body for feeling. I strained to see him, the ache in my head increasing with the effort. At last I saw that he was standing at the end of the bed, near my feet. I couldn't feel anything. I must be able to feel something! *He isn't touching hard enough,* my mind was shouting. Then I felt some tingling in one of my legs like pins and needles. I saw that he was probing further up one of my legs.

He asked me if I could move my feet. I tried, but nothing happened. *I have to try harder, I'm not trying hard enough.* Again I tried to move them, but it was as if my legs were no longer connected to my body. I began to panic. *Why can't I move them?* I could hear the doctors conversing at the end of the bed but I couldn't understand the medical jargon they were using.

' . . . a fracture-dislocation at L1,' said one of them.

'Any loss?' his colleague asked.

'Yeah, looks like a T10 incomplete at this stage. We'll have to give it a couple of days to see if it improves.'

'We can only hope.'

'In the meantime we'll maintain full paraplegic protocol. Call the spinal registrar. Looks like this will be one for them.'

I had no idea what they were talking about. My mind was spinning with confusion. I was unable to think clearly. This couldn't be happening to me, it was all a bad dream. *I want to go home . . . please, someone tell me this is just a bad dream!*

I had no choice but to succumb to the mask covering my

face, all my efforts to remove it having failed. I could see the nurse sitting at my bedside and finally managed to get out a few muffled words.

'Please . . . wh-what's wrong?' My pitiful attempt to speak attracted her attention. She partially lifted the mask off my face and I repeated my question.

'Don't worry, Janine, you'll be all right. We're all looking after you. The doctor will be back shortly.'

In desperation I struggled to make myself heard again. 'Pl-please, somebody help me,' I stammered.

'Shhh, Janine, it's all right. You mustn't try to talk. We're going to look after you.'

I looked up to see a figure at my bedside—the doctor. Everything else around him was a blur.

'Please,' I said, 'Wh-what's wrong?' The words took all my strength.

'Janine, you have broken your back. But we're all here to look after you and help you get better. Now you just try and get some rest, OK?' He spoke briefly to the nurse and disappeared from my sight.

I didn't understand. My utter disorientation stopped me asking any more questions. Nothing was making sense. I just wanted someone to take away the pain, but nobody could. I closed my eyes once more. The voices faded and the room grew black.

Time stood still. Hours and days blurred together into one, day and night no longer separated. I was unaware of how many days had passed as I drifted in and out of consciousness. My world became a series of nightmares and hallucinations which were both disturbing and frightening. The happenings around me no longer mattered. The world inside my head was all I knew.

On one side of me everything was black and cold, yet on the other there was a strange white glow emanating a warmth which seemed to heat my entire body. Inside the glow I could make out two faces. Mum and Dad. Everything else around them was a blur.

I became aware of a dark and sinister presence around me which beckoned me to follow. It was a macabre apparition, surrounding me and overpowering me, there was no escape. Amid the dark figures there was one more ominous than the rest. It was calling me closer, tempting me to follow. I tried to fight, but it was difficult and at times almost impossible to resist.

In my own way I knew that I had reached that fine line between life and death. The pain had reached an intolerable level. It consumed my body, it ate into my mind. I had no choice. I had to let go, I couldn't take this any more.

The faces began to fade. Where had my parents gone? I panicked, crying out in the darkness.

'Mum, Dad . . .'

During those first days my condition deteriorated. The team of neurosurgeons, orthopaedic surgeons, intensive care and spinal surgeons were on stand-by around the clock.

My parents maintained a bedside vigil, waiting for the latest prognosis about my condition.

'Mr and Mrs Shepherd,' Dr Kerr said to them hesitantly. 'Janine has broken her neck as well as her back, but that is not our main concern right now. She has very serious internal bleeding which we're not able to stop. We still don't know exactly where it's coming from.'

'How serious is it?' my father asked.

'I can't say. We're having trouble stabilising her blood pressure and she is steadily losing blood. All we can do is wait and see if it stops.'

Although the spinal injuries were serious, they were not in themselves life-threatening. The internal bleeding, however, was critical.

For Mum and Dad it was a time of great anxiety. Everything was out of their hands and all they could do was wait. They had difficulty coming to terms with the events of the previous few days. It was all so sudden and such an incredible shock.

One minute their lives were trouble-free—the next they had been thrown into turmoil. On the day of the accident, they had been out looking at landscape gardens for the dream house they planned to build in the near future. When they arrived home the phone was ringing. It was my friend John. He told them that I had been involved in an accident, and that they should go to the hospital right away. He didn't want them to panic or worry as they had a two-hour drive to get there, so he assured them that I was OK. Mum and Dad had no idea what was in store for them when they arrived. At the hospital, they were greeted by some of my friends who had gone there to see how I was. It was then that they learnt how serious things were.

While they were at the hospital, my blood pressure dropped. The doctors had to try to stabilise it before they could even consider transferring me to a larger hospital. Units of blood were flown up from Sydney to provide the supply I now needed.

Mum went into a state of shock. The doctors offered her some sedatives to calm her down, but she refused. She wanted to keep a clear mind in case the worst happened.

When at last the helicopter lifted off from the local oval, Mum and Dad were told that I was being transferred to Westmead hospital for emergency surgery. Mum, Dad and Chris then drove to Westmead to meet me. It would take them another two hours, each of them silently contemplating what might happen before they reached me. The situation was critical, and they knew it.

They arrived to be greeted with confusion. The staff had no idea where I was. They immediately panicked. What had gone wrong? Finally they were informed that the helicopter had gone straight to another hospital—Prince Henry, on the other side of the city.

It took them another hour in the car to find a hospital they had never been to before. By now their anxiety was almost unbearable. On arrival, they were ushered into the ward to face another agonising wait as the doctors battled to stabilise my condition. Overcome by the sense of their own powerlessness, they fought to keep a grip on their emotions as their child lay motionless in the bed before them. They could do nothing to help their baby.

The staff knew that for them to be any help to me it was imperative that they too get some rest, and arranged for them to spend the night in the nurses' quarters on the hospital grounds. Mum and Dad were reluctant to take up the offer, as they didn't want to leave my side in case the worst happened. But they were on the point of collapse and the staff assured them that if anything changed in the night, they would come and get them.

At last they agreed and, numb with exhaustion, turned in for the night. Mum made a futile attempt to sleep, but she was sick with worry and could only lie in bed trying to come to grips with the events of the past few hours. Surely this was a parent's worst nightmare? The night dragged on interminably. Then, in the early hours of the morning, Mum heard a voice echoing down the hall.

'Mr Shepherd, Mrs Shepherd, can you hear me?' The voice rang out loudly in the early hours of the morning. 'Mr Shepherd, are you awake?'

Mum sat up in bed, afraid to move. All she could think

was, *They said that if something went wrong they would come and get us ...* Surely this was the moment they had dreaded.

'Yes, we're awake,' my father said as he met the nurse at the doorway.

'The doctor asked if you could come up to the ward straight-away.'

'What is it, what's happened?' he asked anxiously.

'It's all right. It's just that Janine is calling for you. The doctor thinks that it would help her if you came up right now.'

Thank God! Another chance.

'Oh, yes, of course, we'll come right away,' my mother almost cried with relief. They told me later they wondered how they would ever survive the whole ordeal. But there was no choice, they knew, they had to be my strength.

'Dad ... Dad ...' I opened my eyes to see his face surrounded by a light.

'I'm right here, I won't leave you, darling.'

'Wh-where's Mum?' The muffled words were barely audible from under the mask.

'She's here, right beside you,' Dad answered, straining to keep his words coherent.

'Help me ...'

'Shhh, don't try to talk, sweetheart. The doctors are looking after you. Everything will be all right. Mum and I are with you now, and we're not leaving you.'

I could feel my father take my hand in his as he began to stroke my forehead. His grip was strong; it made me feel safe and secure. *Nothing can hurt me now, Mum and Dad will look after me, and nothing is going to take me away from them ... nothing. I'm not going to give in, I'm not ready to go.*

For me, time meant nothing, but for the staff that fought to keep me alive it was all-important. After five days of uncertainty, the bleeding finally stopped. The first battle had been won. Mum would later tell me that it was around this time that I began to become coherent and regain lucidity.

It was as if someone had turned on the lights. The darkness faded, giving way to a warmth and brightness that filled the room. I was able to focus on the faces around me, the room now clear. I didn't know where I had been, but I knew I never wanted to return there again.

The only respite I had from the excruciating pain was provided by the morphine drip attached to my arm. It pumped the powerful narcotic through my body, enabling me periodically to drift off to sleep. As it started to wear off, I would wake up again, bathed in perspiration, and I would have to lie in agony until my dose of morphine was topped up again.

With the bleeding now under control, the next worry was the spinal injuries and the paralysis in my legs, which was gradually getting worse. The next question was whether I would walk again. Each time Mum and Dad confronted my doctors, the list of injuries seemed to grow.

I still had significant abdominal trauma and internal injuries which needed constant monitoring. My back and neck were broken in four places, which explained the paralysis and loss of sensation in my legs and feet. So were my right arm, five ribs on my left side, my collarbone and several bones in my feet. I had head injuries—my head had been stitched across the forehead and at the back. I had contusions, or bleeding from the kidneys, which caused my urine to be stained with blood. I had massive lacerations to my abdominal area and to my right leg, which had been ripped open and was filled with gravel. The area where I had been hit by the utility, on my lower back and buttocks, was covered with a massive haematoma and the muscle had been torn away.

The haematoma caused the medical staff a great deal of anxiety, as well as a great deal of pain and discomfort for me. There was a serious risk of developing a blood clot, which was life-threatening in itself. It was therefore necessary for the medical staff to apply ultrasound to the area twice a day to try to circulate the blood and reduce the swelling. The area was black with the pooling of blood and extremely swollen, and as I was forced to lie flat on my back it was absolutely agonising.

As the days went by, my thoughts became more coherent. I could absorb a certain amount of information, yet I was still existing on a high level of drugs which tended to cloud my thoughts and make me extremely drowsy. When I was awake I would take in what I could about the room I was in. As I was lying flat on my back, I relied on other people's observations to form my perceptions.

Through snippets of conversation between the medical staff and their instructions to each other I learnt I was in ICU, or Intensive Care Unit, the ward reserved for more serious cases. Normally, spinal injuries were treated in a special unit in the hospital, but as I had multiple life-threatening injuries, I was put in Intensive Care.

The rules and regulations in ICU were a lot stricter than in other wards in the hospital. They only allowed immediate family and a few close friends to visit the patient and you could have only two visitors at a time. These visits were at certain times and for short periods, because of the strain on the patient, not to mention the overworked staff. Even though Mum and Dad were generally able to stay for longer periods, there were times when even they were not allowed to see me.

My accident was reported on the radio, in the press and on

television. As a result, many of my friends heard about it and were soon waiting outside ICU to hear how I was. However, I have no recollection of anyone being at my side except Mum and Dad.

While I was in ICU it was necessary for two or three hospital orderlies to come by every two hours to 'turn' me. One of the greatest dangers for a spinal victim is for a blood clot, to develop in some part of the body. To avoid this, the patient has to be turned onto his or her side so that the blood has a chance to circulate. It was an incredible relief for me to be off my back and not to be lying on the haematoma that was causing me so much discomfort and pain. It is imperative for the spine to be kept in alignment during the process and every precaution was taken to ensure that this was done with the utmost care. Two men would stand at one side while one would brace my head and neck, and on the count of three they would coordinate their actions to turn me in one smooth movement.

Many years ago a device called a Stryker frame was used for the same purpose. This was a canvas frame that fitted over the patient like a sandwich. All the staff had to do every few hours was to place a frame on top of the patient and then turn the bed over. The patient would then spend the next two hours upside down. I was very fortunate that they no longer used these contraptions!

I was oblivious to the paraphernalia that had become part of my existence. The oxygen mask over my face was eventually removed but the nasogastric tube in my nose and the orogastric tube in my mouth remained in place. The tube into my stomach was to decompress the bowel so as to prevent vomiting and encourage the flow of blood to damaged areas of the spinal cord. I still had ECG attachments on my chest and I was reliant on the IV (intravenous) line that was pumping vital blood into my body. The tubes for the drip anchored one arm, while the other was kept immobile by the makeshift plaster slab I was now wearing. I was also reliant on the catheter in my bladder that drained body wastes and poisons from my body. I was wearing a brace around my neck and my head had numerous stitches across it. My body was covered in cuts and abrasions. A sheet was draped over me to help me preserve some degree of dignity.

For Mum and Dad the waiting game continued. Each day there was something new to worry about. Dad told me he would walk around the hospital grounds to get some fresh air and clear his mind. He would go down to the small chapel in the hospital and look out at the sea. Next to the chapel there was a wishing well. Each day he would throw in a coin and say a silent prayer for my recovery. He would then return to the ward in the hope that the nightmare would soon be over, wondering if things would ever be 'normal' again.

I lived in my own world, unaware of what my family were going through. My only concern was to try to control the pain that I was in. Anything else was inconsequential. I was only told what I needed to know, the doctors believing this gave me the best chance of surviving and coping with the situation. They told Mum and Dad not to tell me anything about my condition until I asked, as I would when I was ready to know. I had enough problems and there was no point in burdening me with too much at once. I was unaware of this at the time and when they told me everything would be all right, I tended to believe them. This was partly because of the drugs I was given and partly due to my disbelief that this could really be happening to me.

One day when the doctors were doing their rounds I was ready to ask some more questions.

'Dr Kerr,' I said, stuttering in my half-drugged voice, 'when will I be able to go home?'

'Well, Janine, first we have to get you better . . .'

'But I have to start training, I have to get home.'

'Janine,' he spoke gently, 'it might take you a while before you can train again. Let's just think about getting better, OK?'

'Will I go home soon?'

'Well, Janine, it will be a while before you can go home, but don't think about that now, all you need to do is rest so that we can get you better, OK?' Dr Kerr left and I wondered how long it would really be before I could leave the hospital. My thoughts began to wander.

I thought about the pain. How could I escape it? I thought about my injuries, those I knew about. And I thought about my feet and legs, constantly trying to move them, but it was useless. *Will I ski again, will I walk again? Maybe this is worse than I think.* I began to torment myself with worries of what might be. In the physical sense I had become a prisoner to my injuries, but my mind was still able to control what I saw, or chose to see, as my destiny.

Chapter 2

I FOUND THAT WHEN I drifted into sleep, the hallucinogenic effect of the drugs allowed me to escape the pain of the present and escape back in time. I would dream of things as they were before the accident and imagine things as I wanted them to be. My dreams involved my friends and family as I recalled pleasant events in my life.

I was the youngest of three girls in my family. When Mum became pregnant with me, it was no secret that Dad would have liked a boy after the two daughters they already had. As it turned out he wasn't disappointed at all and it was a bonus for him that I was the little tomboy of the family and possessed a passion and talent for all kinds of sports.

From an early age I was involved in sport, in particular athletics. I joined the Little Athletics Association and each weekend was taken up with competitions of some sort. I was a natural all-rounder and every week I would enter as many events as I could. I developed an early enthusiasm for sprinting and by the age of ten I had already notched up several wins in national championships and my athletics career was on its way.

One day a visiting coach came to our local club meeting to demonstrate a new event—race walking. I had never seen or heard of it before and thought it looked rather odd. Nevertheless, I decided to give it a go and after a bit of practice with all the other kids I entered the walking race he arranged that day.

It was a mixed race, with boys and girls together, and I ended up winning! I was pretty pleased with myself. Beating the boys was pretty cool, I thought. Then the coach came up to speak to Mum and me.

'Janine, that was well done. You picked it up really quickly.'

'Thank you,' I said politely.

'How would you like to come and train with me?' he asked, his question directed more to Mum than me.

'Yes, Mum, can I?'

His name was Frank and he was already a very respected coach in athletics. It was a real honour just to be invited to join his squad, as he made a point of selecting the kids he wanted to train. Mum really didn't have much of a chance of saying no to my request, and for the next five years my life would revolve around athletics.

Three nights a week Mum or Dad would drive me to the oval where I would spend the best part of three hours going through the paces with at least twenty other athletes. I continued to keep up with the other events in Little Athletics—middle-distance running, high jump, and the odd throwing event. However, I was enjoying race walking so much it seemed to dominate all my time and effort.

My weekends were spent at various athletic venues and more and more of Mum's and Dad's time was spent looking after my needs and juggling the demands of being parents to two other daughters.

We travelled around the country together attending all the State competitions and national championships. My two older sisters, Kim and Kelley, were pretty fed up with being dragged all over the place. They didn't appreciate having to leave their friends to go and watch me all the time and couldn't wait until they were old enough to stay at home by themselves.

In between athletics commitments there were other equally important engagements, like netball, softball and numerous other activities. My trophy cabinet, which became the centre-piece of my room, was becoming quite large.

Mum and Dad gave all of us the opportunity to develop any natural sporting talent we had, but they never pushed or prodded us in any way. Participating in sport was my choice entirely and Mum and Dad wouldn't have questioned me if I had told them I no longer wanted to participate. Of course, they were proud of my achievements, but as long as I was enjoying myself, that was enough for them.

There were naturally times when I wished I could have had the freedom all my friends had. Training and competing five to six days a week at such an early age started to take its toll after a while. I remember one day, when I was about eleven years old, I was invited to a slumber party by one of my school friends. All my friends would be there, and I didn't want to miss out. However, I had a State athletics carnival the next day and Mum said that I couldn't go. I pestered her so much that we came to an agreement. I could only go if I promised her that I would be in bed by nine o'clock. Can you imagine the embarrassment when my friend's mother came to get me just when the party was hotting up to tell me I had to go to bed! But at least I got to go to the party, or part of it anyway.

By the time I reached high school I had accumulated a swag of national records in athletics. I lived for my sport and wasn't happy unless I was running around an oval somewhere, catching a ball or riding my skate-board. I was full of energy and nothing seemed to slow me down.

However, things were to change when I reached those all-too-difficult teen years. I started to resent the fact that when my school friends were out at parties, having what appeared to be fun, I was forced to go to training and missed out on all the action. One day one of the physical education teachers pinned a news clipping of me up on the school notice board. I was only thirteen and I found the attention all too much. Instead of taking it as a compliment I became very embarrassed, and ended up in tears. I just wanted to be like everyone else, and I didn't want to be signalled out for any special attention.

In the end I gave up my athletics career and spent the rest of my school years competing at recreational level in different sports. I turned my attention to more important matters— catching up on lost time, doing all the things my friends were doing. I really enjoyed the break from competition as it had taken up so much of my youth. In retrospect, I think I had probably been too competitive at too young an age, but on the other hand it gave me a lot of qualities I would need to fall back on later in my life.

Fortunately, I eventually settled down, putting my head in the books during my final years at school and passing my HSC with enough marks to study law. Wanting a break before embarking on a long road of study, I deferred my first year at university and travelled overseas to France to work as an 'au pair', or nanny. Living in Paris at such a young age was a fantastic experience, not to say an eye-opener. I was responsible for the care of four young children aged between one and six, which was quite a responsibility for an eighteen-year-old! I returned home determined that it would be some time before I ever had children of my own. However, I did become quite fluent in French during my stay, and not wanting to lose this, I changed my mind about studying law and instead enrolled to study languages.

I commenced my degree at university and kept up my sporting interests. I began to spend a lot of time distance running and as the university was surrounded by bush, I found a great outlet from study running through the maze of bush tracks in my breaks from class. After two years of study the pull of sport gripped me again and I decided to change to another tertiary institution to pursue a career in physical education. My ambition was to become a sports physiologist, which was offered as a post-graduate course to those who had already completed a related course in sports studies.

However, it was while I was at university I met someone and began what was to be my first serious romance—my first 'real' love. His name was Daven Timms and he was a second-year law student when I was in first year. We met through mutual friends and would bump into each other in the library from time to time and nervously chat to each other. Eventually, Daven plucked up the courage to ask me out on our first official date—for a game of squash! I was playing competition squash at the time, and Daven was a little taken aback when his date beat him on the courts. I guess he didn't take it too much to heart however as he did ask me out again that very same night.

After we'd been out together a couple of times, Daven took me home to meet his mother. His younger sister, Trish, who was only six at the time, came up to me and said, 'Boy, you must really like Daven, this is the second time you've gone out with him!' I was left totally embarrassed. The rest of the family had a good laugh.

Daven was a dedicated student, as his academic record confirmed. He was a straight 'A' achiever and he always joked that he only got a 'B' after he met me. Not only was he a brilliant student, he was also a gifted athlete.

Daven had been a member of the Australian downhill ski team for several years before I met him. Originally from Canada, he had donned his first pair of skis at the age of two. I can still remember the first time I saw him on skis, thinking how natural he looked, not only because he was obviously a very skilled athlete but because he had a style and grace that were apparent even when he was tearing down a mountain-side at breakneck speed.

Daven and I spent all of our spare time together, playing squash or running through the university grounds. We were quickly becoming an item and couldn't bear to be apart for any length of time. In fact, we used to see each other every day and speak on the phone every night. For Daven, not only did he have a girlfriend but he had an admirable adversary when it came to training. He improved his game of squash very quickly and our matches on the court became quite a challenge, for both of us.

When we weren't studying or training, we earned a bit of extra cash doing rubbish removals. Daven and his brothers had bought a utility and started up a business doing anything from removing garden refuse and building materials to helping people move house. In fact, there was nothing they didn't do. I was Daven's offsider and after a hard day's work he used to give me my share of the takings. I was no slouch and always used to pull my weight. We'd be amused at people's reactions when Daven turned up at a job with a 'girl'. Most people doubted that I helped him with the heavy lifting, but he always responded, 'Don't worry, mate, she's an athlete—she's strong!'

Each job was amusing in its own way. One day we had a call from an elderly lady wanting us to remove a tap root from her garden. The only problem was that we had to get the root out of the ground first, which was no easy task. It was an extremely hot day, and as the lady only had one pitchfork, we decided to take it in turns—one of us did the digging while the other sat in the shade of a tree waiting to take over. Whenever the lady came outside to refill our drinks, it just happened to be my turn to dig, and Daven would be sitting under the tree sipping his drink and saying, just loud enough for her to hear: 'Come on, you're slacking off!'

Daven used to ride his bike to university each day, and he persuaded me to do the same. He helped me choose a new racing bike and then we rode from my house to the university a few times to work out the best way to avoid the heaviest traffic. We timed the track so that I could use it for training purposes. Each day I would clock my time and compare my progress. We parked our bikes together and I would often ride home to Daven's place and have dinner with his family, I would then stay the night and ride to university with him next day. I was quickly becoming part of the Timms family and I felt as much at home in their house as I did in mine.

Although I had been skiing for quite a few years already, it was Daven who was responsible for introducing me to the sport in a big way. We joined the university ski club and Daven was soon elected president. Through the ski club we formed many friendships and despite the demands of studying, we all found plenty of time to socialise.

While at university I travelled to Austria with a tour company which organised ski trips from Australia, and deferred my studies for six months so that I could have an extended stay in Europe. I worked as a ski guide, which involved taking Australian tourists around the different runs in the Austrian alps and showing them where they could find the best snow. It was hard to imagine that I was being paid to have such a great time! It also gave me a chance to brush up my German.

I lived in a village called Scheffau, near the venue of the most famous downhill run in the world—Kitzbuhel. I lived in a *gasthof* owned by a local woman named Inge and her husband Gunter. We became great friends and I would sit with Inge in her kitchen for hours after I returned from skiing, talking about all sorts of things. She taught me how to speak the local dialect and I taught her how to say 'G'day, mate'.

Daven was also overseas at the time with the Australian ski team and between events he would come to Scheffau to visit me and to have a well-deserved break from the racing circuit. We missed each other greatly while we were apart and would count down the days until we'd be together again. We spent many fun-filled days skiing on the nearby glaciers and slopes, where Daven taught me how to ski in real European powder, not like the heavy powder substitute we had back home.

Each day was filled with exciting adventures, whether we were racing down the mountain to see who could be the first down (Daven always gave me a head start) or trekking through the woods in the pitch dark to lead a tourist party to 'Cafe Rosemary', a tiny establishment on the other side of the forest. There you could buy the most enormous ice-creams, some of them up to a litre, topped with sparklers.

Most days in Scheffau we would don our tracksuits and run up one of the magnificent mountains which surrounded the village. At the top some hungry-looking mountain goats were grazing, which we used to feed with slices of bread we brought with us. At night we'd go rodelling (tobogganing), or join in a strange sort of game similar to lawn bowls but played on ice.

When Daven finally had to leave the village to rejoin the skiing circuit, we kept in touch by letters and phone calls until we met up again in Sweden, where we had arranged to spend some time with some of his friends. It was then that we donned our first pair of cross-country skis and headed off for a weekend trekking into Lapland. It was a wonderful but quite challenging experience. We got lost in snowstorms, and had to find our way with contour maps. At one point we stopped to get our bearings and when the cloud cleared we discovered we were standing on the edge of a sheer cliff—a bit too close for comfort!

We went on to Finland and then Denmark before finally making our way home. We had a fantastic time together, and it was impossible to ever think of being apart. We were so much in love I couldn't have wished for a happier life.

We returned home and back to the 'real' world—university and exams. I got a part-time job as an aerobics instructor to bring in a bit of extra pocket money. I worked at various gyms around the place and at the university, sometimes doing as many as three classes a day, which became a bit hectic with my study commitments and the rest of my training. Daven would always try to make it to my class if he was free, making a point of standing right at the front of the class. He was my keenest pupil!

Along with several of my friends I started to become involved in triathlons. I was strong in both the running and cycling legs and I only needed to work on my swimming to complement them, so I spent every day at the pool swimming laps and doing intervals. The rest of the time I'd go cycling or running to relieve the boredom of concentrating on a single sport. I started competing on the triathlon circuit and it wasn't long before I won the NSW championships and with it my first cash prize, a racing bike, along with a swag of trophies.

Daven and I used to train together and with Daven's background we were soon drawn into competitive cross-country ski racing. By now Daven had had enough of downhill skiing and we both enjoyed the freedom of getting away from the crowded slopes and heading out on the range on our cross-country skis.

I had the ideal build for cross-country skiing, which required one similar to that of a marathon runner but with a great amount of strength in the arms and legs. It also required an extremely high level of aerobic fitness, and with my background of athletics at such an early age I met this prerequisite with flying colours. All I needed to do was to master the cross-country skiing technique and I would be on my way.

When I entered the scene most of the other skiers hadn't heard of me. In my first competitive season in Australia I entered a race in the NSW town of Cabramurra, which was one of the lead-ups for the State championships. I was the dark horse in the line-up but went on to win a long way ahead of the top State skier at the time, in a time that was comparable with those recorded overseas for the same distance. After the race, one of the interstate visitors came over and asked me when I would be returning to the United States.

'What do you mean?' I asked.

'Oh,' he exclaimed, 'you're Australian!' He couldn't believe the time that I had done and assumed I was from overseas.

I quickly progressed to a level where I was in contention for the national team and although I would have been satisfied with selection in the B team I was delighted to learn I had made the A team for an extended overseas tour.

First stop was the United States to compete in the lead-up races to the European circuit. As the Australian team was so small, we decided to start the tour in separate groups and join up again later. I travelled to America with two male skiers, Chris Heberle and Michael Welsh, having arranged to meet the rest of the team in Europe after Christmas.

The cross-country skiing circuit consists of two main events, the Europa Cup and the more prestigious World Cup. To compete in the World Cup, skiers had to record certain minimum qualifying times. There were no Australian female skiers then on the World Cup circuit and I was keen to qualify as soon as possible. After only a few races I notched up a result that made me eligible for World Cup competition, and soon after was accorded official endorsement from the Australian Ski Federation.

We made our way to Europe and I could feel my standard improve dramatically. My technique was getting better all the time and the experience of training with Chris and Michael was proving invaluable. I achieved results which were more than promising, winning a major tour race in Italy, the Dolimetenlauf, a 25 km event which I entered as a training run, and I gained a third and a fourth place in the Lowlander championships in Denmark. My World Cup results were improving with each race and the experience of competing against the best skiers in the world was starting to pay off. By the end of the season I was full of confidence in my ability and was excited at what the future held.

I had never doubted my ability to pit myself against the best skiers in the world. Nor was I deterred by the fact that I came from a country which had no deep tradition of winter sports. I was a totally dedicated athlete who trained hard and was very single-minded about getting what I wanted.

In Europe we met up with another member of the A team, James Hamilton, and two of our top male skiers, Dave and Rod Hislop. The men took me under their wing. I was the fledgling on the tour, and as I was the only woman in the team they looked after me and gave me all sorts of helpful tips.

I became friendly with girls in other teams on the circuit, especially the Canadians. We had spent some time with them in America, and then met up with them during the races in Europe. I got on with all of them, but there were some I really hit it off with. One day, after we had finished racing, the Canadian coach, Marty Hall, invited me to join him and the girls for lunch at a pizza restaurant. We spent hours talking and eating pizza while I filled them in about life in Australia.

The Canadians were one of the top ski teams in the world and were to be the hosts at the next Olympics in Calgary. They travelled with an entourage of assistants, doctors, coaches, physiotherapists, ski technicians and many more. We were entirely by ourselves, which placed a lot of pressure on us and made it very difficult to compete with the other teams.

One day, while we were attending an award ceremony, Marty approached me with an offer that was too good to be true.

'Janine, what are your plans for the future?' he said as we sat waiting for the ceremony to begin.

'Well, when I return home I'll go back to university and finish my studies before returning to Europe next year with the team.'

'You know, if you really want to make it in skiing you'll have to put your studies on hold until the Olympics are over. You Aussies are crazy. It's not so difficult for the guys—at least there are a few of them, they travel together and they can give each other support. But you—you're alone. You don't even have a women's team, it's impossible to break into the top.'

'But what choice have I got?' I asked.

'I really think you can make it,' Marty said. 'I think you have got what it takes, but your only chance is to join up with another team. What I'm saying is this . . .'

He went on to offer me the chance to train as part of the Canadian team for the following season leading up to the Olympics. I would meet up with them in the States in early November and then travel to Europe with them. I would have full use of their facilities and resources.

I couldn't believe my ears. This was the chance of a lifetime!

'Marty, I'd love to come over with your team,' I told him.

'I really want to get to the top, and I would love to join up with your girls. I want to put Australia on the map as a force to be reckoned with, to show the world that we can really ski, even if we are on the other side of the world.'

'I don't think you have a choice, Janine, if you want to make it in this sport. You can't do it as a lone Aussie—you need the support that we can offer you. You don't have any time to waste. You have to make up your mind what you really want, the Olympics are just around the corner, you know.'

I knew he was right. I had no choice. I made my decision then and there. I would join up with my new friends as soon as possible. I told him I would gratefully accept and began to make the necessary arrangements back home to defer my studies for a couple of years.

I returned home in late March, four weeks late for the start of a new term at university, so I had a lot of catching up to do. I managed to transfer my studies for that year to Canberra University so I could be close to the snowfields and the Australian Institute of Sport (AIS). Although cross-country skiing was not yet a fully integrated sport at the AIS, which meant that no skiing scholarships were offered, team members were allowed to take full advantage of its facilities and the help of its staff.

We all took part in a camp in early May, in which we were tested for our aerobic endurance and strength, specifically for skiing. I tested way above any of the girls at the camp, and most of the males as well. My oxygen uptake, or VO2 max (a prerequisite for success in any endurance sport), was one of the highest levels for women they had ever tested, and my body fat was so low that it was less than that of most of the males.

I was, as we would say in the skiing fraternity, psyched! This was just the beginning and I could feel great things were out there waiting for me. I couldn't wait to get back on the snow.

But now things were different. I was lying in bed, my body broken, unable to move my legs or perform even the most basic of human functions.

It was a nightmare. How could this be happening to me?

Chapter 3

WITH THE BLEEDING under control and the treatment of my spinal injuries the next worry, it was time for the doctors to think about transferring me to the acute spinal injuries ward. I was wheeled out of ICU for the next stage of my recovery. But the process had only just commenced.

The acute spinal injuries ward—or 'Acute', as it was called for short—was located in a building next to ICU. Most spinal patients were taken there immediately if there was no need to undergo intensive care. This was my new 'home'.

It exuded all the musty hospital smells that I had become accustomed to. It had six beds in it and I was assigned to bed number two. There was a silver railing going around each bed with a striped dull green curtain attached to it, the sort of thing that you could only find in a hospital. There was a nurses' station at one end, to my left, which would have been impossible to see had it not been for the mirror strategically placed above my head. On my right was a door with two large plastic panels in it leading to the next ward.

'Acute' was for high-dependency cases and the nurse-to-patient ratio was at least one to three, except at night when it was one to six. There was always one 'floating' nurse who would rotate between the wards and if any extra help was needed they would be sent to Acute.

It was a strange feeling to drift off to sleep and then wake to find myself in new surroundings. I was still connected to some of the paraphernalia I had had in ICU. Some of the equipment had disappeared, but I had appropriated many other 'necessary' items. There were the 'TED' (Thrombo-Embolic Deterrent) stockings that fitted tightly over both of my legs. They were necessary to maintain blood pressure in my veins and reduce the risk of blood clots. To help prevent clotting, which was a serious threat, I had to have three injections a day of an anticoagulant called calciparine to thin the blood. The stockings and the calciparine were both unavoidable for any patient who had to spend long periods of bed rest. By now my right arm was firmly encased in a plaster cast that finished just below my right shoulder. My neck was in a brace which was kept firmly in place by sand-bags on either side of my head.

My broken back was a greater worry than the breaks in my neck and my doctors decided it wasn't necessary to put my neck in traction using callipers. Instead, the sandbags were used to achieve the same function. I was 'fortunate' that I was spared the procedure of drilling into my skull, which is the usual treatment for a broken neck. Although it is performed under local anaesthetic and there is therefore no pain, the psychological effect is apparently most disturbing. Either way, my neck was held firmly in place and there was no way that I was able to move it.

The drip still remained, by now pumping pethidine into my body instead of the more potent morphine. It not only provided me with much-needed pain relief but served as my only source of sustenance, as I was still unable to eat anything.

Eating was the last thing on my mind, not just because of the intense pain that I was in but because I was feeling so sick from the drugs. It was ironic that the one thing that was helping me to cope with my horrendous injuries was also making it impossible for me to replenish my reserves and give my body what it so desperately needed to mend itself.

I still had a catheter in my bladder, which was attached to a bottle underneath my bed. This was something I was totally unaware of and it wasn't until some time later that I actually started to wonder why I hadn't been to the bathroom for a long time!

The end result was that the only part of my body that I could move was my left arm, but this was still made difficult as this was the arm with the drip attachments.

I not only became accustomed to the pethidine but I also became tolerant of the level of pain that I was in. It was always with me and though the drugs never actually deadened it, what it did was obliterate a level of consciousness. In other words, I didn't care about it. However, it left me in a state of feeling that what was happening to me was not real, as if I was standing back and watching detachedly.

To keep my neck in perfect alignment, I was required to lie absolutely flat, without any pillows, so that all I could do was gaze up at the ceiling. My back also had to be kept in alignment, but this was simple as I was unable to move the lower part of my body anyway.

Most of my knowledge of the ward was therefore formed from what Mum and Dad told me about it.

I learnt that I was sharing the room with five other people who had also suffered spinal injuries of some degree. There were three beds on either side of the room facing each other and there was one nurse who was on duty at all times. I could just reach the mirror above my head with my left hand, which enabled me to see certain parts of the room. Limited though my range of vision was, the mirror helped to enlarge my world beyond the immediate area of my bed.

A young man named John was in the bed to the right of mine. He had been thrown off a horse he was riding on the same day as my accident, but had been brought straight to 'Acute' ward whereas I had gone to ICU. He hadn't suffered multiple injuries like mine, but he had broken his back in exactly the same place as I had. I could imagine the pain he must have been in, as he too was forced to lie flat on his back. At night I would hear him moan in agony as he cried out for relief. I knew what he was going through.

On the other side of the ward to my left was a young girl named Natalie. She was only seventeen years old and had been involved in a car accident with a group of friends. She had gone to a party with her boyfriend and they had accepted a lift home with someone who had been drinking. Natalie was asleep in the back when the driver lost control and collided with another car. Her worst injury was a broken neck and she was placed in traction.

The night that Matthew came into hospital remains vivid in my mind. It was late and Mum and Dad had gone home. I could hear the footsteps of the staff as they shuffled in and out of the ward and the groans of the other patients as they settled down for another night of pain. Suddenly there was a commotion outside the ward and then I heard the doors open. I moved my mirror and could just see the outline of two ambulance officers who were pushing a trolley. The patient groaned as they lifted him off the trolley and into his bed, and I felt a terrible sense of sadness that someone else had become a victim. It was Matthew.

It seemed to take forever as the nurses fussed over him before a doctor arrived on the scene. The next thing I heard was a loud drilling noise as they bored through Matthew's skull to put the callipers in place. I could hear the staff trying to comfort Matthew and explain what they were doing. I knew that everybody else in the ward was awake, even though I couldn't hear anyone. Then John's voice broke the silence.

'Poor guy, sounds like he's having a rough time.'

'Yeah,' I said. 'I wonder what happened to him?' The procedure continued for most of the night before the staff settled Matthew, and he eventually fell asleep. After the drilling ceased there were many other things to attend to and we were a captive audience, unable to escape the grim reminder of what we were all trying to forget.

In the bed next to Matthew was an elderly woman named Thelma who, like Natalie, had been involved in a car accident, suffering what was called a 'hangman's break' of her neck. She was very lucky to have survived, especially since she was at an age where muscles and ligaments were not at their strongest. She had also broken her pelvis which caused much pain as well.

The final bed in the ward was a sort of transient stop. It was occupied by several different people who generally had less serious injuries than the rest of us. They would come into our ward for a few weeks before being moved to another part of the hospital.

The other patients in 'Acute' became my new 'friends'. Although we couldn't see each other, we constantly talked, often simply to relieve the boredom. Our families brought in photos of us so that we could see what one another looked like and put a face to the voice. We depended on each other for support, especially during the night. With no visitors or distractions to divert from the pain, the night signalled a time of loneliness and terror which one couldn't escape.

When I had the accident, Daven was still overseas and wasn't due to return for a few weeks. Apparently I asked Daven's father not to let him see me. I had no memory of this and can only assume that I didn't want to worry him. His father had phoned him to tell him the news, but knowing that there was little he could do from the other side of the world, he assured Daven that I would be all right until he arrived home.

Just before I went overseas, Daven and I had been through quite an emotional time together. I had come to a point where I had serious doubts about our relationship and the strength of our mutual commitment. We had been together constantly for five years, and for the first time I felt I needed a break. I wanted to be alone.

My decision to end our relationship, even for a short time, upset Daven greatly. He couldn't understand what had happened, what had gone wrong. He had gone on holidays just before I left for the States, saying that he would stand by and wait no matter what I finally decided. He wanted to work things out and if that meant giving me time and space on my own, he would do it.

Although it was a difficult decision for me, I felt inside that I was doing the right thing. I wanted some time to think things out and I really wanted to concentrate one hundred per cent on my skiing without any emotional concerns that could distract me from my goal.

Our paths crossed quite a few times overseas, and we spent the last few weeks together before I returned to Australia. It was to be another two months until we would see each other again and that gave me enough time to think about how I really felt about our relationship. We spoke on the phone only days before the accident, and we were both excited at the prospect of seeing each other again. The time apart had been good, for both of us, and I was looking forward to seeing him again.

C*hapter 4*

By now there were a few more doctors on the scene, comprising neurosurgeons, orthopaedic surgeons and rehabilitation specialists. They were all part of the team responsible for my progress and their daily visits became a ritual I would look forward to with both anticipation and anxiety. Dr Blum, my neurosurgeon, would do the daily rounds with a few other, less prominent, doctors. Each visit he would continue with his pin-pricking routine to see if there had been any significant neurological improvement overnight.

Days and finally weeks passed and then what seemed to be the miraculous happened. One day when I was lying there trying to move my feet, I thought I could feel them respond a bit more than they had before. I couldn't believe it. This was the sign that I was going to recover, I thought. *I knew it would happen, I will be able to ski again!*

My parents and the doctors were delighted and we all clung to the belief that each day would bring new progress. Things could only get better from now on! I never gave up hope of recovering and regaining full use of my legs. This hope spurred me on and helped me to overlook the other, not so positive, things that were happening. The feeling in my feet still hadn't returned—in fact, I had no feeling or sensation from the buttocks down to my feet—but this didn't deter me. I was determined that I would recover.

I felt more and more positive with each passing day. I practised moving my feet as much as possible. I couldn't feel much progress, but I believed it would happen eventually, if only I could just hang in there.

As my accident received a lot of news coverage, it was only a matter of time before a television station decided to do a story on me. I wasn't quite prepared for what was in store when the cameras came rolling in for Channel 9's *Today* show and I wondered whether they knew that I was 'high' as a kite when they interviewed me!

They asked me about the accident, and I told them what I had been told. I still had no recollection of the day it occurred. My doctors later told me that I had post-traumatic amnesia. This was something the body did as a way of protecting itself from painful or harmful memories.

They also asked me how I saw my future in skiing, and I told them that I would still be aiming to reach the Olympics. Of course, this accident would put my training behind somewhat, and the road ahead would be long, but I was confident of returning to skiing. After all, I was improving with each day. It was only a matter of time before I would be allowed home!

Various other stories appeared in the press and the resulting mail took me by surprise. Messages of support and encouragement overwhelmed me. Letters and cards came from all over the world—Norway, America, Africa, everywhere. Mum would read them to me. Many of them were from people I had never even met. Some would write to tell me about someone dear to them who had also had an accident and how it had devastated them. They urged me to hang on and keep going, with their prayers and best wishes for a speedy recovery. To the end of my days, I will never forget the kind words that flooded in to me. The generosity of the human spirit will never fail to amaze me.

The mirror over my bed which I was able to manipulate with my one good arm to see around the room proved an invaluable asset. Later on, when I was able to watch television, I used it to see the screen behind my head. Now Mum pinned my letters on the wall behind me so that if I tilted the mirror I could read them.

One day a letter arrived at the hospital addressed to Mum. It was from a lady named Elizabeth Etherington. Inside was a note and a poem. She wanted Mum to know that her thoughts were with her, that she herself had three children of her own and that she felt for the terrible pain that Mum must be going through. Her reason for writing was that by some incredible coincidence she had been at the scene of the accident. The poem read as follows:

Lying there lost in pain a comforting hand to hold.
The rocks beneath, the gasping breath, my story must be told.
The right leg moves when her name I mention—her hand moves to her face.
Then while with calm and care I speak her fists clench full of tension.
Then suddenly, though her eyes don't see, from the grass her head she raises.
While underneath the coats and rug her body bleeds with grazes.
But even as she lies there with her body torn and broken
She gives to me an inner strength, though not a word to me she's spoken.
The time I spent beside her seemed like hours stretching, tight,
The seconds when heart beat I lost did fill me full of fright.
But all the time I spoke her name and sometimes Nevin's too

I never doubted that with her mind she'd make herself pull through.
I know that she knew I was there, her hand grip told me so. And as the
ambulance drove up the hill, fellow-feeling with her did go.
There'll be many times when we'll look back upon that fateful day
When life gave to all of us a reason why we pray.
To many it may be very hard when life is hurt so deep
But with the days of passing time think of all the love she'll reap.
No-one has a reason why we're tested in this way
But one thing is for certain that Janine fought hard that day.
I hope these words of mine I've shared, with you and all who care
Have in some very tiny way eased some worries you may bare.
My thoughts, my prayers, are with you, though many miles away,
And hope the road ahead of you will shorten with each day.

As Mum was reading the poem to me I noticed the tears rolling down her cheeks. I was crying too. It was so close to home, so personal. It would be much later that I would eventually meet this person called Elizabeth, and learn why the day of my accident would stay clear in her mind forever.

After having spent some time in the city, Elizabeth, her husband Larry and two of their friends were driving home to Mudgee. Elizabeth was dozing off in the back seat when they started to climb the steep incline of the mountains road.

Suddenly a loud bang snapped her awake. She looked around to see something flying through the air. It looked like a body, but that was impossible, she thought—not that high in the air. They screeched to a stop and jumped out.

Elizabeth ran back to where she had seen the 'thing' flying through the air and was horrified by the scene that confronted her. A body lay in the dirt on the side of the road—my body. A few people had already gathered around. She noticed three men about to pick me up, one lifting me under the arms, the others by the feet.

'What do you think you're doing?' she screamed as she ran down to where they were standing.

'We're going to put her in the car and take her to hospital,' one of them replied.

'Just leave her where she is,' Elizabeth told them. 'Someone call an ambulance—quick!'

For the next few minutes until the ambulance arrived, Elizabeth tried desperately to comfort me. My friends John and Nevin soon reached the scene to find me lying on the side of the road. Elizabeth placed some pieces of clothing over my injured body to keep me warm, holding my hand and speaking to me in an effort to calm and console me. As she gazed down at me, she was sickened by the sight.

I was covered in blood, my face lacerated by cuts and abrasions. The skin on my forehead had been pushed back from my scalp like a carpet, exposing the skull underneath. My eyes seemed to have rolled back in my head, glazed and unfocusing. I was thrashing about convulsively, moaning in pain, and frothing at the mouth. I was bleeding profusely from gashes in my legs and torso. My clothes were torn and stained with blood and gravel.

When the ambulance arrived they placed me on the spinal board, put me inside and carefully cut the clothes from my body. As Elizabeth watched them drive off, she thought it would be the last time that she would ever see me.

Hearing Elizabeth's story some time later, it was difficult to imagine that she was actually talking about me. It was an eerie sensation. Once again I felt as if I was looking down, watching from a distance. When I read her poem today, I am no less moved than when Mum first read it to me. It brings a flood of emotions to the surface, not just all the hurt and pain, but all the love and sharing that accompanied it. And when I read it, I am grateful that God brought Elizabeth into my life that day.

Chapter 5

It SEEMED TO happen so suddenly. The improvement in my legs and feet began to recede, until finally I lost all movement. The alarm bells rang. Something was definitely wrong.

Dr Blum had hoped that any neurological improvement I had so far made would continue, but the sudden regression indicated that this wasn't the case. It would now be necessary to carry out some further tests to ascertain what the problem was.

Mum and Dad were greatly upset by the news. It seemed that everything was going so well and that the worst was over, but now they were thrown into uncertainty again.

Dr Blum told them I would have a test called a myelogram the following day. When I was told about the tests, I didn't understand how urgent they were. I wasn't concerned about the loss of movement—in fact, I hardly even noticed it. After all, as far as I was concerned it would only be a matter of time till I was allowed to go home and commence training again. Surely this was just one of those routine tests we all had to go through in 'Acute'.

I was taken to the X-ray department the following morning. I was so excited at the thought of leaving the ward for a few hours I wasn't even thinking about what was in store for me. As the orderlies wheeled my bed outside to the ambulance, I had my first taste of sunlight in two weeks. After having been exposed almost constantly to the artificial lights of the wards, the intensity of the sun took me by surprise and I was forced to close my eyes for a moment against the glare. The heat felt so good beating down on my face. Just as they were loading me into the ambulance I opened my eyes to the most wonderful sight I had seen in a long time—a clear blue sky and not a cloud to be seen. It felt good to be alive!

Down in the X-ray department, however, it was another story altogether. It seemed the test I was about to have wasn't as simple as I had thought and turned out to be a very painful procedure. After being transferred to a bed so hard it felt as if it was made from rock, I was carefully tilted so that they could work on my back. I could see the staff preparing the equipment. First they had to inject a large needle into my spine to anaesthetise the area. Then they used a very large hypodermic needle to inject a special dye right into the spinal cavity. This was the most painful part. An uncomfortable pressure or throbbing sensation ran through my back as the dye made its way up through the spinal cavity. Then the bed was tilted so that my head was lower than my feet. This was to ensure that the dye could penetrate the length of the spinal cord.

While I was in this position, a series of X-ray pictures was taken of my back to see if the dye made its way up through the cord unobstructed or if there was something which was causing a blockage.

The whole procedure was very unpleasant and I couldn't wait till it was over. Even then, it took some time to recover from the tests. One side-effect of the treatment was a dreadful headache, a metallic taste in the mouth and an overall feeling of nausea.

I was never so glad to be back in the familiar surroundings that had now become my home. I was utterly exhausted and just wanted to sleep.

Early next morning Dr Blum made an unscheduled visit. Mum and Dad were already there sitting by my bed. Dr Blum was always friendly and I liked him a lot. But today he was serious.

'We've been looking over the results of Janine's myelogram,' he said, 'and it doesn't look good. She has a burst fracture in her back and there are a lot of bony fragments which are compressing the spinal chord. We need to operate on the back to decompress the spine and then we'll need to do a bone graft in order to make it solid again.'

'When will you need to do the operation?' Mum asked.

'Well, it's important that we do it sooner than later,' he said.

'Do we have any choice?'

'Unfortunately, no. If Janine decides to go ahead with the operation there's a chance she might walk again. If we don't operate, she will almost certainly end up in a wheelchair. But I have to let you know I am talking about major surgery, involving a very delicate part of the body, so there are some risks involved.'

I just lay in my bed trying to take in what Dr Blum was saying. It didn't seem like much of a choice to me. Either way I might never walk again! I didn't like those sort of odds.

I didn't like what I was hearing. It made me feel ill. All this time I had believed I was making progress and that everything would be all right, but now it seemed like I had been wrong. For the first time since my accident I was confronted with the severity of my injuries and I couldn't come to terms with it.

Dr Blum took my parents outside to discuss the details of

the operation. The feeling of nausea increased. 'Please, someone, help me,' I called.

The nurse on duty rushed over to my bed, saw that I was shaking uncontrollably and called for help. Just as they turned me on my side, someone got a pan under my mouth and I vomited violently.

When I had finished, one of the nurses washed my face with cold water, trying to settle me down. When she left, I lay and stared at the ceiling wondering how this could have happened. It just wasn't fair. As the tears rolled down my cheeks, I closed my eyes as the pethidine started to take effect.

The operation was scheduled in two days' time, exactly four weeks after my accident. Initially, the doctors had told me that I would be spending eight weeks in bed and with only four weeks to go I was counting the days. However, things were different now. After the operation I would have to spend at least another eight weeks on my back, which meant a total of twelve weeks in bed. This was such a depressing prospect I felt as if I had been robbed. They had promised me it would be only another four weeks, and now it was eight. How was I going to last that long?

The night before the operation I was feeling tense and nervous. I knew it could go either way and the thought of someone cutting me open and tampering with my spinal cord filled me with apprehension. The procedure wasn't exactly reassuring, I thought. They would be operating with a neurosurgical team as well as an orthopaedic team. The orthopaedic surgeon, Dr Stephen, would start the operation, making his way to the spinal cord, and then Dr Blum would take over. This was the delicate part of the operation when one false move could cause more damage to the injured spinal cord. After removing the shattered fragments of bone, they would then use one of my broken ribs to form a graft over the vertebral column to stabilise and strengthen it. As I went over the procedure in my head, I began to feel more and more tense.

As I stared up at the ceiling, for the first time since my accident I tried to put things in a wider context. Until now, I hadn't realised the situation was as bad as it was. Now I began to ask the inevitable question. *Why?* Why has this all happened? And why to me? And for what reason—if there was one? What good could possibly come out of this?

I couldn't sleep that night. Not even the drugs seemed to have any effect. What would happen if the operation went wrong? What would I do if I wasn't able to ski again, or play sport? I was an athlete: my body was everything to me. If I didn't have that, what did I have? I couldn't escape my thoughts. It was as if I was in some sort of void as I tried to ponder what the future held.

Next morning the staff began preparing me for the operation. I was given a pre-med injection, which made me shiver. Mum and Dad had already arrived by the time the orderlies came to collect me. They kissed me goodbye and said they would be waiting for me when I came out. I knew they were being brave for me, but I could see the worry on their faces. Now it was my turn to be strong. 'Don't worry, I'll be OK,' I assured them.

Chapter 6

COMING OUT OF the blackness, I recognised the familiar bright lights of Intensive Care. I went to take a breath but was stopped by a sharp stabbing pain in my chest. *I can't breathe, what's wrong?* The pain gripped my body like a vice. The pressure started to build up. *I'm going to have to breathe ... I don't want to ... it hurts too much.* I opened my mouth again and took a breath. *Oh, my chest ... what have they done to me?*

I reached down to where the pain was coming from. My entire chest area had been tightly bandaged. I wrapped my left arm instinctively around my chest, pressing firmly on my side. I didn't know what else to do. I took another breath. For some reason the pressure I was applying seemed to ease the pain slightly. I took a few small, shallow breaths.

I felt drowsy. The anaesthetic had barely worn off. My eyelids felt heavy and I strained to keep them open. Through the blur around me I could just make out Mum's and Dad's faces. I held out my hand.

'Hi, sweetheart, it's all over,' Mum assured me as she took my hand.

I didn't want to speak. The discomfort was too great.

'Dr Blum said everything went well,' she said. 'You just try to get some rest.'

I tried to take a few deep breaths but it was too painful. I felt as if all my internal organs were about to spill out. The only relief came from pressing even tighter on my side.

When the nurse came over, I tried to speak but could only manage a whisper.

'I'm so sore . . .'

'Janine, it's all right, it's normal to feel very sore after an operation like you've had.'

I tightened my grip on my side.

'You have to be careful not to move too much,' she said, pointing to my stomach. 'You have a drain in your side which will stay for a few days.' She attended to some routine tasks and went away.

Not long after two orderlies arrived. I knew their job was to turn the patients, but surely they wouldn't be attempting to turn me? The mere thought of it was unbearable. My chest was now throbbing with each breath.

'How're you going, love, ready to be turned?' one of them asked as they positioned themselves on either side of me.

'Please don't move me, I'm too sore,' I whimpered.

'Sorry, love, but we have to turn you, regulations you know.'

'Please, please, can't you miss it for once, please . . .' I must have looked so much in agony that they relented.

'Well, OK, I guess it'll be all right. We'll be back in two hours anyway.' They moved on to the next bed. I was so grateful. I closed my eyes and tried to think of anything but the pain in my chest.

Sometime later Dr Blum came by to see how I was getting

on. I was still groggy from the anaesthetic, but I was pleased to see his smiling face.

'Well then, young lady, how are you feeling? A bit sore they tell me.' That was an understatement. 'Let's see if you have any more movement in your feet now.'

This was a bit scary. I hadn't even tried to move them yet. What if I couldn't? Oh well, I had to try sooner or later. I did, and thought I could feel them move.

'Did you see that?' I said excitedly. 'I think they moved a bit.'

'I think you're right,' said Dr Blum, smiling.

'I'll be able to ski, won't I?' I asked. In my excitement I only caught part of what he was saying, but that was enough for me.

'I'm pleased with the operation, it couldn't have gone better. I'll be back tomorrow to check up on you. Keep up the good work.' He smiled again and wiggled my feet affectionately before he left the ward.

It couldn't have gone better. That's what he said. I heard him. I'd be back to normal in no time. It'd just be a matter of time before I'd be able to go home and start training again. What news! I couldn't wait to tell my friends. Sure I would have a lot of hard work, a lot of catching up to do, but I would be going to the Olympics, I was sure of it!

I closed my eyes and images of skiing filled my mind. I was so happy. Everything was going to be all right after all. I was startled by a voice at my side.

'Good morning, Janine, how are we today? My name is Jenny and I am your physiotherapist.'

I wasn't expecting a physiotherapist. What could she possibly want?

'I will be looking after you while you are in Intensive Care. We have to give your lungs and chest some exercise as they've been through quite a bit of trauma during the operation. We need to keep them free from any infections.'

She handed me a strange blue contraption with some little balls inside and told me I had to blow into it and make the balls rise. I was supposed to keep them up for as long as possible.

She has got to be kidding, I thought. I couldn't envisage inhaling enough breath to blow into anything. I was flat out just trying to breathe to keep alive! I looked at her and I could tell she was serious. *How on earth was I going to do this?*

I held the container in my hand and tried to take a deep breath. It was impossible. I exhaled pathetically into the container. I'm sure she couldn't even see that I had taken a breath at all.

'Come on, Janine, you've got to try and lift the balls. Have another go.'

I tried again. This time at least she saw I was making an effort. But there was absolutely no way I could make any of the balls move even slightly.

As if that wasn't enough, she had more torture in store for me. Now she wanted me to practise coughing! I tried to appease her with a few miserable wheezes, but didn't succeed.

This physiotherapy routine was carried out regularly each day to make sure my lungs stayed clear and didn't collapse. It was a rigorous grind that I looked forward to with considerable trepidation. But I knew it was a necessary part of my recovery, and the sooner I got better the sooner I could go home.

'Janine's back,' said Dave. He was the nurse on duty in Acute when I returned.

I was greeted by all my friends in the ward. 'Hi, Janine . . .

G'day ... How are you feeling ...' They were all keen to find out how everything had gone.

I couldn't speak loud enough for everyone to hear as I still had the drain in my side so I had Mum do all the talking for me. I was still very tired, but I was glad to be back with my friends in familiar surroundings. The little patch of ceiling above my head still needed a paint, but at least I knew where I was!

It was important to keep up with my physiotherapy and the daily ritual of blowing the balls and coughing continued for some time. The drain in my side was a bit uncomfortable, but I wasn't looking forward to having it removed as it was taped firmly to my side with thick plaster and I knew it would really hurt. I was right. When the nurse did come to take it off she tried to be as gentle as possible, but it was like pulling the world's biggest and stickiest bandaid from my body!

With the plaster finally off, and my chest a little the worse for wear, it was time to pull the drain out. It was the weirdest feeling. I could actually feel the drain moving inside of me, and when the nurse showed it to me I was surprised at how long and thick it was. I thought I must have had a huge gaping hole in my side after it was removed, but luckily I couldn't see that far! The nurse carefully bandaged the area again, taking a lot more care than the doctors did.

A few days later I was due to have the stitches removed. While I was waiting for the doctor to take them out, one of the orderlies came around to talk to me. I really liked him and used to call him Uncle Jim because he was a bit of a character. He used to traipse around in a daggy old tracksuit and runners and would lounge about my bed for hours on end talking.

As usual he sat down beside my bed. I was pleased to see him.

'Well,' he said, 'you look good. The operation went well.'

I wondered how he knew. He must have been talking to my doctors. That was nice of him to take an interest.

'It only took five hours all up and, boy, do you have a great stitching job!'

I was even more puzzled. 'How do you know so much about the stitching, Uncle Jim? You haven't even seen it yet.'

He looked at me indignantly. 'What do you mean I haven't seen it! I did it!'

I couldn't believe my ears. Since when did orderlies start helping out in the theatre? Something's not right here.

'And I did a damn neat job, if I say so myself,' he continued. 'Took an hour to finish. I wanted to give you a scar you could be proud of.'

Was I in for a shock! It seemed that all this time I had thought he was an orderly, but he was actually one of my surgeons. And I had been calling him Uncle Jim! I couldn't believe it. I was embarrassed, but not disappointed. I was glad he had stitched me up. He was my friend, and what better person to do the job? And I didn't stop calling him Uncle Jim!

I was still quite sore for some time. It not only hurt to talk but to laugh as well, which was a bit of a problem as laughter was an essential ingredient for survival in the ward.

There wasn't much you could do lying flat on your back twenty-four hours a day. There never seemed anything worth watching on television and I soon got tired of it. But luckily my sister Kelley came to the rescue. She worked as an editor for a TV station and one day she brought me in a video recorder and put it on top of the television set. Now I could watch anything I wanted at my pleasure. It wasn't standard practice in the hospital at the time, but no-one seemed to mind. After a while the nurses on duty would sit by my bed and watch whatever I had on, which was company for me. I felt as if I was entertaining for the night.

Kelley brought in lots of videos for me to watch—movies, serials and so forth. The one I really liked was a British comedy series called *The Young Ones*. It was the most ridiculous, outrageous show, but I loved it. For a patient lying in a spinal ward, it was just what the doctor ordered. The only problem was that it was absolute torture to watch as I still couldn't laugh—it hurt too much. Eventually I had to ask Kelley to take the tape off as I couldn't stand it any more. I would have to wait till my chest healed up.

Mum spent every day and most of the night at the hospital. Dad would come in after work and then they would drive home together. They became very familiar with hospital life and it started to feel like home to them. Judy, Natalie's mother, and John's mother Gwen also came to the ward every day, and they all became great friends. The patients weren't the only ones whose lives had been turned upside down. The same had happened to their parents and it was comforting for them to be able to share their thoughts and fears with each other. They would all chat together across the ward or go outside and sit on the grass drinking cups of coffee and talking about our progress.

John had had his operation weeks before me. He had broken his back in a similar place to mine and had the same kind of graft as I had. However, he was fortunate to have escaped the multiple injuries that I had sustained. As he hadn't broken his neck he was allowed to sleep with a pillow, which was a luxury I couldn't wait to have. Natalie had also been operated on before me, but her surgery was on her neck for something called central cord quadriplegia, which meant there was damage to the centre of the spinal cord. These patients usually progressed well, the usual prognosis being that they would walk but often suffer quite extensive loss of movement in their hands.

As the bones of the neck are a lot smaller than those in the back, they heal much more quickly. This meant that Natalie would be able to get out of bed a lot sooner than either John or myself. Although I had broken my neck, it wasn't as severe as the break in my back. I was able to get by with the sandbags on either side of my head instead of callipers like Natalie, who had to have her head shaved as a result. She was in those all-too-difficult teen years and was a bit self-conscious about what her friends would say about her new hairstyle.

We all started to feel like one big family—whenever one of the mothers was a bit late getting to the ward, the others would play the surrogate mum and help us with whatever we needed, even if it was just giving comfort by having a chat.

Six weeks after the accident I was still on pethidine, although it was no longer administered intravenously but by injection. Together with the fact that I was flat on my back, this meant that it was very difficult for me to eat. I had completely lost my appetite and the mere thought of food repulsed me. As a result, my weight was spiralling downwards and it started to worry everyone.

The hospital nutritionist came to see why I wasn't eating, concerned that I wouldn't have the strength to recover.

'Janine, is there anything we can cook for you that you would particularly like?' she asked.

'I'm just not hungry,' I told her. 'The sight of food makes me sick.'

'But you have to eat something, or the doctors will have to put you back on the drip,' she said.

Not the drip again! I would at least have to agree to try some food. 'OK, I'll try but I can't guarantee anything,' I said. 'My favourite food is chicken.'

'Great, that's a start. I'll tell the cooks.'

Sure enough, at dinnertime, there was my chicken. I took one look at it and felt absolutely nauseous. I couldn't eat a thing and next day the nutritionist came to see me again.

She was worried because my weight had plummeted and I was losing an incredible amount of muscle as well. She told me that every day I spent in bed without moving I was losing one per cent of my muscle mass, which meant that I had already lost over 42 per cent of it. When I looked at my left arm I could see it was wasting away and I knew I had lost a large amount of weight.

So I agreed to make one last attempt to eat before I was put on the drip again, and I was given a liquid meal which tasted a bit like a chocolate drink. I tried my very best to digest it, but it is not the easiest thing to eat anything while lying flat on your back.

Mum tried her best to help too. She would go home each night and cook my favourite meals. I had always loved pasta and Mum made oodles of it for me. I tried my best to eat it, knowing the trouble she'd gone to, but it usually made me sick. Most of it ended up being eaten by Daven or one of my other friends. But Mum kept making me meals undeterred until the day I finally left hospital.

However, I was able to stomach most liquids. Mum used to sit by my bed and feed me soup while she was talking to Gwen or Judy. Soup's not easy to eat lying down and as Mum was not always looking where she put the spoon, I ended up wearing more of the soup than I ate!

One day Gwen brought John a bag of iced doughnuts. She offered me one and not wanting to offend her I took it. I was never very keen on junk food, but this doughnut tasted fabulous and I gobbled it down. It probably wasn't the most nutritious thing to eat at the time but it was better than having soup spilled all down my front! From then on Gwen always made sure she brought a bag of doughnuts with her.

Chapter 7

A FEW WEEKS after the operation my side was feeling a lot better. We were all well accustomed to the routine of the ward by now, and instead of running our day by the clock, we knew what time it was by what the nurses were doing.

The routine was necessary to ensure the smooth running of the ward, but no matter how necessary it was, it still made one yearn for the day when life didn't have to be so regimented. To adapt to the system required a complete loss of independence, and just for once I wished I could do something in my own good time.

The day usually started around 5.30 am, when we were woken up whether we liked it or not. We used to stay up late watching television and just as we were getting to sleep, it seemed, the lights would go on, signalling the beginning of a new day. As the ward was understaffed, the nurses had to get going early to make sure everything would be done.

By now there would be two nurses on duty as opposed to one during the night. They would invariably wake us with a bright and cheerful, 'Good morning, everyone, how are we this morning? Did we all sleep well?' They obviously got more sleep than we did!

Next came the morning wash, or sponge. This was no easy task. Not only did each patient have to be washed and turned, but the bed linen had to be changed as well. This took two orderlies to turn the patient and two nurses to attend to the washing and changing the linen. One nurse would hold my head still while the two men stabilised my back, and the other nurse would wash my back and the more inaccessible parts of my body. While the men kept holding me on my side she would then somehow slip the sheet from under me and replace it with a fresh one. How she managed to do this I could never quite work out, but it was almost a contortionist's act which required the cooperation of all four members of the team.

Whenever I had any contact with the hospital staff, I would always take the opportunity to talk as much as possible. Always hungry for conversation, I tried to keep up to date with what was going on outside the ward. It lessened the feeling of isolation from the world. So with all five of us talking it became a rather social event!

After they had been around the ward and washed everyone's back it was time to go around once more, this time to sponge our fronts. While the nurse was sponging my legs and arms I usually washed my face with my good left arm. Needless to say, the entire procedure was a lengthy one.

Bathtime over, it was now time for breakfast, which came around about 7.30 am. As I wasn't able to feed myself I had to wait for a nurse to spoon-feed me. I still hadn't regained my appetite but I usually managed to keep down a few bites of soggy toast and some tea, which I had to drink out of a straw.

The nurses then finished off the job they had started earlier, by brushing our teeth for us, combing our hair and looking after anything else we needed doing in the hygiene department. This was extremely important for us, as being clean helped us to feel a little more human.

Next it was time for the physiotherapists, who arrived between eight and eight-thirty. They came twice a day and I really looked forward to seeing them. Their job was to administer 'passive movements', which kept the joints mobile and flexible through a series of exercises to strengthen the wasted muscles. There were always two of them doing the manipulation and it felt great to have someone move my legs for me. The put us through a series of stretches which really hurt, because the muscles and ligaments had contracted so much while lying still for so long, and it was important that they didn't tighten up any further.

I enjoyed this tactile stimulation. As we couldn't even touch our own bodies it was good to be massaged by someone else. Physical touch was a great healer of both the body and the mind. In addition to the physiotherapy, Mum used to rub my feet each day with moisturiser. I still had no sensation in my feet but it did wonders for the circulation.

Then came the X-ray technicians. Patients in Acute had to be X-rayed at least once a week, so each day there was always someone to be zapped by their machines.

Between all this we had to take our medication, which was given at five o'clock and eleven o'clock, and in the evening again at five and eleven. We all had a lot of tablets to take, and I always made a point of finding out exactly what each one was for. They came in all shapes and sizes, colour-coded for convenience.

After medication, the nurses would attend to patients who had drips in their arms, refilling solutions that had run out and replenishing antibiotics, as well as emptying catheters and checking for infections. If an infection developed we were placed on antibiotics and made to drink water till we almost burst!

Mum always arrived either before breakfast or while we were being washed. She'd try to ease the burden of the staff by looking after me as much as she could. After she had put the food she'd cooked the night before away in the fridge in the kitchen for later in the day, she would sit and talk, brush my hair, read to me, massage my feet, attend to my needs— you name it, she did it. Mum was extremely organised and I don't know what I would have done without her.

Daven's mother Jenny was worried about my nutrition, and brought me in a juice squeezer. She felt that if I couldn't eat very much, then at least I could get some much-needed vitamins from a range of fruit and vegetables. She was very thoughtful. She would often sit by my bed for hours, talking and knitting, which gave Mum a welcome break.

After lunch there was more physio, more turning, more medication and of course more injections of calciparine, and then finally dinner—at four-thirty! How anyone could want dinner at this time was beyond me, but that was the rule. Fortunately, I had Mum's meals to fall back on for some variation from the uninspiring hospital menu.

There were always doctors doing their rounds. I was visited by the spinal registrar and a hospital resident once a day, while my surgeons came at least twice a week to check up on my progress. Often they would arrive with a group of medical students who would gather at the foot of the bed and talk about you as if you weren't there. This used to annoy me, as I had a fair knowledge of anatomy and thought they should have included me in the discussion.

'Right, here we have a young girl, previously an athlete, who has been involved in a major accident on her pushbike,' the doctor would say, giving a brief summary of my symptoms and asking what they would have done in such a situation. The fledgling doctors would all stand sheepishly, not knowing what to say, and perhaps a little intimidated by the manner of the surgeon. Of course I was supposed to lie there like a dummy while they all discussed me.

Quite often I would find the suspense too much and decide to give them a bit of a hand, blurting out the answers when they took too long to answer. I was never a great one for patience! They would all look aghast—how dare the patient answer, she should be seen and not heard ... but that's definitely not in my nature!

There were many positive things about life in the ward— the helpful staff, the visitors who turned up day after day, the companionship of the other patients. But for all these good points there were many more depressingly negative ones. Chief among them was the loss of identity. After a while, you began to feel like just another number in the system, and that the whole purpose of the day was to make sure you were washed, fed and medicated in a certain time.

My body was at the disposal of the system and I was continually obliged to submit to procedures that could only be described as humiliating. As my body had no way of emptying itself of the wastes that accumulated in the bowel, I had to have them removed manually by the nursing staff. In the early days of my hospital stay I was too sick and in too much pain to worry about this, but as the months rolled on it became the thing I dreaded most. After the nurses had finished and moved on to the next patient, I would quietly shed a few tears, the procedure having stripped me of my last shred of self-respect.

Looking back, I know it was something that had to be done, but that did nothing to lessen the indignity at the time. Most of the nurses did their utmost to make the process as quick as possible, knowing how embarrassing it was, but occasionally you would get a nurse who lacked any compassion or sensitivity. They would leave the curtain open ever so slightly while they were doing their task, not thinking that anyone walking past could see what was happening. Or they would carry on a conversation with someone on the other side. I found this inconsiderate and disrespectful. Fortunately, such nurses were few.

It wasn't easy living in circumstances that offered so little privacy. The hospital was extremely run-down and very dirty. The walls needed a coat of paint, the curtains should have been replaced—in fact, the whole place could have done with a complete refurbishment. You could hear everything going on in the ward. If someone was having their bowels attended to or their catheters changed, it was all done for the benefit of the other five people who shared the room. There was absolutely no privacy, and there was nothing you could do about it.

Without denying that certain things had to be done, it's still important to remember that patients are people, with a genuine need to maintain some degree of privacy and dignity. We had all been through considerable trauma and we needed as much personalised and individual care as possible. We needed to know that we still had some rights and we needed to have them respected. Sometimes it would have helped if the 'routine' could have been thrown out the window for a while.

I was determined to maintain a bit of 'self' by discarding the standard white gown we were supposed to wear. I was helped in this by a very special person whom I used to call Uncle Darryl.

I first met Darryl when I was initially admitted to Intensive Care, although he was only a name to me then. He was one of the orderlies who looked after me. Apparently I complained that my mouth was very dry and the doctors told the staff to give me ice cubes to suck on. Darryl used to supply me with my ice cubes and from then on I used to cry out in the night,

'Uncle Darryl, Uncle Darryl ... more ice cubes ... more ice cubes.'

When I was moved to Acute, Darryl came and introduced himself. He was like a huge teddy bear, with a soft voice and gentle nature. But the thing I remember most was that he always wore one of the gowns from the children's ward, covered in little ducks, rabbits or teddy bears. It looked really funny, and I loved it.

When I said how much I liked them, he offered to get me one. I immediately threw away my standard 'whites' and started wearing the cute little gowns he kept supplying me with. It was my way of being a bit different and saying I was a person, not just another patient number.

Uncle Darryl remained my loyal friend while I was in hospital, always visiting me whenever he could. He also became great friends with my family, especially with Dad. He even brought in a television set for Mum and Dad to use while they were staying in the nurses' quarters on weekends. He was a very kind and thoughtful man. He would even come and visit me on his days off or while he was on holidays, and then go and sit on the grass outside with Dad and talk for ages. He became a good mate to all of us.

When our visitors and families departed at the end of each day, there came a new challenge—the loneliness of the night. I never wanted Mum or Dad to leave me and missed them terribly when they finally had to go home. As the staff wound down for the day and there was only one nurse on duty, I used to feel a terrible sense of isolation at being left alone in the ward and it would get worse as the night wore on.

Television provided some comfort and feeling of companionship. We all usually watched the same programs and we would discuss anything that was of interest. We watched anything that was going—mini-series, news, sport, or just plain rubbish. It didn't matter as long as it was noise. I was fortunate that the Commonwealth Games and the World Cup soccer were on during my stay. I followed them intently, waiting for them to start each night.

Mum had discovered some time earlier that there was a phone connection next to my bed. The nursing staff allowed me to bring in my own phone so that I could make my own calls. This was a great boon and helped to lessen my sense of isolation. I would mainly use it at night when I felt most lonely, ringing Mum and Dad to see if they had got home all right. It became my lifeline to the world outside.

I got calls from all over the country, and even one from Zimbabwe. It was Daven's cousin David, whom I had met some years earlier when he came to stay with Daven's family for a while.

'Howzat, man, it's David here,' he said in his strong Zimbabwe accent. 'Now what's that they tell me about you having an accident. Now you just get better, you hear?'

'OK, David, I'll do as you say.'

'And promise me you'll give those nurses a hard time, right, man?' His accent always made me laugh, and it never seemed so out of place as in the middle of a hospital spinal ward. They say laughter is the best medicine, and on this occasion they were absolutely right.

One night the nurse on duty had an idea to relieve the boredom somewhat and lighten up the atmosphere in the ward.

He started threading straws together into a very long row, then stood in the middle of the room and made an announcement.

'Right, everyone, I have decided that to keep us all occupied tonight we are going to have a little competition.' We all listened intently. 'This is how it will work. I've threaded a whole lot of straws together and your job is to guess how many straws I have used. The closest to the number wins.'

Of course the problem for all of us was seeing the straws, but Wayne had an answer for that. He climbed up on some chairs and draped the straws over the curtain railing between each bed! He made sure that they hung down over each of us so that if we reached up we could actually touch the straws.

'Since we all have to spend so much time in this place together, and since we are so far away from each other, I think it is only right that we have a feeling of closeness, that we feel bonded to each other,' he said. The whole thing was getting crazier by the moment, but we loved it!

'When I say go, I want you to reach up and grab the straws above your head. Everyone ready . . . go!'

We did as we were told, and reached up for the straws. It was getting quite odd by now but Wayne was just beginning. He jumped up and shrieked like an American preacher, 'Can't you feel the vibes? We're all touching the straws together!'

Wayne then got rolls and rolls of toilet paper and started to unroll it around the room, over the top of all of us. I don't know where he got it all from—lucky none of us needed it!

'Now, it's time to guess the number of straws. OK, Natalie, you're first, what do you say?'

Wayne wrote down her answer, then went around the room until he got to me. I guessed a number but it was already taken, so I had to pick another. I had judged my bet by counting the number of straws above my head then calculating how many identical metres of straws were around the room, then adding a few for good measure!

After all the scores were collected, Wayne stood in the middle of the room on a chair for the announcement. 'And the winner is . . . ' the suspense was too much . . . 'Janine!'

Everyone cheered—it was getting pretty silly by now.

'We can't have a winner without a prize, now, can we?' Wayne said as he began to collect the toilet paper up from around the room.

Uh-oh, I thought, starting to get suspicious, what does he have in store for me now?

'For coming first in the "Acute" ward straw guessing competition I would like to give Janine her prize.'

Wayne walked over to my bed with all the toilet paper he had collected from around the room and dumped it right on top of me. I couldn't stop laughing as he proceeded to cover me completely with the paper ... fortunately it was unused!

It took some time for Wayne to clean up the ward and the great straw competition became a talking point for some time. We all laughed about it as we recalled the night to our parents and friends. It mightn't sound like much now, but it was just so good to be able to laugh. It rejuvenated the soul and made the depressing elements of life in the ward less prevalent, and it was something that no-one could take away from us.

One night while I was watching television, I started to get some pains in my chest. At first I paid little attention to them, but as they got progressively worse I thought I'd better tell someone. I called out to the nurse who was on duty, who happened to be Wayne. He came over and had a look at me and immediately called the night registrar.

In no time at all, the doctor arrived and began to examine me. To my surprise, it turned out to be very serious. I had the first symptoms of a pulmonary embolism, or a blood clot in the lungs. This was a major threat for any spinal victim and the staff were always on the lookout for any such development. I later learnt that six patients had recently died from pulmonary embolisms in the Acute ward alone. Those most at risk were people with multiple fractures—like me.

The doctor said he was going to put me on a heparin drip, which would thin the blood, and first thing in the morning I would be transferred to another hospital for further tests.

He then began to look for a vein in my arm to take the drip line. It proved to be more difficult than he anticipated. After five fruitless attempts my hand started throbbing, and I was getting quite frustrated. When I asked him what the problem was, he said the veins in my arms were traumatised from all the drips I had already had. He then began to get a bit worried himself, which did nothing to quell my anxiety, and left to fetch another doctor.

Wayne had seen the ordeal that I was going through and when the doctor had gone he told me to hang my arm over the side of the bed. This helped to pool the blood in the veins and when the other doctor finally arrived he found the spot straightaway. I was forever grateful to Wayne.

The first hint of daylight brought another doctor to my side, this time a woman, to take some more blood for laboratory testing. But when she looked at my arm she said that there was no way she could get any blood from it. Apparently the first doctor before her had made such a mess of it there was nowhere left to try. Since my right arm was still in plaster, the only other place to take blood from was my foot. It wasn't the most convenient place to have blood taken from, but she was far more gentle than the doctor the night before.

Then came yet another doctor, a small and cheerful man of Chinese descent who introduced himself as Allan. He filled me in on the details of the tests I would be having. They would be taking me to Prince of Wales hospital, which was nearby. Apparently Prince Henry didn't have the right facilities to do them.

By the time the orderlies came to get me, I was quite excited at the prospect of an outing for the day. In the ambulance I looked around trying to imagine what it would have been like the day of my accident, of which I still had no recollection. I was still wearing a neck brace and couldn't move my head, but I tried to see as far as possible. I asked the paramedic sitting in the back with me what it was like outside and he gave me a running description of the streets and suburbs we were passing through and what we were doing—turning left or right or stopping at traffic lights. It helped give me a sense of orientation.

When we arrived at the hospital I was wheeled to the X-ray department for a ventilation-perfusion scan (also called a radio-isotope lung scan). This involved putting a tube into my mouth through which I inhaled a radioactive gas to check air circulation and enable the doctors to see if all the areas of the lungs were functioning properly. Then a radioactive compound was injected into the drip in my arm which coursed through the bloodstream to ensure that blood was being circulated to all areas of the lungs.

The test seemed to take forever, but finally I was given the all-clear by the doctors. The ambulance men then came to take me back to Prince Henry. I felt a little nauseous after the tests, but they assured me that was normal. However, this little inconvenience was outweighed by the fact that I had been out for the day, and I really enjoyed the break from the ward routine.

Mum wasn't aware that I had been taken away for tests and when she arrived to find my bed empty, she immediately feared the worst. Before she had the chance to ask what had happened to me, she overheard a doctor talking to a nurse nearby.

'Where's Janine?' he asked.

'It's not good news,' the nurse replied. 'She's been taken to Prince of Wales—suspected pulmonary embolism.'

'Oh well, you win some, you lose some.' His tactless comment fell on the wrong ears.

Mum sat down, the words echoing in her mind. *You win some, you lose some.* She had heard about the danger of pulmonary embolisms, but this took her completely by surprise. She sat and waited anxiously for the rest of the day until I was returned safely to my bed.

It was some time later that Mum recalled this event to me, and it made me acutely aware of the pain and suffering that Mum and Dad and my family went through. Although they were not the patient, their suffering was as intense as mine.

Though my lungs were all right, they still had to clear me of the possibility of clots in the legs. This was done with a machine called a 'Doppler', usually operated by a technician known as the 'Doppler lady'. However, the 'Doppler lady' was on holidays at the time and wasn't expected back for another two days, so that meant I had to wait until then to be completely cleared. At last she arrived at my bedside with her machine in hand. First I had to have the 'TED' stockings removed, which wasn't easy as they were extremely tight and it was like trying to remove a layer of skin.

She then covered my legs with a jelly-like substance and ran a probe over them, which was about the size of a toilet roll. This probe was connected to a speaker through which the 'Doppler lady' listened. She told me she could hear the blood flowing through the veins. This was then calibrated with different readings from other parts of my legs. By doing this she could tell whether or not there were any clots present.

Fortunately there was no sign of any and I was given the all-clear, for the time being anyway. It seemed there was always something to worry about, and I had to be thankful for any blessing, no matter how small.

Chapter 8

SEVEN WEEKS AFTER my accident and three since my operation, I had the plaster cast removed from my right arm. It was now time for the physiotherapists to begin working on my arm and wrist to get some mobility back. I had naively believed that when the plaster came off I would be able to use the arm, but that wasn't the case. The plaster had reached from my fingertips to just below my shoulder, and consequently the entire arm had been completely immobile the entire time I had been in hospital.

At first it was as if my arm was glued in position, and it was very painful trying to move it. The physios explained that this was due to the fibrous tissue that had developed in the joints and that after a while it would break down and the pain would disappear. However, it would take at least another two weeks until I had full use of the arm again.

Once it was functioning properly, I wanted to build it up as much as possible. It had wasted quite a lot since the accident, and I wanted to prevent any further deterioration. I asked Mum to bring in some of my hand weights from home so that I could exercise it. The staff must have thought I was a bit of a fanatic when they saw me doing my 'sets' lying flat on my back in bed. I felt the strength come back quite quickly, which was a good sign and made me work even harder.

At the same time as my arm improved, I became concerned that my legs weren't as strong as they should have been. In fact, without the help of the physios I couldn't even lift my legs off the bed. I drew on all my reserves to try to move them, concentrating with all my might, but to no avail. The message just didn't reach them. They felt like lead weights.

Try as I might to remain positive, it was getting more and more difficult. I wondered if I had heard Dr Blum correctly when he had said the operation had been successful. I had taken this to mean that I would recover completely and that my life would return to normal. But things weren't looking promising. Shouldn't I be a lot stronger by now? Shouldn't my progress be quicker? I knew I would be very weak from all the time I had spent in bed rest, but this was quite different. It didn't seem like just a weakness in my legs, but as if I had no control over them. And what about the numbness and lack of sensation in my lower body? What did he really say? Did I just hear what I wanted to hear?

The doctors continued to do their rounds, checking to see if I had made any improvement. However, it was one particular doctor, the rehabilitation specialist, who was to be the bearer of bad news. She was a down-to-earth woman who believed, like most doctors, that it was wrong to give a patient false hope. She always painted the worst possible scenario, so that anything better would be a blessing.

In retrospect, I can understand such a clinically rational approach. Doctors have to avoid giving a misleading impression. But who is to say even then that this is the right attitude? For patients in a spinal ward, most of them victims of some horrific accident, to cling to hope of any sort, however slim, can't be that bad. Hope is their only defence against the onslaught of depression—Hope of recovery, hope that their lives may once again return to normal, hope that they will again be happy, and for me hope that I would walk and ski again. Once that is lost, the spirit is crushed.

It was during one of this specialist's visits that Dad thought to ask her if there was any doubt that I would be able to have children in the future. This hadn't even crossed my mind—I just wanted to walk! She said it was too early to tell at this stage. I had suffered extensive internal injuries and the situation would only be clarified when they had healed. I wasn't too concerned about this. I was only thinking about my legs.

One day when she was doing her rounds, the conversation took another turn.

'Janine, it might be a good idea to start thinking about what you will do with yourself when you return home,' she said matter-of-factly.

I didn't know what she was alluding to.

'You will have to make some changes to your life, you won't be able to do the things you did before,' she continued.

'What do you mean' I said. 'I intend to return to finish my course. I'm in my last year of my P.E. degree, I have to finish it off.'

She looked at me sympathetically, sensing the apprehension in my voice.

'Well, that might be a bit unrealistic. Your injuries are permanent, Janine, you will never be able to do the things you did before. Once we get you up, we're still not sure how well you will be able to walk. You may need to use a walking frame or wear callipers on your legs to help you.'

Callipers ... walking frame ... I couldn't believe what I was hearing.

'But what about my skiing?' I asked.

'Janine, it takes time to assess how much normal function

you will get back, but you will always have some level of neurological loss. You will have to make some adjustments to your life.'

I could only just see her, but her words were clear in my head.

'You may always need to rely on the use of a catheter in the future. We will have to wait and see.'

In just a few short minutes, my dreams were beginning to evaporate. Everything I had worked for had been taken away from me in an instant—my studies, my career, my sport, my body, my life, all of it gone. Why hadn't someone told me earlier? Had everyone been stringing me along all this time? Could I believe them any more?

I felt numb. I couldn't think, I couldn't speak, I didn't want to, anyway. Images and words flooded through my head. Words that had previously not been in my vocabulary. Callipers, walking frames, catheters ... other plans, permanent injuries, never be the same again. I wanted to run away. No, I wanted to fight, I wanted to prove them wrong ... But I couldn't even move.

From that day, I began to slip into a deep depression. It became a struggle to put on a brave face for my family and friends. I hid my doubts and anxieties from them—they had travelled so far to see me I didn't want to depress or worry them. Consequently, they all thought that things were a lot better than they really were. I would always tell them that I was progressing well, that it wouldn't be long before I would be out of hospital and home again.

But the strain started to take its toll on me. When my visitors had left for the day, I would slip back into depression, often crying myself to sleep. I missed them all so much, I missed my home, and the pain of watching them go was immense.

It was almost ten weeks since the accident and I was still

in Acute. I had seen both Natalie and Matthew get out of bed for the first time, and how excited they were about it. When Natalie first came over to my bed in her wheelchair, the first thing I noticed was the smile on her pretty face. I couldn't help but share in her happiness. But eventually Natalie and Matthew both left the hospital, then John was moved into the next ward, and I was left on my own.

I felt as if I wasn't making any progress. No-one gave me any indication of when I would be moved, when I would get out of bed, or when I would go home. The frustration of lying in bed and not being able to move began to build up inside me. *When will this all come to an end? I've had enough.* I had to get out of bed, I had to see if I could walk, I had to find out now, I couldn't wait any longer.

The nurse on duty that night was Dominic. Dom had become my good friend and we always chatted through the night. He knew this night was different, sensing that something was bothering me. He turned around to see that I was trying to move the sandbags from either side of my head.

'Janine, what are you doing?' he asked as he rushed over.

'I've had enough, Dom. I can't stand this any more. I can't stay still any longer, it's driving me crazy. I have to find out if I can walk, I have to know.'

'You can't do that, you know that. If you try to move you'll destroy all the work you've done. It'll all be wasted.'

'I don't care, I have to move, Dom,' I begged.

'Please, Janine, I know it's hard, but don't throw everything away now.'

He was right, I knew, but I didn't care. I felt trapped in my body and there was no way out.

'Dom, I don't know what to do. It's as if nothing matters any more. What can I do?' I started to cry.

'I know it must be terrible lying there like that, Janine,' he said. 'I really do. But you must keep trying. Now why don't you let me get some water and I'll wash your face and arms. That might make you feel a bit better, OK?'

There was nothing I could do. I lay in bed and just stared at the ceiling, exhausted from the whole ordeal. Dom was a kind and caring man, and he sat at my bed most of the night, washing my face and talking. He helped me through what was to be my worst night in Acute. For that I will always be grateful.

But my despondency refused to go away. I found it impossible to remain positive. There seemed to be no hope. The medical staff became concerned and one of my doctors came to discuss my problem. He prescribed some anti-depressant drugs and as a last resort I agreed to take them. They made me extremely tired, and I spent much of the next few days asleep.

Realising that the best medicine for me would be to have a goal to aim for, they decided to move me into the neighbouring ward as soon as possible. Dr Stephen, one of my orthopaedic surgeons, promised me that it would only be another two weeks until I was allowed out of bed. This was enough to lift my spirits and at last I felt I could see some light at the end of the tunnel. Now at least I had something to look forward to and I began to count the days.

Moving into the next ward, which was called 'South', was a great boost for me. I was finally getting a bit closer to going home. One of the first things the doctors did was to have my neck brace removed. The whole time I had been in hospital, my head had been held flat on the bed. Now I would be allowed to have a pillow. What a luxury, I thought!

They started me off with a very small pillow. Initially, I was reluctant to move my neck at all. It was so long since I had done so, it felt weak and fragile. What if it hadn't healed? I had to take it very slowly, moving it only very slightly, and it was extremely stiff. However, I was now able to do without my mirror, which had been so important for me but would no longer be needed. When the nurse came to take it away, I wondered who would be using it next, and hoped it would be as useful for them as it had been for me.

While I was still in Acute I heard about some of the patients in South ward. One of them was a young girl named Maria. She was only seventeen when she had a serious accident, and like most young people until then had been happy and carefree. When she left school, she took a job for a while at a McDonald's restaurant, aiming to start studying art at college the following year. Having been accepted for the course, she then took a well-deserved break.

The festive season was in full swing and a group of her fellow workers had organised a party shortly after New Year's Day to which Maria and her boyfriend were invited. One of their friends offered to drive everyone back to McDonald's to continue the party and they all piled into his panel van. There were ten of them all told and seven of them had to travel in the back, including Maria and her boyfriend.

They were going along in all good spirits, when the driver's door swung open as they went around a bend on the high side of a split road. He leant over to grab the door and suddenly lost control. The van swerved across and plunged down the embankment to the other lane below, where it landed upside down.

Maria was taken to Prince Henry along with some of the other survivors. Tragically, Maria's boyfriend wasn't amongst them. He was sixteen years old. Maria was in a coma for two weeks. She woke up on her eighteenth birthday to find herself a quadriplegic.

I thought about her a lot when I was in Acute, wondering what she looked like, what was going through her mind, how she was coping. It wasn't long before I found out because when I was moved to South, I was put in the bed next to hers.

The previous patient in my bed had been an elderly woman, and the staff thought it would be good for Maria to have someone around her own age next to her. Her bed looked as if she had been in hospital for years, surrounded by toys and covered by a brightly coloured doona her sister had brought her. On the floor beside it were fluffy slippers in the shape of a dog.

When I first saw her, Maria was sitting in a wheelchair beside her bed, strapped in by a large belt as she was unable to hold herself upright. She could move her head reasonably freely and one arm very slightly, but that was all. She was now able to speak, but it was still difficult to understand her.

As the days progressed, I picked up more and more of what she was saying and eventually I hardly missed a word. Her wheelchair was straight out of a science fiction movie with knobs and switches all over it. A long lever stretched up in front of her to around neck-level, which she activated with her chin to propel herself along. She could have done with a few lessons on road safety, as she was always crashing into something or someone—she was such a cheeky thing and I'm sure she did it on purpose most of the time!

On my left was a young Frenchman named Jean-Claude who was from Noumea and spoke no English. When the staff found out I could speak French they decided that it would be a good idea to put us together, in the hope that it would help Jean-Claude feel less isolated.

He was a good-looking young man, in his mid-twenties, who I guessed would have been quite tall before his accident.

He was still well-tanned and looked as if he would have been the outdoors type.

Back in Noumea, he had gone out for the night with a group of friends. They were driving home in a jeep when it overturned, throwing Jean-Claude out onto the road. He broke his back and became a paraplegic. Noumea was unable to offer the same standard of specialised care as Australia, so he was sent here for treatment, like a number of New Caledonians suffering from spinal and other such severe injuries.

One of the common problems we all faced was the threat of bed sores from being immobilised for so long. The constant pressure on the skin caused it to break out in blisters which would eventually ulcerate and become extremely painful. They were difficult to treat, but the best method was to place the patient on a water bed, which distributed the pressure evenly over the body and off the affected area and distributed it evenly over the body.

Jean-Claude had suffered very bad bed sores while in hospital in Noumea, which was another reason why he had been sent here, so that he could have them treated. He was so badly affected that the whole time I spent in South he was in a water bed. It was a long time before he graduated to a wheelchair, as his sores made it impossible for him to sit.

I had quite a soft spot for Jean-Claude. It was lonely enough being in a spinal unit, but to be in another country without any friends and unable to speak the language must have been frightening. I spoke to him in French, but he was very shy and didn't talk much. Apart from me, the only other person he spoke to was a French woman whom the hospital had evidently arranged to visit him every few days. When the staff needed to ask him something, they usually enlisted my help as interpreter.

Across the room from Maria, Jean-Claude and myself was

Little Athletics, aged 9 and 10.

Winning the Australian
championships at age 12 and
setting a record that still stands.

My first triathlon.

Relaxing with Daven after winning the NSW Triathlon Championships.

Packing up after a triathlon in Wollongong.

A university ski trip. From left: Daven, Bob, Erica, me and Quentin.

Olympic skier Dave Hislop gives me a split time in the Australian Cross Country Championships.

Europa Cup, Admont, 1986. Me with the Chinese ski team.

*The Australian cross country ski team at the Lowlanders
Championship in Norway.*

From left: Alan, Michael, me and Chris in Sun Valley, Idaho.

Packing up to go to another race. From left, Ben, me, Rod and Dave. The trophy on the bonnet is the one I won in the Dolimentenlauf.

Receiving my University Blue from the Honourable Justice Michael Kirby.

Four weeks before the accident at the Australian Institute of Sport Training Camp.

Just before the accident. Chillingly, the poster on the door reads, 'What Would You Like to be When You Grow Up? Alive!'

At home after the operation on my legs only weeks before the accident.

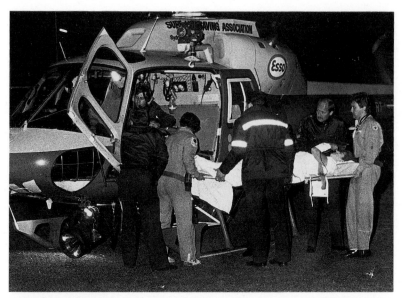

Being airlifted from Katoomba Base Hospital by the Westpac helicopter (photo John Falloon). I have no memory of any of this, but apparently I kept trying to remove the oxygen mask.

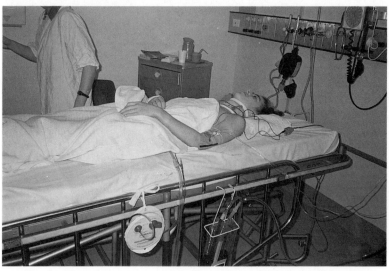

In the Intensive Care Unit after the operation. Note the drain in my left side.

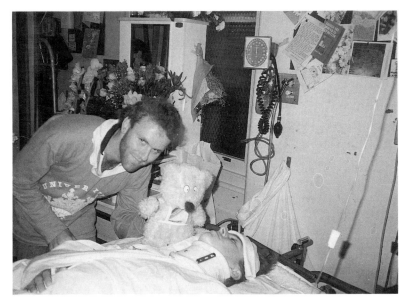

Four weeks after the accident with Stuart, a friend. I was to stay in this position for twelve weeks.

From left: Rod, Daven, Tim and Stuart keeping me amused.

Mum and Dad spent every day at the hospital.

Learning to walk in hospital. Crouching at the front is John, who was riding with me the day of the accident. On my right is Dom, one of the nurses.

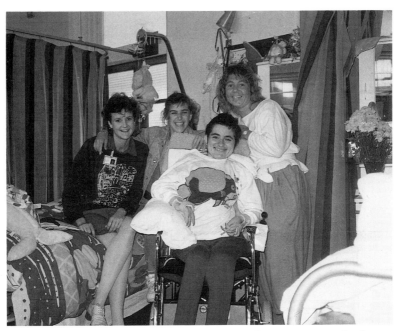

Sitting on Maria's bed. My bed is on the right. Maria is at the front.

At home in my first cast with my friend Pauline.

At home on the makeshift bed with Trish (front), Quentin and Marissa.

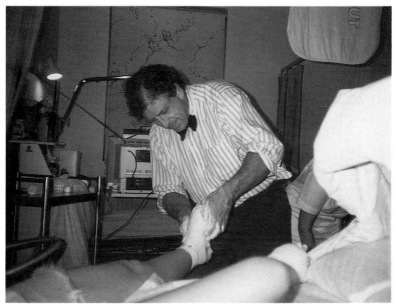

Dr Stephen putting plaster on Cecile's leg as I watch and wait for my turn.

With Dr Adrian Cohen (Ado) at the Richmond Air Show.

Friends for life! With Elizabeth, the woman who arrived at the accident scene and prevented me from being moved. If she hadn't intervened, I wouldn't be able to walk now.

a woman we referred to as 'the crazy lady'. This was probably a bit cruel, but it fitted her well, poor soul. Maria gave her the nickname the night she was brought into the ward. There was a lot of yelling and commotion which woke everyone up.

'Leave me alone, you bastards, leave me alone!' she was shouting. 'What do you think you are doing? Stop it! Help me, someone!'

'It's all right, Mrs Smith,' we heard the nurses trying to soothe her. 'We're here to help you. Just relax, everything will be OK.'

'Get away, you, you're trying to kill me. Where are the police? They'll arrest you all. Get your hands off me.'

This sounded interesting and the whole ward was riveted.

'Someone help me! Can you hear me, this man is trying to rape me!' she screamed at the top of her voice.

More staff arrived on the scene. There must have been at least five nurses around her, but that still wasn't enough to hold her down. She was a huge woman, and she was thrashing about in a frenzy.

'Mrs Smith, now please calm down, we're here to help you,' they repeated. 'Now we've got a needle here to give you that will help you feel a little calmer.'

'No, don't you dare touch me, you rapist! They're trying to drug me! Help ... help ... HELP!'

There was a lot more commotion before the nurses managed to jab her with a needle which eventually settled her down. We called one of the nurses over, to find out what on earth was going on. She told us the woman had slipped down some stairs at her house and broken her back, though fortunately only the vertebra with no damage to the spinal cord. Such patients were normally taken to the orthopaedic ward, but as there were no beds available there she had been brought to the spinal ward.

To compound things, she suffered from serious mental

problems which required daily medication. But she had been brought in without the medication and the staff didn't know what prescription she was on. Someone was contacting her next of kin to find her medical records so that they could give her the correct medication. In the meantime, she had to be watched closely.

After they settled the poor woman down for the night, all but one of the nurses left to return to their wards. For the moment, all was quiet, but not for long. I heard an unfamiliar noise and I strained my head to see Mrs Smith getting out of bed and making her way to the nurses' station. It would have been funny if it wasn't so pathetic. This huge woman was bent over and shuffling along at a snail's pace, dragging her catheter bottle behind her! I saw her trying to use the phone and thinking there might be some trouble rang my buzzer for the nurse. Unfortunately, it was a male nurse—or in Mrs Smith's demented mind a sex maniac in disguise.

'Mrs Smith, what do you think you are doing?' he said. 'Now you just get straight back to bed.' He must have grabbed her by the arm to lead her back, for she went completely hysterical.

'Stop!' she screamed. 'Get your hands off me you filthy man! Help! He's trying to rape me! I know what you want, but you won't succeed! Help, someone, help.'

There was quite a scuffle before more nurses arrived to restrain her and give her another needle. She had to be tied to the bed and even then kept calling for help until at last she lapsed into unconsciousness.

This was only the beginning. The uproar continued for three nights until they finally managed to contact her son. He brought her pills in, which thankfully put an end to her wild behaviour and the rest of us were able to get some sleep. Mrs Smith actually turned out to be quite a nice person, once she started taking her pills.

One of the positive features of being in a ward with so many other people was that you formed friendships in a very short time. I found myself mixing with people I would never otherwise have had the opportunity to meet. Most of my friends were either full-time athletes or at least heavily involved in sport. My life had revolved around training, and I didn't have much time for anything else.

One person I would never have met if it hadn't been for the accident was a young man named Michael. He was in his mid-twenties and was of Greek origin. He was a colourful character who brightened the ward and made everyone laugh.

Michael was an extremely keen football player and played at a very high level in the local Sydney competition. For all my love of sport, I wasn't much of a football fan. When I was young my father, who was coaching football at the time, used to drag me and my sisters to watch it every weekend. This was probably the best way of turning me off the game he could have thought of. Had Michael and I not been sharing a hospital ward, I'm sure our paths would never have crossed.

Of course Michael hit it off splendidly with Dad and the two of them became great football mates, listening to it on the radio, watching it on TV and talking about it all the time the way men do.

Actually, if it wasn't for football, Michael wouldn't have been in hospital. He had broken his neck in a tackle, but like Mrs Smith he escaped without any spinal damage.

He was allowed out of bed quite soon after the accident and was able to walk around, although he had to wear a brace on his neck. Someone had given him a pair of extremely brief pink underpants and he used to parade around the ward in them, which along with the brace made quite a sight!

He was very friendly and outgoing, and used to help out around the ward as much as possible, even to the extent of fetching a bedpan for a woman patient in urgent need when there was no nurse on hand and emptying it when she was finished. She was very relieved, in more ways than one.

As my health began to improve, my appetite gradually returned. I'd usually get through Mum's dinners by lunchtime, which meant that I had to fall back on the dreaded hospital food in the evening. One day Michael suggested we order a pizza from a restaurant he knew of nearby that made home deliveries. The restaurant didn't mind delivering to a hospital and Michael took the pizza around the ward, sharing it with anyone who wanted a piece. It made a great change from our standard fare.

John had been moved into South ward a few weeks before me, though at the other end from me, so that we had to raise our voices a bit to talk to each other across the beds. Next to him was a woman schoolteacher who was very quiet and kept mostly to herself. She found the experience very traumatic and had difficulty coming to terms with the consequences of the accident she had suffered. She wondered if she would ever be able to return to teaching, which was her whole life, and how the children would react to her if she did.

Next to her was a Turkish woman who spoke absolutely no English. She had been involved in some sort of altercation in her homeland and had been shot. The bullet had lodged in her spinal cord and she was a paraplegic. Like Jean-Claude, she was unable to receive the specialised treatment she needed and was brought out to Australia for her care.

Thanks again to Maria, the Turkish lady earned the nickname of the 'Moaner'. She used to moan and wail at the top of her voice all night, saying the one word of English she knew—'Help ... oh ... oh ... oh ... help.' There was little we could do to help her in her agony. It wasn't just the occasional wail, it went on and on and on, and no-one could get any sleep. Once she'd start for the night Maria would say, 'Oh no, here goes the moaner again.' We all felt sorry for her, but it was the most obnoxious sound! It even drove the staff crazy!

Then there was Ron. As the saying goes, they threw away the mould when they made him! Ron was a middle-aged man of small build, with a bald patch separating the hair on either side of his head. Like Michael, he had escaped spinal damage and was soon up and about. He used to walk around wearing a brace around his neck and striped shortie PJs and visit the patients for a bit of a gossip, never without some story of his own.

I had first heard about Ron when I was in Acute. Someone told me about this character who used to sit in bed drinking beer out of a straw! When I first met him he greeted me in his usual manner, 'G'day, sweetheart, how are ya today?' With a cigarette hanging out of his mouth, his PJs and thongs and his can of beer, he was quite a sight!

'Hi, Ron, how are you?' I said.

'Oh, I'm bloody great, love, having the time of my life, bit of a holiday really. But what about you, hey, had a bit of a rough trot they tell me.'

'Oh well, I'm OK. What about you though, you're up and about quite soon after your operation. Didn't they have you on a drip?'

'Listen, love, the only drip they're goin' to put me on is one with beer in it!' he exclaimed, taking another puff on his cigarette.

He was stopped in mid-draw by an irate nurse passing by.

'Put that cigarette out this moment, Ron,' she told him.

'Yeah, yeah, just about to stub it out anyway.' He stuffed the butt inside the beer can and made a quick retreat back to bed.

After Ron had been in hospital for some time, the doctors allowed him out on day leave as long as he didn't go too far away and came back at a reasonable hour. I think they were glad to get rid of him for a while, actually!

Ron and one of his female friends would go down to the bowling club in the hospital grounds. The patrons must have had a bit of a giggle as he used to go down in his PJs and thongs!

One day I got a phone call late in the afternoon. It was Ron.

'G'day, love, it's old Ron here. Listen, I was just wondering if you could do me a favour?' I suspected there might be trouble.

'I'm at the club and I thought I might stay out tonight. I was thinkin' maybe you could have a word to the doctor and see if it's all right, OK?'

'Well, Ron, I don't like your chances, maybe you should get yourself back here before they find out you're still out,' I said.

'Oh, I'll be all right, love, it's just that it's getting a bit late. Please, love, just have a word to the doc, OK?'

I did as he asked and I was right. The doctor on duty absolutely flipped. It was Allan, the Chinese. He grabbed the phone from me and spoke to Ron directly.

'Ron, you listen to me. You better get yourself back here quick smart, you hear me!' He hung up and just shook his head. That was Ron's last outing until he finally left hospital.

There we were, so many different people from such diverse backgrounds, yet for now we had so much in common, so much to share. It made me all the more aware that pain and suffering doesn't discriminate. It can, and does, happen to anyone.

Along with my 'new' friends in South, I was still surrounded by my 'old' friends. In fact, my visitors were my salvation. From the first days following my accident, they came to offer support and encouragement. Friends from skiing, friends from past sporting days, friends from university and college, friends from school, friends of the family, relatives, people I hadn't seen for years. Nothing kept them away.

One of those who came regularly was a family friend named Brian Hannan, better known as Hap. He was what I would call an honorary member of my family—the brother I never had. As soon as he heard what had happened to me, he was on the steps of ICU, comforting the rest of my family. He used to stop by every morning on his way to work with a bag of croissants for everyone and they would sit on the grass outside the ward, waiting for news of my condition. It was only after I had been in hospital for some time that I looked up one day to see Hap standing by my bed.

A little annoyed that he hadn't been to see me, I exclaimed, 'Hap, where have you been, why haven't you been here yet?'

Hap wasn't very amused. He must have thought I was joking, but I really had no memory of him being there before.

From what I've heard about my delirious ramblings, visiting me during my initial time in hospital must have been quite funny, although it might not have seemed so at the time. One day, my sister Kim was standing by my bed brushing my hair when I said, 'Kim, get your pen out and write this down. One cup of flour and water, cook the pastry, add the sultanas and nuts and don't forget the pepper. Please write it down, it is really important.'

Kim actually got it all down on paper which she later showed me when I was out of hospital. I couldn't believe the ridiculous things that I had said to everyone, but with the powerful drugs and a tortured mind, it's not such a surprise.

As I began to improve and the pain eased off, I became more concerned about my physical appearance. I had never been overly concerned about how I looked. I never wore make-up and always dressed in a casual manner, mainly in track pants, runners and shorts.

However, lying in a hospital bed, attached to a catheter bottle and various other devices, it was difficult to tell whether I was male or female. After a while I found that I very much wanted to look and feel like a woman. Mum used to brush my hair each day and put a ribbon in it—a small gesture but an important one.

Although the nurses would wash everyone's hair every now and then, they were far too busy to spend much time on any one patient. It was a very time-consuming task, as the bed had to be raised at the end so that the water would run off into a dish. Then plastic had to be carefully slid under the head so that the sheets didn't get wet. One of my regular visitors, Jo, was a nurse herself and I seized the chance to enlist her help.

'Could my friend Jo please wash my hair today?' I asked the nurse on duty. 'She's a nurse and she knows how to do it properly.'

'Sure, I'll just get you what you need.' She was pleased to be relieved of the job and moved on to the next patient. This was a real treat for me as Jo would not only spend a lot longer washing my hair but massage my head for ages as well, which I absolutely loved. It became a regular appointment for Jo every time she came. Fortunately, she was more than happy to oblige.

One of my other visitors, Sue, was a beautician, and she offered to give me a facial. What a treat! She got all her products and set about covering my face with a clay mask. In addition to the facial, she gave me a full make-over. This was pampering at its best!

Mum finished it off with a brush and a ribbon in my hair and I felt on top of the world. Sue left some make-up with me and a mirror, so that Mum would be able to do my face for me from now on.

By now I had lost so much weight, the bones were protruding from my teddy-bear gown, but the make-up and the ribbons made me feel as if I could still be attractive, despite the obvious deficiencies in my appearance.

If good things come out of every situation, the most valuable thing I got from my hospital stay was the support of my friends and family. They rallied around me with such strength and love it gave me a reason to fight on and something to want to go home for. They came at all times of the day—and night—often staying for hours. Sometimes so many turned up at once that some of them had to wait outside for their turn to see me.

Despite an overwhelming sense of fatigue, especially in the early days, never once did I wish they hadn't come. Although I knew I had to get as much rest as possible, it was far more important to have the emotional support of those I loved. My accident became a team effort. I wanted to get over it as much for my friends as for myself. It made me realise how special they were to me.

Chapter 9

DR STEPHEN, the orthopaedic surgeon assisted by Dr Blum
at my operation, visited me quite often immediately afterwards, but at that stage I was too disoriented to take in what
he said.

It was in South ward that he described the course of the
operation in detail. Both doctors worked as a team, and could
only decide what to do about my spine when they saw how
much damage there actually was. Once they reached the area
of the break, they were confronted by a vertebral column
which had been completely crushed. (I was later told that it
looked like a peanut that had been squashed to a pulp.) As
there was nothing left to attach to a rod or a plate, they
decided to use one of my broken ribs to fuse the back
together. The bone from the shattered vertebra was carefully
removed from the spinal cord and the rib was inserted to prop
the resulting gap apart. They then packed the space with the
rib and fragments of bone to form one large replacement
vertebra. The rest of the rib was then used to form a splint
on either side of the fusion to strengthen it.

To this day, the details of the operation never cease to amaze me!

Dr Stephen was a dapper and even rather eccentric man. Under his white coat he always wore a brightly coloured bow-tie and a smart shirt. I could tell from the outset that he was no run-of-the-mill doctor. He came at all hours, sometimes starting at the crack of dawn, and I often saw him wandering around the ward late at night. Both he and Dr Blum were dedicated and extremely hard-working, and I was fortunate to have had them on my side. As far as I was concerned, they were the best of the best.

Dr Stephen was an outdoors type who loved sailing and skiing, and we hit it off immediately. He would do his rounds of the ward, checking on his charges' progress, but when he got to my bed he would invariably stay for a chat.

'Well, Janine, how are we today?' he would begin. 'Have you heard there was a good snowfall this weekend? I think I might head down and take a look at it.'

'Oh thanks, rub it in,' I would joke. 'When are you going to let me out of here so I can go down too?'

One day he came with the best news I had had since I was first admitted. He would be letting me out of bed in a few days' time! But the first thing I had to do was to have a plaster body cast fitted to me which would support my back when I was upright.

I was taken to Prince of Wales hospital to have the cast fitted because Prince Henry didn't have the special bed required to fit the mould. I was collected by the orderlies who placed me on a Jordan frame, the normal device used to move spinal patients. It was formed by sliding hard plastic straps under the patient and connecting them to a special metal frame which was clasped into place and the patient was lifted onto a trolley. The frame was then disassembled until the patient needed to be lifted again.

This trip to Prince of Wales was a bit more enjoyable than the last one. I didn't have my neck brace on so I was able to look around and see where I was going. I was surprised at how modern Prince of Wales looked, compared with the shabbiness of Prince Henry. And whereas Prince Henry was a sprawling, scattered collection of hut-like blocks, the Wales was housed in one relatively new multi-storeyed building.

I was wheeled into an elevator which rose swiftly to one of the top floors. The other people in the lift looked at me for a moment and quickly turned away as if they were trying to avoid contact with me. I felt uncomfortable and self-conscious. Then the doors slid open and I was wheeled down a corridor to a smallish room full of the sort of materials and utensils you'd expect to find in an artist's studio. There were white sheets on the tables which were covered in something white, which I later concluded was dried-up plaster.

I was greeted by a man wearing, appropriately, a white coat.

'Hi, you must be Janine. Are we going to give you a wonderful new outfit today to take home with you,' he said in a friendly voice. I looked at his hands and noticed that they were covered in plaster.

'First we need to get you onto this bed so that we can work the plaster around you.' He pointed to a strange-looking bed in the middle of the room.

Using the Jordan frame, the orderlies lifted me onto the centre of the so-called bed. It was more like a horizontal crucifix made of steel, with plastic straps across it similar to those in the Jordan frame. I had difficulty keeping myself balanced on it while the man in white and the nurse assisting him went to work on me.

Before they could put the plaster on they had to place my body in a tube of stretch material, like a body stocking, to stop the plaster from sticking to my skin.

When the nurse began to put the stocking on she couldn't

believe how thin I was. I was like a skeleton, with bones sticking out everywhere. She said that she would have to pad me up quite a bit before the plaster went on, otherwise it would press on the bones causing pressure spots, not to mention a lot of pain.

The stocking was so tight it felt as if it was cutting off my circulation. However, that was nothing compared with what else was in store for me. It was now time to put the plaster on, which had to be done quickly so that it didn't dry before they had finished. It actually went over the plastic straps that were under me, which were then quickly slid out of the way. They ended up wrapping so much of the stuff around me from my collarbone to my hips I thought they were going to mummify me! It just went on and on. It was so tight when they finished I felt as though I'd never breathe properly again. My only thought was *what am I going to do when I put on weight?*

By the time I returned to Prince Henry I found that my bed had been replaced by a specially designed model that could be tilted from a horizontal to a vertical position and was used to prepare the patient for eventually getting out of bed for the first time.

Dr Stephen had instructed the staff that I was to remain in bed for another twenty-four hours to allow the plaster cast to set. I was so excited I couldn't believe it—After thirteen weeks of lying flat on my back, I was actually going to get out of bed. This whole thing would soon be over, and I would be going home!

That night I could hardly sleep. All I could think about was getting out of bed. By the time morning came I was jumping out of my skin. The head sister, whom we called Sam, walked into the ward and I almost knocked her over with my excitement.

'Hey Sam, did you hear I'll be getting up today?' I said elatedly.

'Yeah, I'd better tell the physios to watch out, it won't be long before you're down at rehab driving them crazy,' she laughed. She had a great sense of humour and was always joking, but I think she was serious this time.

'Yeah, I can't wait to get my hands on the weights and do a few sets.' It had already become a bit of a joke with the staff that the physios were dreading the day that I started rehabilitation. They thought I might go overboard with enthusiasm and break the machines!

However, my enthusiasm was short-lived. Later that morning I was visited by the registrar.

'Hi Greg, have you come to check on my plaster? I'm getting up today, you know,' I said, just to rub in the fact.

'Sorry, Janine, I've got some bad news.' He paused. 'Dr Stephen just rang to say he wants you to stay in bed for another day. He doesn't think that your plaster is strong enough yet to support your back.'

I couldn't believe it. He must have got it wrong.

'No, that's not right,' I protested. 'He said I would be able to get up today. He promised.'

'I'm really sorry, Janine, I know how much you've been looking forward to this, but Dr Stephen is the boss and he knows what's best for your back,' he said sympathetically, and left me to myself.

A moment later Mum walked in, looking as excited as I had a few minutes earlier.

'Hi sweetheart, all ready for the big day?' she said as she put her bag down beside my bed.

I couldn't hold my disappointment in any longer. I felt as if I was letting her down as well as myself.

'No, I ... I ... won't be ... getting up today,' I said, and started to cry. 'Dr Stephen said I have to stay in bed another day, to let the plaster set.'

Mum was naturally very upset for me. She knew how much

I had been looking forward to it. But she tried to put it into perspective.

'I know it doesn't seem fair, but I guess Dr Stephen is only doing what is best for you,' she said. 'It'll only be another day and then you'll be up, and you'll forget all about it.'

I knew she was right, but it was such a great disappointment. The past three months had made me emotionally vulnerable and it didn't take much to push me over the edge. Thirteen weeks seemed like nothing compared to the extra day I had to spend in bed. I felt as if everyone had let me down. I wondered if I was ever going to get out of hospital.

Mum left to talk to the nurse. I just wanted to forget all about this place. I closed my eyes and filled my mind with pleasant memories.

Five, four, three, two, one ... GO!

I blasted out of the timing gates and started to push along the straight. I could see the next competitor just ahead of me and knew that it was the Danish girl. I put my head down and continued to push, each pole digging into the snow to get maximum acceleration. Push, push, my thoughts clear in my head. My breath quickened as I began to narrow the gap between us.

Out of the corner of my eye I could just see the outline of the ski-jump that dominated the starting area enclosure. I put my head down again and saw the snow disappear beneath my skis. I was oblivious of the task that lay ahead of me—ten kilometres of snow-covered tracks that would test my endurance to the limit.

The race was the Lowlanders Championship for cross-country skiers from countries that didn't have year-round snow coverage or who lived more than three hours from permanent snow. Principally, this meant countries such as

France, Italy, Holland, Denmark, Britain, Spain and Australia, as well as southern Sweden. It excluded skiers from places like Norway and northern Sweden, who spent the entire year on the snow and consequently dominated the sport. It was held in Norway, at one of the most famous ski resorts in the world, the Holmenkollen.

We were starting to approach the hills, and pulled off to the side of the tracks to skate along the groomed snow. 'Track,' I called to the competitor ahead of me, knowing she would follow the rules and move over to let me pass. The track had narrowed as trees pressed in close on either side, making it even more difficult to pass.

'Come on, Janine! Push, push! You're looking good, you're ten seconds up on number seven—go!' I knew the voices. It was the boys from the team scattered along the track. Competitors set off at staggered starting times, so it was difficult to know how you were going in relation to other skiers. The boys took the times of my rivals at various points along the track and then relayed them to me so I could gauge how I was doing.

I was breathing heavily but still in control, well within my limits I thought. 'Track,' I called again and passed the skier in front and could see the next target ahead.

We continued to weave up through the trees, up the demanding hills. My shins began to ache. It became more and more painful. I'll have to pull out, I thought, I can't keep my feet up. Concentrate, Janine, concentrate, I told myself, glide.

I had anticipated that this might happen. Over the past three months I had developed a chronic case of compartment syndrome, a condition where shin muscles became overdeveloped. This meant that when blood was pumped to the legs, the muscle inflated and placed the sheath surrounding the muscle under extreme pressure. The associated pain was so great that it became impossible to hold your foot up and you experienced what is commonly called 'foot drop'. With a recent change in the rules of cross-country racing to allow the skating technique, many racers had been afflicted by this condition.

My condition had become so bad that the only solution was to have an operation on my legs when I returned home. One of the Canadian girls had already undergone the operation successfully, so I had no qualms about having the problem attended to. But this was the last race of the season and, despite the pain, I thought my legs would hold up for just one more competition.

I turned the corner to head for the most challenging hill on the course. The pain in my legs was getting worse and again I thought I would have to pull out. I began to exaggerate the skating motion as I tried to lift my legs higher to compensate for the foot drop.

'Nene ... go ... go!' It was Daven, running alongside the track.

'Dav, my legs have gone. I don't think I can finish. They're really hurting,' I gasped.

'Keep going, Nene, you're doing really well.' He looked at the stopwatch in his hand. 'I've got you down only five seconds behind the leader. That puts you in third place so far. You can do it. Hang in there, Nene!'

I couldn't speak any longer. The hill was starting to take its toll. I put my head down and focused on the task ahead. Just one step at a time, that was all I had to concentrate on for now. I knew that if I thought about the five kilometres that lay ahead I would throw the towel in. The pain was now excruciating and I found it hard to think of anything else. One step at a time, the next hill ... then I'll worry about the next one, I told myself.

It seemed to work and before I knew it I was turning the

corner for the straight. I had dropped off the pace, my time would be slow, but at least I had finished.

I double-poled up to the finish and over the line. My legs, or more precisely my shins, were utterly numb. I kept moving, because I knew that to stop would bring on cramp. Daven had skied back to the finishing line to meet me.

'I'm so proud of you, Nene,' he said. 'You did really well.'

'I didn't think I'd finish, Dav. I think my legs have gone. Looks like I'll be having the operation sooner than I thought.'

Daven helped me off the track. I took my skis off and tried to walk. It was impossible even to lift my feet. I limped over to the side of the track and sat down as the last of the racers were heading up the straight.

'Janine!' Chris came running over excitedly. 'I've got you down in third place and all the top skiers have finished. That's great, well done!' Chris had been taking the split times and writing them down to compare them.

'Third! You must be kidding!' I sat up and watched the last competitors pushing over the line.

He wasn't kidding. Much to my surprise, I had come third. Two French girls had beaten me but I had come in ahead of their third skier. It was a wonderful way to finish the season.

'Hey, Nino, how're you going?'

I opened my eyes to see my friend Tim standing at my bedside.

'Oh, hi, Tim.' I looked around wondering where Mum had gone. 'Where's Mum?'

'She just went down to the shop. She said to come straight in and see you.'

I looked at Tim and couldn't hide my feelings.

'I'm not feeling that good today, Tim. Did Mum tell you the news?'

'Yes, that you're not allowed to get up yet. I'm sorry, Nino. I know you've been looking forward to this for so long.' He pulled up a chair and sat down beside me.

'Tim, I feel so low, so depressed. I don't know what it will be like when I go home. I just can't see any end to this whole thing. All I want is to go home with you guys and have my life back. Is that so much to ask?'

At that moment I knew everything I had bottled up inside for so long was about to spill out all over the place. I put my hands to my face and tears started running down my cheeks. For so long I had hidden my true feelings, my doubts, my fears, from my friends. I wanted to be as positive and cheery as possible, I didn't want them to think that coming to see me was a drag. But I was sick of being brave. There was only so much that a person could take.

Tim sat and looked at me, not quite knowing what to say. After all, what could he say—that everything would be all right? And what if he was wrong? He took my hand and listened as I continued to pour out my pent-up feelings.

'Tim, I still can't work out why it had to happen to me. I'm trying to fit God into the picture. It's the only way I can make any sense out of it, but I still haven't come up with any answers.'

Tim listened and I talked. It was good to finally let someone in to share my pain and talk about these things that were now of such great importance to me. There was so much on my mind, so many questions.

I was obsessed by the thought that if the accident had occurred for no reason, there was no purpose to existence and no point in carrying on. However, if there was some plan, some meaning to it all, then maybe that would give me a reason to keep going.

Despite my efforts to fight back, inwardly I knew that I would be leaving the hospital a different person from the one who had been brought here so long ago, not only physically but emotionally. However, the road ahead was obviously a long one, and I wondered what I would do with myself once I did get home.

Something that had been weighing on me of late was a profound sense of guilt. I felt responsible for putting my parents through such an ordeal and making them suffer so much. I felt I was to blame.

I had recently received a letter from the driver of the car that hit me. I couldn't get it out of my mind. It was causing me a lot of heartache.

'Dear Miss Lee,' it had begun. (My middle name was Lee—he couldn't even get my name right!)

'I am the driver of the car with which your bike collided,' he wrote. (He had hit me from behind—how could I have possibly collided with him?) 'I have looked into the circumstances of the accident and fail to see that I was at any fault . . . ' Towards the end he added: 'But I'm sorry you were hurt and hope you get better soon.'

The fact was that when that young man ran into me on that warm May day so many months ago, he didn't think about the consequences it would have on my life. Or afterwards about my shattered dreams, my shattered body, left on the road where he had hit me. He had never come to see me, never even phoned to find out if I had lived or died—he just didn't care. His only thought was of saving his skin when he had to face court.

All I had wanted was for him to show some concern, to say he was sorry. Was that really too much to ask?

Chapter 10

IT WAS AN EARLY start for the ward the next day, but not early enough for me. I knew Dr Stephen wouldn't dare tell me I couldn't get out of bed and try to put it off again. If he did, I would keep on pestering him until he finally said yes.

'Good morning, Dom, today's the day, isn't it?' I said, knowing the answer all too well.

'Yep, you bet. We've come to raise the bed. It'll be a long day for you, might as well get started early.'

'How long will it take until I'm actually out of bed?' I asked.

'It depends on how well you adjust to being upright, but it usually takes most of the day.'

'You're joking. I wanted to be up before Dad gets here this morning.'

'Sorry, Janine, it'll take a bit longer than that.'

I couldn't see why it should take so long, so Dom went on to explain the reasons.

'Because you've been horizontal for so long, your body has adjusted to this position. If we just raised the bed in one go you would get dizzy and probably black out. Your body has to remember how to function as it did before and how to pump the blood back to your brain when you're upright. That's why we have to take it slowly.'

I was keen to get started and wasn't going to let anything dampen my spirits this day. Dom turned a lever on the side of my bed and I heard the noise of the motor as it strained to lift me.

'Wow, this is fantastic!' I couldn't help yelling out in my excitement. 'Hey, everyone, I'm getting up today and it's so great! I can see you all!'

'Good on you, Janine! Well done ... Yippeee!' came a chorus of responses from the rest of the ward at the sight of one of their friends finally getting up. But the bed had barely risen any distance when it stopped.

'Is this as far as you're going to lift me?' I cried out in frustration.

'Let's just take it one step at a time, eh?' Dom replied. 'I'll leave it here for an hour or so and see how you go. If you feel OK then I'll raise it a bit more.'

Oh well, I thought. I might as well enjoy the view while I can. It was the most I had seen of the ward for the whole time I had been there.

Dad arrived for the day while Mum caught up on a few things at home, and was happy to see that I was finally on my way.

A few hours passed and I was still feeling good. Time to go up a bit higher, I thought. I called out to the nurse who had replaced Dom.

'Hey, Fran, I'm feeling great, do you think you could move me up a little higher?' I pleaded.

'Are you sure you're OK?' she asked.

'I'm fine, really!'

'All right, I'll raise you a bit higher, but you tell me if you start to get dizzy, OK?' She turned the lever a bit more and the bed groaned as it pushed me a bit further towards the vertical.

I could feel the blood rushing to my feet and started to get a little light-headed, but there was no way I was going to let on. I didn't want to stop for anything.

By lunchtime I was actually feeling quite hungry. The thought of food was no longer repulsive as I started to imagine what it would be like to eat upright instead of flat on my back. Dad had brought me in some pasta that Mum had made so I tried my hand at eating in my new position. I felt so normal!

As the day continued I was steadily lifted higher and higher. At about forty-five degrees, the staff put a strap around my waist to make sure I didn't fall out. By late in the afternoon I was due to be lifted for the final time—to the vertical.

The nurse raised the lever for the last time and the bed lurched upwards, until it could go no further.

'Oh wow, this is great!' I exclaimed. I looked around and couldn't believe how different everything seemed. It was over three months since I had seen anything or anyone from a normal upright perspective. I could see John in the far corner of the room, and down the other end the doors leading into the Acute ward.

I kept trying to take in as much as possible. The staff were wandering around doing their duties and there I was strapped to my bed looking at them for once on an even level. The strange thing was that everyone seemed a lot fatter than I had imagined, but I didn't think they would appreciate me telling them that!

Not long after I had been raised, my feet began to ache. There was a wooden board along the bottom of the bed so that my feet had something to rest on, but the pressure on them was intense. The staff told me it was just a consequence of not being on my feet for such a long time and I would soon get used to it. Well, I had an answer for that. Mum had brought in some running shoes for me to wear when I was finally allowed up. I asked Dad to put them on my feet so that I had some cushioning under them. When he put them on, however, I couldn't actually feel them, as I still had no sensation in my feet.

Just as Dad had put my shoes on, Daven walked in. He knew that this was the big day, but he was totally unprepared for the scene that greeted him.

'Hey, Dav, look at me!' I shrieked as he approached. 'I'm up here.'

I must have looked quite a sight. I was wearing my teddy bear gown, my sandshoes and a ribbon in my hair, strapped to a bed towering over everyone around. Daven couldn't help laughing.

'Hey, Nene, that's great. How's the view up there?'

'How do you like my shoes, Dav?' I said, gesturing to my feet. 'I thought I would go and run a few kilometres once I was up—just getting warmed up.'

One of the doctors happened to walk past and he smiled and shook his head when he saw me.

'Hey, Allan, do you think I'll be up in time to do a few laps with Daven today?' I called.

He laughed. 'Oh sure, Janine, no problem, as long as you're back for dinner.'

A few more hours passed and I was still feeling well. Daven had ridden his bike in and had to start making tracks before the traffic got too bad. It was getting late by the time my friend Wayne came on duty to lower the bed so that they could get me up.

He brought the bed back to its original position and I began to get nervous at the prospect of what I had been waiting for actually occurring. Wayne explained what they were going to do.

'OK, this is what'll be happening. Two of us will lift you up by the arms until you're in the sitting position. Then we'll leave you there for a while so that you can get used to it, OK?'

'Yes.' I was listening intently.

'Once you're all right in the sitting position, we'll lift you to a standing position. But remember, it's been a long time since you've been upright, it will feel really strange. If you feel sick at all, make sure you tell us.'

'OK, I'm ready, let's do it!' I said, trying to hide my nervousness. Suddenly the mere thought of moving my body scared me. *What if the plaster doesn't hold up? What if they drop me and I fall on the floor?*

Wayne and Alison held me by the arms and lifted me slowly to the sitting position. Dad stood back and watched silently.

'OK, Janine, can you slide your legs around so they're hanging over the side of the bed?' Wayne asked.

'I'll try,' I said, as I clumsily attempted to comply. 'I think you'll have to give me a bit of a hand, Wayne, it's very difficult.'

Wayne helped me swing my legs over the side of the bed, and suddenly there I was—*sitting!* It was such a strange and foreign sensation.

'Can you try to sit upright?' Wayne asked.

'But I am sitting straight, aren't I?'

'No, you're leaning back at quite an angle. Just try to move forward slightly.'

I realised my senses must have been all out of kilter. I felt as if I was sitting completely vertically, but in fact I was leaning back considerably. If the two nurses holding me had let go I would have fallen straight back on the bed. They pulled me forward and I felt as if I was about to topple over the bed.

'Hold it, guys, that's too far. Now I'm going to fall forwards!' I said in alarm.

'No, it's all right, Janine, you're actually sitting straight now,' Wayne said. 'I know it feels a little strange but you'll soon adjust.'

I felt as if I was drunk and just about to keel over.

'You look great! How does it feel?' Dad asked as he looked on.

'Pretty strange,' I said. They held me in the sitting position for a while until I felt a bit more at ease. I looked down at my little legs. They seemed so frail and weak. I wondered how they were ever going to support me.

'How are you feeling, Janine? Do you want to try to stand up?' Wayne asked.

'I guess so,' I said tentatively. This is it, I thought.

Wayne and Alison took a firm hold of my arms and lifted me to my feet. I felt totally disoriented, as if I was standing on someone else's legs. I could feel intense pressure pushing up through my feet and my weight being supported by both nurses. Please don't drop me, I prayed silently.

We stood there for quite a while. I couldn't stop looking down at my feet. I wasn't quite sure what to do next.

'How are you feeling, now?' Alison inquired. 'Would you like to sit down in your chair for a while?'

'No, let's try a few steps, please.' I had to see if I could move my feet.

'OK, but let's take it slowly. Just try to move one leg first. Concentrate on lifting the foot and moving it forward.'

I looked down at my feet again. I couldn't remember how to move them. They didn't feel like they were part of my body. I was trying to move my foot but nothing was happening. And yet it should have been happening naturally.

'Wayne, this just isn't working,' I said. 'My legs won't move.'

'It's OK, Janine, it'll come, it just takes some time. Try again.'

I shut my eyes and tried to visualise how I used to walk. *Right, Janine, let's concentrate, I told myself. Lift the left leg and move it forward, away from the body. Focus!*

I looked down and saw that I had slid my left foot forward. It had actually moved! It was only a few centimetres but that didn't matter, I was walking! I waited a bit longer while I concentrated even more, then slid my right foot forward. Two steps! I looked at Dad and saw that he was beaming. He couldn't believe it either.

Two more small steps and I collapsed into the wheelchair that Dad had put behind me. It had been a long day, but well worth waiting for. I was exhausted and needed to rest. Four steps today ... I'll do even more tomorrow. I knew this was just the beginning.

Sitting in my chair, I didn't want to get back into bed. I wanted to go outside while it was still light, to see what it looked like outside the ward.

'Wayne, is it all right if Dad takes me outside to have a look around?' I asked.

'Well ... I guess it's OK, but not for long. It's been a long day and you don't want to overdo it. You'll start to get tired and probably a bit nauseous as well, so take it easy and make sure you don't go too far from the ward, OK?'

'Thanks, Wayne, we won't be long,' I said gratefully.

Dad put a blanket over my legs and pushed me out the door, out of the confines of the ward. Although it was now late afternoon, the sun was still strong enough to warm my body through. I could feel its warmth on my face and I looked up and absorbed its rays. It felt so good. I looked around me, taking in all I could. Everything felt so intense, so real, I wanted to reach out and touch everything around me.

The seasons had passed while I had been inside. Winter was almost over and there was a breath of early spring in the air, bringing the scents and sounds that I used to take so much for granted. I breathed in deeply, savouring the fragrance of the wattle in full bloom and the sight of flowers breaking out of bud. Birds were chirping happily in the trees, singing their message that the spring had arrived.

I felt as if the world had stopped and was suddenly now starting up again. It was these little things that I had missed—the sun, the birds, the flowers, the fresh air. I wanted to take in as much as I could.

Dad wheeled me further down the path. I was oblivious to the buildings around me as I let my face soak up the sunshine and enjoyed the simple beauties of nature around me. As we got further away from the ward, I saw the most fantastic sight I had seen in a long time. The hospital was situated on the coast, a prime piece of land, and Dad had pushed me down far enough for me to catch sight of the magnificent coastline below.

Tears ran down my cheeks as the past four months flashed through my mind. So much had changed, would it or could it ever be the same again? There was so much to work out, so many questions still to be answered. But now wasn't the time. I was tired and drained. Tomorrow would bring even more challenges. For today, at least, I had done enough.

Chapter 11

ONCE PATIENTS EMBARKED upon the road to recovery, their schedule revolved around rehabilitation and occupational therapy. This was to prepare them for the day they would eventually leave the hospital to face the outside world again. Depending on their level of disability, it was important for them to learn certain skills, so that they could lead independent lives once out of the hospital environment. It meant a total readjustment, not only physically but emotionally as well.

Physiotherapy and occupational therapy—or OT for short—were conducted every morning and afternoon, and you had to go to one session of both each day. I was allocated to the morning shift for physio, but was eventually excused from OT in the afternoon, which suited me as I wasn't really interested in it very much.

Going to the gym for rehab meant that I had to be dressed each day. I was able to say goodbye to my hospital gowns, which I wasn't exactly unhappy about. Mum had brought me in some tracksuits and loose clothes to wear, which had to be big to go over the plaster cast I was still encased in. Getting dressed was no easy matter, as the plaster made it almost impossible to move. I think it weighed more than I did!

The day after I first got out of bed I awoke nice and early in anticipation of going to the gym. I could hardly wait to get down there and on the program. I was determined to get my legs and feet working again as soon as possible.

A nurse came and dressed me in my tracksuit and gymshoes, and then another helped me get out of bed and into my wheelchair. After breakfast, Dr Stephen stopped by to see how I was going. He had a look at the plaster and said that it was OK to start rehab, but he didn't want me to spend too much time upright for a couple of days. He was still worried that my back wasn't stable enough.

After he left an orderly named Bob arrived to collect the patients going to the gym that morning. He wheeled me outside and left me sitting there while he went to get the others. Some of the regular rehab patients wheeled themselves out and joined me to wait while Bob brought the others outside.

'G'day, you joining us today?' one of them asked.

'Yes, what's it like down there?' I asked.

'It's not too bad, but they work you pretty hard.'

'Yes, that's what they told me inside, and I can't wait,' I laughed.

'Well, looks like we better get into the cattle truck,' he said, pointing to a large van nearby.

'That's our transport?' I asked.

'Sure is, they squeeze us in one by one,' he said with a laugh.

By this time Bob had returned with the last patient, making nine of us all told. He opened the back of the van and wheeled the first three in, putting them in a row in front, then came back to get the rest of us.

'OK, champ,' he said to me. 'Ready to go on board?'

'Sure, as ready as I'll ever be,' I answered.

He pushed me up the ramp into the van, then shunted the rest in beside and behind me and shut the doors. It really was like being packed in a cattle truck going off to slaughter!

Bob started up the engine and drove through the grounds to the rehab department, a low white building like all the rest whose only distinguishing feature was a sign saying 'Rehabilitation'. We then went through a similar procedure to be unloaded one by one and those who could manage it made their own way inside. Bob wheeled me up the ramp and down a long corridor with vinyl floors. Like the rest of the hospital, the place could do with a coat of paint, I thought. At the end of the corridor Bob pushed my chair through a large set of glass doors into the gym.

'OK, Janine,' he said. 'Enjoy your first day. I'll be back in a few hours to pick you up. Be good.'

I looked around and was impressed by what I saw. This was what I'd been waiting for, real gym equipment. There were all sorts of machines and contraptions to put life back into our wasted muscles and limbs. Most of the equipment looked run-down and due to be replaced, but as long as it did its purpose, I didn't mind.

I was greeted by Stephanie, one of the physios whom I already knew from the ward. 'Hi Janine,' she said cheerily. 'We've been waiting for you. I hope you're ready for some hard work?'

'The harder the better,' I laughed.

She started off by wheeling me around the gym, showing me over the equipment and what it was used for. There were two sets of horizontal bars along the walls, as in a ballet studio, except that these ones were to teach people how to walk, not dance. A few people were already working out on them, pulling themselves slowly along them. Stephanie wheeled me over and positioned my chair between two of the bars.

'OK, Janine, what we're going to concentrate on today is getting you standing up all by yourself, so that you can support your own weight,' she said, taking my hands and helping me to the standing position.

'Good, now I want you to grip the bars so that you are holding yourself up.' I did as I was told. It took quite a lot of effort in the upper body to stay upright, as my legs were unable to support me. All the strength had to come from my arms.

We practised this a few times until I was able to get myself up on my feet, with my wheelchair right behind me. While I was standing, feeling very pleased with myself, I happened to look around and for a moment I was shocked by what I saw. On the wall at the end of the bars was a large mirror, in which the patients could watch themselves walking, as a sort of learning aid. It was the first time since the accident that I had actually seen myself in full view, and I was amazed at the figure staring back at me. I hardly recognised myself.

My once muscular body had been reduced to a bag of bones. The clothes I was wearing hung on me like a sack. My legs were like little pegs, weak and thin. I looked terrible. I knew I had lost weight, but this was unbelievable. I could only stare at the strange person who was supposed to be me.

'It's a bit of a shock, seeing yourself for the first time, isn't it?' Stephanie said.

'Yes, I can't believe it's me,' I said sadly. 'I must have lost so much weight—and muscle.'

'Don't worry, now that you're up you'll start putting on weight quite quickly,' she said reassuringly. 'And the muscle will come back after you've been working out here for a while.'

At that moment Mum walked through the door, having been sent down to the gym to find me by the nurses in the ward. She had missed seeing me get out of bed the day before, and this was the first time she had seen me on my own feet in almost four months.

Our eyes met and I could see the tears slowly falling down her cheeks. I could also feel tears welling in my eyes. I knew what must have been going through her mind—that she would never see this day. I had the same thought.

As she came closer, the smile on her face broadened.

'Hi, Mum,' I said as she stood beside me. 'How do I look?'

She leant over and kissed me on the cheek. 'You look fantastic!'

Seeing Mum face to face, looking straight into her face, was a wonderful sensation. She had only missed one visit to the hospital the whole time I had been there. She and Dad had given me more support and love than I could ever have wished for. I couldn't have done it without them. This was for both of them, for all they had done for me. Just to see the smile on Mum's face made it all seem worth the effort.

'OK, Janine,' said Stephanie. 'Now I want you to try to move your foot forward while you're holding onto the bars. I'll walk behind you with the wheelchair so that when you want to sit down it will be right here.'

I looked down at my feet and concentrated. Calling on all my strength, I managed to move one of my legs forward a fraction.

'Janine, you're looking at your feet,' Stephanie said sharply. 'I want you to try to look up at the mirror when you walk. OK?'

'OK, it's hard, though. I feel I need to look down at them to see where they're going.'

'I know, but that's what the mirror is for. See if you can do that.'

I looked up at the mirror and tried again. It was difficult and took a lot of concentration. I could see my feet flopping around—I had no control over them. I couldn't believe that something that I had always taken for granted could be so hard. I collapsed into my chair. My legs were tired and my arms were aching from holding me up.

As a result of losing what is termed proprioception, I had no control over my feet. This is a sense in which the mind knows exactly where a certain part of the body—in this case the feet—is in relation to the rest of the body. That's how we can walk without looking at our feet—we just know instinctively where they are. But I had no idea where they were and had to look down to know where to put them.

Stephanie stayed with me for most of the morning while I practised my walking and then we all stopped for a well-earned tea break. There were many patients in the gym I didn't know, some of them from North ward which was the one next to ours. This was mainly for patients who had been in the hospital for over six months or who were being treated for some complaint they had acquired after being discharged previously, like bed sores or urinary tract infections.

Most of the patients in the gym were from other areas of the hospital than the spinal unit. There were several amputees and a few people suffering from brain injuries. I shared the bars with some of the amputees, who had to learn how to walk and balance with crutches. As well as bar work, many patients would spend their time doing body exercises on a floormat or catching a large medicine ball the physios tossed to them.

Within a few days I had John for company. He too had finally got himself a plaster casing and made the great leap out of bed. We would spend hours on the bars practising walking and standing or trying to catch the medicine ball without falling over. Considering our lack of balance and the slabs of plaster we were carrying, it was a difficult task.

We would also do various other exercises on the weight machines and similar routines. On one occasion Stephanie made us stand against a rail on the far wall to exercise our calf muscles by trying to stand on our toes. It should have been easy, I thought, but try as I might, I couldn't generate even a flicker of movement. How could I not even stand on my toes? I tried again, but still nothing happened.

'Why can't I move?' I asked helplessly.

'We weren't sure if you would be able to do this, Janine,' Stephanie replied. 'You've lost a lot of strength, but you've also suffered a lot of nerve damage. There may be some muscles that never regain their normal function. We'll just have to keep working on it and see how much we can get back.'

I dismissed out of hand the idea of never regaining the use of my leg muscles. I was still convinced that eventually I would be walking normally, and even able to take up skiing again, no matter what anyone said to the contrary. Now that I was on my feet, I felt in control. No-one was going to tell me what I could or couldn't do. Sure, I had a lot of work ahead of me. Learning to walk again would be quite a challenge, but it was just a matter of trying and the results would follow. I would not only walk, I would run and ski and do all the things that I had done before. I wouldn't stop until I could.

Each day in rehab was filled with a new challenge, to do a little better than the day before. The van came every morning to shuttle us down to the gym. We went through each of the activities and I didn't stop until I was exhausted. After a break for morning tea we went back to work until it was time to return to the ward for lunch. Mum would come down to the gym each morning and watch me go through my paces. Sometimes, instead of coming back to the ward with us in the van, she would push me up the hill in my wheelchair.

Not long after I started in rehab, I learnt they had exercise bikes there. Somewhat to my own and everyone else's surprise, I found I could manage them quite effectively and move the pedals around by myself. This gave me a great sense of achievement and it was great fun as well. It became my favourite activity, and from then on I spent a lot of time on the bike.

One day I noticed a man on the bike next to me I hadn't seen before.

'Hi,' I said, trying to strike up a conversation. 'You're going well.' He was a good-looking man, probably in his late twenties to early thirties. I was surprised that he was pedalling so fast and there didn't seem to be anything wrong with him. I wondered why he was in the gym.

'Hello, y-yes, this is my favourite. My name is Paul,' he said with a slur.

'I'm Janine,' I replied, and we continued our chat.

I soon learnt Paul's story from one of the physiotherapists. He was a diver with the water police. One day he had to dive to recover a weapon of some sort when his equipment failed. He was stranded underwater without oxygen for a considerable period and suffered serious brain damage, which left him with a severe speech impairment and extensive memory loss.

He had a beautiful wife and two gorgeous little children. They would visit him each day and watch him do his exercises, but when they returned next day he couldn't remember that they had been to see him. In fact, he hardly had any recollection of his family at all. It was terribly sad to see his wife sitting patiently with their children as he went through his routine.

Each day I went to the gym I worked on the bike next to Paul. Each time I had to reintroduce myself, as he never remembered my name or having met me before. Then suddenly he stopped coming to the gym, I think because he went somewhere else for more rehabilitation. I missed him and hoped that things improved for him and his family.

I liked all the staff down in the gym. Stephanie had a colleague who was also named Stephanie. This became a bit confusing at times, so one became Steph and the other Stephanie. Steph was darker in complexion than her namesake, a little more solidly built and much more extroverted. There were also two male physios named Craig and Tim whom I had already got to know when doing 'passive' movements in the ward. In fact, I already knew most of the staff.

I also got to know a lot of the other patients from the other wards, some of whom I remembered more than others, especially a young man we called RJ.

RJ had been involved in a motor accident. When it first happened he was completely paralysed and the doctors believed that he had little hope of recovering. He surprised them all by gradually regaining the use of his hands and his legs. He was now walking with the help of a walking frame. He would spend most of his time in the gym, walking along the bars like the rest of us but keeping mostly to himself. He had incredible determination and I greatly admired his spirit.

He had been in hospital months longer than I had and was a regular in the gym. He would wheel himself there each day and back again. To get back to his ward he had to push up a very steep hill and as a result his upper arms were extremely well-developed and very strong. He had his hands wrapped in plaster to protect them from blisters that had already formed on his skin.

The weeks passed and I continued with my exercises in the

gym. Most of the time I managed either to spend two sessions in the gym or I would practise walking with Dad in the hall outside the ward. I had improved to the point where I could now walk with the support of another person. I still needed something or someone to give myself purchase, otherwise I would have ended up flat on my face.

When I say walk, it wasn't the conventional gait of one foot following the other, it was more like a shuffle. I had to take one step forward with one foot, then bring the other foot up to meet it. I was amazed that my skinny legs even carried me, with my feet flopping all over the place. It was a tedious process but it worked, nevertheless.

Once I had got to this stage with my rehab, the physios put me to work on a set of dummy stairs outside the gym. I thought walking along the bars was difficult, but that was nothing compared with climbing stairs!

Up to this point I had managed to cope with moving my legs forward, but to move them upwards was another thing altogether. I just didn't have the strength in my legs to lift myself up and it took some time for me to manage even one stair, and even then I had to use most of my upper body to do so. I couldn't believe how much I had taken for granted before this accident. Now even the smallest tasks became huge obstacles which had to be confronted daily.

I wanted to improve my walking as quickly as possible. I still needed support when I walked and when there was no-one around I was stuck. I soon discovered that I could get the support I needed by pushing my wheelchair instead of sitting in it.

'Hey, Janine, you're meant to sit IN the chair, you know,' the nurses would say.

'I know, but if I sit in it, how am I ever going to learn how to walk?' From then on I was rarely ever in my chair. I was always pushing it empty around the ward.

Daven started to bring his rollerskis to the hospital with him. These resembled cut-off metal skis with wheels attached underneath that could be used on asphalt or similar surfaces to train when there was no snow available. Daven used to ski around the car park and I would sit in my chair and watch him.

One day, when Daven was rollerskiing, I wheeled myself outside with Dad to watch him. Mum stayed inside and watched out the window.

'Hey, Mr Shep, how about a race?' Daven said as he whizzed past.

'Oh yeah, come on, Dad, let's go,' I said.

With that Dad started pushing my wheelchair and it didn't take us long till we were fast on Dav's heels.

'Ha, think you're pretty fast, catch us if you can,' I yelled as we overtook Daven on a corner. My chair went up on one wheel and I had to lean the other way to stop it overbalancing.

This was the most fun I had had for ages. Dad was having a ball too. But when Mum caught a glimpse of what we were doing through the ward window, she couldn't believe it, and came running out, yelling.

'What do you think you're doing? You stop that right now!' she shouted at Dad. We slowed down, feeling a bit guilty at giving her such a fright. But I caught Dad's eye and saw that he had enjoyed it as much as I had.

Then I noticed my little car sitting in the car park. I had lent it to Daven to use while I was in hospital as he didn't have one of his own. After all, I didn't have much use for it for the moment. I got Dad to wheel me over to it.

I got close enough to see inside the back and there were my things just as I had left them—rollerskis, tracksuits, running shoes, still as messy as ever. I wondered how long it would be till I would be able to use them again.

It was getting late and Daven had to get home. Dad left us

together and went back inside the ward. It was the first time we had been alone in such a long time. It was impossible to have any time in privacy when you are sharing a ward with so many other people. Our relationship had taken a back seat while I was in hospital, but soon I would be getting home, I thought, and what then?

Daven kissed me goodbye and I watched as he drove my little car out of the hospital gates. My heart went with him. I wanted so much to jump in the car and go home with him, but I couldn't. I turned my wheelchair around and headed back inside the ward with Mum and Dad.

Sam dropped in one morning to say that one of the local television stations wanted to come and do a story on my accident for the evening news in a few days' time. I agreed to do it the following day in the hospital grounds. They wanted to talk to me and then get a few shots of me walking.

The film crew duly arrived the next day and we went outside to choose a scenic spot to get the shots they wanted. The reporter started the interview while I was sitting in my wheelchair:

'Janine Shepherd, Australia's top female cross-country skier, was tragically knocked down while on her bicycle in the Blue Mountains in May this year. She broke her neck and back in seven places, she broke her arm, five ribs, she suffered head injuries, internal injuries, the list goes on. Her hopes to represent Australia at the 1988 Winter Olympics were shattered. However, her courage and determination have helped her in her bid to get back on her feet ... Janine, can you tell us what happened the day of your accident ...'

After going through the details of the accident, he asked me what my hopes were in regard to my skiing career. I answered almost offhandedly.

'Oh no, I'll ski again, I'm sure I'll ski again, I have no doubts about that. It's just a matter of how well I will ski.'

'What would you do if you couldn't ski again?' he asked.

'Oh well, I'd do something else. I'd swim I guess,' I joked. *Of course I will ski again, it will just take some time, but I'll do it.*

The interview finished with me walking or rather limping along, with the reporter holding me up. The poor man, I think it exhausted him! They finished off the story with the words: 'Janine now hobbles along like her own grandmother, unable to walk unless she is supported ... but she wins a gold medal for her courage.'

I watched the story on the news a night or two later, along with the rest of the ward. It was the first time that I had actually seen myself walking from another person's perspective, and it looked very strange. It made me even more determined to get back on my feet and back into training as soon as possible. I didn't care how hard I had to work, or what it would take, I just knew I had to keep pushing my body even further.

Chapter 12

DR STEPHEN'S REGISTRAR dropped by one morning to check up on the patients on their list. Mum and Stephanie were standing at my bed, when they spotted him at the nurses' station.

Mum couldn't help noticing him, 'Wow, Janine, you should see your doctor, he's very good-looking,' she said.

Stephanie took one look at him and turned to me. 'I think I might hang around for a while, just in case he needs a hand,' she said cheekily.

He walked over and introduced himself. 'Good morning, Janine. My name is Adrian Cohen. I'm Dr Stephen's registrar.'

'Good morning, Dr Cohen,' I said. I could see Mum and Stephanie standing behind him with big smiles on their faces.

'Oh, please call me Adrian,' he said. 'I've just come by to make sure everything is OK. How is the cast going?'

Mum was right. He was handsome! He was tall and solidly built with dark hair, and very snappily dressed in smart pants and shirt, finished off with a thin black leather tie. He must have been taking lessons from Dr Stephen, I thought.

'Well, actually my cast is starting to hurt my back,' I said. 'There's a bone pushing against it'.

'Let me have a look.' He pressed the plaster until I let out a yelp. 'Is that where it hurts?'

'Yes, it's getting very uncomfortable. Can you do anything about it?'

He examined the plaster a bit more closely.

'What I can do is drill a little hole in the cast, like a window, so that the bone doesn't press on the plaster. I'll have a word to the boss and we should be able to do it tomorrow. OK?'

'That'd be great. What time will you be here?' I asked.

'In the morning. If you have any more trouble before then, just get one of the nurses to give me a call and I'll come up and see you.'

What a bonus, I thought, as he moved on to his next patient. My own doctor on call!

Next morning he returned with his drill and told me to sit up so that he could find a good place to make a hole, then turned on the drill and started to press on the plaster. I could feel the pressure on the cast, hoping he'd stop before he went right through.

'That should do it,' he said, holding up the piece of plaster he had removed. 'Does that feel better?'

I moved around a bit, but I could still feel the bones pressing on the plaster.

'Could you take away a little more?' I asked.

'I can't take away too much, Janine, or you won't have any cast left.'

That didn't sound like such a bad idea. 'Just a little bit, please ...'

'All right, I'll take a bit more off, but that's it. OK?'

He drilled away again until I had a large hole in the middle of my back. This exposed the bones protruding from the operation. They were quite large and, being so thin, it actually made the situation worse

I had no idea at this stage that I would be seeing a lot more of Adrian in the future.

Despite my obvious disabilities, I was actually feeling quite well. My appetite was returning and I was starting to enjoy my food much more.

While I was bedridden, Dad used to bring me in a regular supply of strawberries that he'd buy at Dural on his way in and often I'd eat a whole punnet in one go. Maria also liked them and Dad used to bring in extra punnets for her. For some reason I started to crave all sorts of food, not all of it of the most healthy variety. I took a liking to the pies they sold at the hospital shop. Dad used to buy me one each day and I'd swamp it with tomato sauce. The problem was, however, that though I had the desire to eat enormous quantities, my stomach had shrunk so much I could hardly fit anything in.

As my health improved so did my desire to go home. I felt there was no longer anything they could do at the hospital that I couldn't do for myself, and besides I was terribly homesick.

On top of this, at the time of my accident Mum and Dad were in the process of moving house. They had been renting a townhouse while they built their dream home. This was a big enough headache without having to worry about a daughter in hospital. To fill me in on how things were going, Daven went over to the house one day with a video camera and filmed the builders at work. With Dad's help he gave a running commentary as he went through the unfinished house, explaining where everything was.

'This is where your bedroom will be, Nene, and if you walk

through the door here you'll notice we're now standing in the bathroom,' he narrated, following Dad outside to give me a guided tour of the garden. It was fun seeing what my new house would look like. It was a single-storey place, which would make it a lot easier for me to get around.

The video made me even more determined to go home. I started pestering Dr Stephen and my rehab doctor to let me go. They finally agreed, but only on certain strict conditions. I had to continue with my rehab at a hospital close to my home, for instance. But before they let me be discharged permanently, I would only be allowed home for weekends until they were sure that everything was under control. If that went smoothly for a few weekends then I would be permitted to go home for good. I didn't really care—the thought of going home for just one day was exciting enough. I felt as if I had been in hospital forever.

Sam came along one afternoon when Mum was there to discuss the details of my first visit home.

'Janine, I just want you to know that things will be pretty hard for you at first,' she said.

'What do you mean, Sam?'

'We usually find that people have trouble adjusting to the change of routine. In hospital, they've been like everyone else, but at home, they're the odd ones out. That can be very upsetting.'

'Not me, Sam. I can't wait to get home.'

'That's fine, but you'll probably find it a bit of a shock to the system. A lot of our patients feel sheltered in here and put off going home as long as possible. I'm just warning you, Janine, it may be difficult at times.'

'Thanks, Sam, but I know I'll be all right,' I said.

I knew that she was only trying to prepare me for what lay ahead but I found it hard to believe that anyone would actually want to stay in hospital any longer than necessary. I listened to what she had to say, but it didn't change my mind. I was ready to go home to be back in my own room with my own belongings, and pick up where I had left off. I had a lot of time to make up for.

All the necessary arrangements were made and I was to leave hospital on a Friday afternoon and return on Sunday afternoon. The doctors had briefed Mum and Dad on any problems that I might have and they insisted that I take my wheelchair home with me. Mum stayed home that day and Dad was to pick me up in the late afternoon. The nurses packed whatever I would need—clothes, medications and other articles—and I waited impatiently for Dad to arrive.

Sam was there to help us and she arranged for Dad to bring his car around to the front of the ward to make it easier for me. Before I left I went around the ward saying goodbye to all of my friends. I was only going for two days but it seemed like a month to me.

I wheeled myself outside while Dad packed my bags into the back of the car. Now came the problem of how to load me into the car. I wanted to sit in the front seat, but when I looked at it I wondered how I would fit into such a tight space. However, it wasn't as hard as I thought. Dad helped me to my feet, lifted me in his arms and carefully placed me inside. It took a bit of trouble to find a comfortable sitting position, what with the plaster cast going from my chin to my hips, but I wiggled around till I got myself settled and after waving goodbye to Sam and the other nurses we set off.

As we drove out the gates, my excitement gave way to apprehension. My little isolated world now left behind me, I remembered what Sam had said. Maybe she was right, maybe I wasn't ready to go home. I was about to tackle the real world, and it was an unnerving prospect.

I looked around taking in the unfamiliar surroundings. I had never been through this part of Sydney before. By now, of course, Mum and Dad knew it like the backs of their hands. Dad gave me a running commentary on the way.

'See over there, that's where the pizzas you ordered came from,' he remarked. I looked at the sign of the pizzeria and their home delivery service and wondered if they would be making a trip to the hospital tonight.

It was peak hour and as we approached the city the streets were full of people scurrying home from work. They all looked so wrapped up in their own little worlds. I wondered how many of them knew of the other world that existed inside the walls of the hospital. Just like me before my accident, I was sure it was the furthest thing from their minds.

I watched them running across the road, analysing their every step. It looked so simple for them, the way they lifted their feet without the slightest effort. I remembered when I too could do that. I knew they never even considered how difficult it really was.

Halfway home I saw a McDonald's sign ahead.

'Oh, Dad, can we stop? I've been dreaming of McDonald's for ages!' I pleaded. All the skiers in the team had extremely large appetites, me included, and it was quite common for us to have a Mac Attack whenever we passed a McDonald's.

Dad could hardly refuse and we pulled in for my usual order, hamburger, fries, thickshake, and sundae. However, my eyes were larger than my stomach and after one bite of the hamburger and a few fries I was forced to dump the rest of my long-awaited treat in the bin.

We set off again and my back began to get very sore. The trip was getting the better of me and I was feeling tired and uncomfortable. I had never really noticed before how rough the roads were, but now each bump seemed to go right through my spine.

Dad stopped at a park and helped me out of the car so that I could stretch my legs. It was situated on the harbour looking back over the city. Cars zoomed past and the water was dotted with pleasure craft out for an early evening's sailing. I thought of the hospital I had just left, my empty bed waiting for my return and my fellow patients. I looked at my watch. Dinnertime at hospital. I knew what everyone would be doing.

When I was feeling up to it again, we got back in the car for the last leg of the journey.

'Well, this is it!' Dad said, as we pulled into the driveway of our new home.

'Oh, it's beautiful, just like in the video,' I said.

No sooner had Dad stopped the engine than Mum had come out to meet us.

'Welcome home,' she said as she gave me a kiss. 'How was the trip?'

'Well, it was a bit tiring,' I said. 'I didn't realise it was such a long way!' It had taken well over an hour and I was looking forward to getting out of the car.

'Let's get inside. We'll get you settled and then have dinner.'

Dad helped me out of the car and slipped his arm around my waist and I slowly made my way to the front door. Even though I had never been to this house before, it was just wonderful to be home with my family.

I was tired but far too excited to miss out on the opportunity of looking around. Dad brought my wheelchair inside and I was thankful there were no stairs.

'Can I see my bedroom first?' I asked. I wanted to see my belongings and the other things I had missed while I had been in hospital.

'OK, first stop, Janine's bedroom,' Dad said like a tour guide, pushing my wheelchair up the hallway.

It was beautiful. Mum had put all of my things away just

as I would have. There was a full-length mirror on the wall and it felt strange seeing myself in it sitting in a wheelchair in my own room. Behind me was my cabinet that Mum had set up with all my trophies.

Mum opened the wardrobe and I looked at the clothes she had hung up for me. I picked up a tracksuit neatly folded on a clothes basket. It had the words 'Australian ski team' embroidered on the front. With Mum's help I put it on and looked at myself in the mirror. I realised how much I had missed my room, my things, my clothes. I had always craved my own space, and loved being alone in my room. *I belong here*, I thought, *I never want to go back to the hospital*.

Dad wheeled me into the kitchen, to be met by the rich smell of a baked chicken dinner with all of my favourite vegetables which Mum had cooked for my homecoming. Dad pushed my chair up to the table and we sat around it for our first dinner as a family for such a long time.

Dad was not normally one to say grace before dinner, but on this occasion there was a lot to be thankful for. We all held hands and he began to give thanks. I looked up and could see the tears in my father's eyes even though his head was lowered, and felt him squeeze my hand. The impact of the accident on my parents was now very real to me, and I could see that the pain and heartache of the past four months had taken its toll on all of us. Holding hands and crying with him, I had never been so glad to be home.

That night I felt closer to my parents than I had ever felt before.

Before Mum helped me into bed that night she showed me the intercom system they had installed, linking the various rooms of the house so she and Dad could hear me if I wanted something or had any problems. Their room was on the other side of the house, but the bathroom was strategically placed close to mine, so it was almost like having my own en suite.

When I was alone in my room, I couldn't help but notice the dark silence that enveloped me. I had waited for this moment so long, to be alone in my own room, but now it was almost too quiet and dark. I had slept in a room with so many other people for what seemed like an eternity, in a ward that was always noisy, and never dark. I suddenly felt very alone. I closed my eyes and tried to sleep, but my mind was racing.

I thought about the last night I had slept in my bed, the night before the accident. I tried to remember the day of the accident itself, but only the morning came back to me; the afternoon was completely erased from my memory. My friend Chris had arrived from his home in Falls Creek the previous afternoon and we had gone on a training run together. That evening we watched a movie on television and then talked late into the night, mainly about our plans for the coming ski season.

Chris was our top male skier at the time, though he always needed a prod when it came to training. I was the opposite— I never stopped. He always said he was pleased to have a woman in the team who was determined to succeed and not afraid to put in the hard work—even if he sometimes seemed a little less than keen on it himself.

Chris had travelled to Sydney the year before with another friend and team member, Michael. I didn't know Michael very well at the time, but that changed in the next few months when the three of us toured the United States together. We all became great friends.

We spent almost two months together in the Yellowstone National Park, which I was already familiar with, having watched Yogi Bear as a child! It was a well-known cross-country training ground and the venue for the American selection races that year, where we met up with an American racer we had got to know in Australia the previous year named Alan. We stayed in a three-bedroom condo, Michael and Chris in one room, Alan in one and I in the other. One of the advantages of being the only woman was that I always got a room on my own!

We had a great time in Yellowstone. It was the most beautiful place, a snow-covered fairyland. The tracks wound through the forest and as we skied around them each morning the snow would still be falling off the trees from the night before. After lunch we'd hit the tracks for another session, then walk into the nearby village, which consisted of a bank, a supermarket and not much else, to stock up on food in case the weather turned bad, as it sometimes did. Some days we would take a break and go off touring or abandon our skis and go for a run through the forests, which was always hard work in the snow.

It was in Yellowstone that I first met a representative of one of the big ski companies. We were such a small country in winter sports by comparison with the rest of the world that none of our skiers received any sponsorship assistance, even in the form of equipment. (This was to change some years later.) He gave me a pair of racing skis he had with him, which had a new type of base and were very fast. When I arrived in Europe a few months later they gave me another two pairs. This was a real break for me, a sign that things could only get better.

Eventually we left our little paradise and made our way north for some events in Canada and then back across the border to America. Once I had qualified for the World Cup circuit we made our way to a race in Giant's Ridge, Biwabik, Minnesota. The temperature plummeted well below freezing and the officials hesitated before deciding to let the races start. Finally we all lined up for the women's 10-kilometre event.

Being inexperienced in such extreme conditions, I began the race without adequate protection for my face. After a while my face started to become numb and I noticed people were yelling at me. I arrived at the top of one of the many hills in the course where an official called out to me, pointing to my face. I didn't know what he meant, but a little further on another official shouted to me that I had frostbite on my face and should stop. By this stage my face was completely numb and I quickly pulled over to the side of the track. Someone wrapped a blanket around me and led me to a tent where there were several other girls who had similarly withdrawn.

My face didn't really begin to hurt until it started to thaw out. I was left with very red cheeks which eventually turned into scabs, but I learnt something that day and I never ventured outside again in such extreme temperatures without proper protection.

I wouldn't be able to go away with the team this year, I told myself as I lay wide awake in my new bedroom with these memories running through my head, but I was determined to work hard and make it the following year.

Morning approached and I had hardly slept. My first night at home had not been the restful experience I expected. I was glad to hear Mum's footsteps coming down the hall.

'Good morning, sweetheart, how did you sleep?' she said.

'Not that well, Mum. It was so quiet, I'm not used to it.'

'Don't worry, dear, it'll be better tonight, I'm sure. Let's get you dressed and have some breakfast. How does that sound?'

'Great,' I said. Anything had to be better than the soggy toast they gave us in the hospital.

The weekend passed all too quickly. I couldn't move around unless someone was there to help me so I spent most of the time lying on a bed in the lounge room that Mum had set up for me. This was a blessing, as the cast was so heavy and uncomfortable I wasn't able to sit for any length of time.

The weather was unusually cold for that time of year and in the evenings Dad lit a fire in the lounge room. After dinner we sat and talked, listening to music and watching the fire. It had a soothing quality about it and seemed to create a void which I was grateful for. We stayed and watched the flames till they had almost disappeared.

I spent the rest of the time relaxing, trying to unwind. I was still very tired and needed to spend a lot of the day sleeping. I wasn't only physically exhausted but emotionally as well.

With Sunday evening approaching, I knew I would soon have to return to hospital. I didn't want to leave and persuaded Mum to ring the hospital to see if they would let me stay one more night. They reluctantly agreed as long as I was back early Monday morning.

Next morning Mum packed my bag to take me back to hospital. I kissed Dad goodbye and watched him wave us off as we drove up the driveway. It would only be a week until I would be home again, but it would be a long week.

I felt as if I had been on weekend leave from gaol and now had to return. Maybe it was more than a coincidence that the hospital was located next door to the notorious Long Bay prison. That might have explained some of the bizarre dreams I used to have in hospital. Once I dreamt that I had escaped and I was running around the grounds in my pyjamas. Noticing my absence, the staff alerted the security guards and alarm bells were ringing. Doctors and nurses were running everywhere looking for me and I spent the night hiding in the bushes waiting for the chance to take off. My pyjamas were no longer covered in teddy bears but stripes.

I wondered if there would be anyone waiting to arrest me when I returned this time!

Chapter 13

DURING MY WEEK back at hospital, I had a visit from some friends who asked if John and I would be allowed to go out for dinner. There was a Chinese restaurant opposite the hospital and they thought it would be a nice break from the hospital food. I couldn't agree more! John and I both got permission to go. There were six of us all told—Ian, Nan, Tom, Biddy and myself and John.

We decided to leave the wheelchairs in the ward and walk over, which was quite a task for John and me. It took some time to get us across the road but we managed to make it safely.

Once inside the restaurant, Ian went over to the counter to get us a table. I was holding onto a chair for support, when the waiter came over to lead us to our seats. I thought I could make it by myself as there looked to be enough chairs and tables on the way to grab onto. I let go and tried to move over to the next chair, and before I could reach it, I lost my balance. I could feel myself falling and there was nothing I could do to stop myself. I went down with a thud.

I lay still, not daring to move. Ian and Nan rushed over to pick me up. 'Are you all right?' they inquired anxiously. 'Did you hurt yourself?' I had given everyone a fright.

'I think I'm OK ... What a stupid thing to do,' I said uncertainly. I didn't want to worry anyone unduly, and I didn't want to go back to the hospital and end everyone's night out. They got me to my feet and put me in a chair. I was quite shaken but I convinced them that I was all right. I didn't even attempt to move by myself for the rest of the night.

Once I was safely back in bed for the night and my visitors had left, I thought I had better tell the staff about the incident. I was worried that I may have hurt my back, as I had fallen so hard. So I told a nurse who filled out an accident form and a doctor came and had a look at me. Fortunately, I was cleared of any serious injuries but the fall was quite a fright and convinced me I should be more careful in future. The last thing I wanted was to end up staying in hospital any longer than I had to.

The week drew to an end and with Friday afternoon fast approaching I packed my things in preparation for the trip home. I was getting excited at the prospect of getting back to my own bedroom. Mum had arranged to come and drive me home. We decided to leave a little earlier to miss the peak-hour traffic. Safely seated in the front, with my wheelchair in the back, I waved my friends goodbye as we once again drove out of the hospital gates.

At home I settled in much more quickly than the previous week now that I knew where everything was. I spent the weekend in much the same way, sitting around in my wheelchair or lying on the bed in the lounge room. I was getting used to sleeping in my own room now, the silence no longer a problem. The weekend passed all too quickly again and after another phone call to the hospital I was allowed to extend my stay to Monday morning.

It turned out to be an auspicious day. When my doctors came around on their morning visit and heard my account of how well I was managing at home on my own, they agreed that I could go home the following weekend for good. They arranged for me to continue with my rehab at Westmead hospital and the staff rang to inform them that I would be starting the following week.

I couldn't believe it. It had been almost four months, but I was finally going home—for good!

My last week in hospital passed even more quickly than I had anticipated. I had two outings which helped speed it on its way, the first a little out of the ordinary.

Michael had left a few weeks earlier, but needed to come back for checkups and would always drop in to see how we were all going, his neck still in a brace, but a cheerful smile on his face as usual.

'How are you going?' he asked. 'How was the weekend at home?'

'Oh, great, Michael,' I replied, but I'm so excited. This weekend I'm going home for good.'

'That's fantastic! Hey, I think we should celebrate, what d'you reckon?'

'Great, what did you have in mind?' I thought he was suggesting we order another pizza.

'Well, you know my cousin I was telling you about, the one who runs the restaurant near here? I thought we could go out for dinner there one night. Reckon they'll let you?'

'I'm sure they will,' I said enthusiastically.

I got the OK from the nursing staff and Michael said he'd pick me up next evening around six o'clock. His cousin had recently opened a restaurant nearby which specialised in seafood. Mum was there in the afternoon to help me get dressed. I hoped the restaurant wasn't too classy, as I didn't exactly look like the belle of the ball in my track pants, a baggy shirt and joggers, but it was all I could wear over my plaster.

'Hey, Janine, looks like you're really going out in style,' Sam said as she came into the ward. 'You should see the car Michael's just arrived in!'

Mum wheeled me outside and to our astonishment, Michael was there in a Rolls Royce!

'Hi, Janine,' he said with exaggerated casualness. 'I borrowed my cousin's car. I thought it would be a bit more comfortable for you.'

I had never been in a Rolls before. Michael helped me out of the chair and into the front seat. He was right, it was comfortable. I waved Mum goodbye and we set off on our regal way. But to my dismay, the first thing I saw at the restaurant was steps—lots of them. I didn't know how on earth I was going to get inside, but that was soon solved, Michael carried me up.

His cousin greeted us at the door and led us to a table, presenting the menu to us with a flourish. Knowing my eyes were bigger than my stomach, I kept my order relatively small, but it was delicious and we had a wonderful time. Michael had me back at the hospital around nine o'clock and helped me inside.

We must have looked an odd couple—Michael with his neck in a brace and me with my plaster cast, unable to walk! But that night served more than one purpose. It made me feel a little more 'normal', just being able to go out like anyone else. And although Michael and I were just friends, it was nice to be asked out by a man. To be appreciated like that was very important, especially now.

With only a day or so to go, I went on an outing with the spinal ward. These excursions were arranged every few weeks to give the long-term patients some contact with the normal world. We were going out to lunch, to a Chinese restaurant.

There were about nine of us in all and two nurses. They loaded us into the hospital bus and off we went. At the restaurant a table had been specially prepared for us. All the chairs had been removed so that our wheelchairs could fit around it.

We spent the afternoon eating and talking, and enjoying the break from hospital routine. Most of the other patients were from North ward, the one next to mine. I had got to know a few of them already from the gym, but there were a few that I hadn't met.

I often wheeled myself into North ward to chat to some of the patients. It was a little larger than mine and had a pool table, which was always being used by someone.

After lunch we set off back to the hospital when Bob, who was driving as usual, suggested stopping off at the beach on the way home. We all agreed and pulled into a car park next to a car full of surfies.

Our bus had the words 'Prince Henry Hospital Spinal Unit' on the side, and in any case we didn't exactly look inconspicuous. While Bob was unloading us, I noticed the boys in the car staring at us. It was very intimidating and I suddenly felt very self-conscious. At the hospital nobody ever stared, so it was a bit of a shock to be gawked at like this. But I soon forgot about them when Bob wheeled me down to the beach and helped me out of the wheelchair.

'Like a little walk on the sand?' he asked. 'It's really good for the feet.'

It was just what I wanted. He took my shoes off for me and helped me down to the sand. It might have been good for the feet, but it was hard work trying to walk on such an uneven surface. I made a mental note to try to get to the beach as much as possible in the future so that I could practise my walking. Then we went back to where we had left my chair and he gave John a turn.

I sat and watched as John struggled to maintain his balance. I knew how difficult it was. Seagulls were walking up and down, looking for some trace of food to scavenge. The afternoon breeze was picking up, blowing spray on my face. This was a great place for rehabilitation, I thought. It sure beat the gym!

Back at the hospital, with only one more day to go till I was home for good, I spent the night talking to Maria, giving her my phone number and address and promising to visit her as soon as possible. Maria was also leaving soon, to go to a special nursing home for quadriplegics.

The next morning couldn't come quickly enough. Mum arrived early and packed up my belongings. I had collected quite a lot of things during my stay, including a bagful of cards and letters I had kept. There was also a sheepskin my friends at college had bought me, as well as my soft toys, some flowers that had arrived a few days earlier, my clothes and all the medications I needed.

There was, however, one item missing from the list—my wheelchair. I had decided to leave it behind me. I knew that would mean giving up a bit of independence, but I was determined to make do without it. I would just have to learn to get around the house on my own two feet.

Just as I was about to leave, Adrian stopped by to say goodbye. He asked if he could ring me when I got home, as he had some tickets for a show in a few weeks and would like me to come. I was flattered by the invitation but more than a little surprised. If I hadn't known better it almost sounded like a serious 'date'! I didn't exactly seem the ideal candidate for this kind of proposal, and he was my doctor. Wasn't this somewhat unethical? And what about Daven? He was still my boyfriend, after all.

I liked Adrian a lot and enjoyed his company, but I had to decline his offer. He insisted on taking my number nevertheless, despite my telling him that I wouldn't be able to go out with him. I told him that he was welcome to ring but that was it: I was already spoken for. He laughed and somehow I doubted that he took my refusal seriously. He didn't seem the kind to give in without a fight.

With my goodbyes complete, I drove out of the hospital gates for the last time. I knew that there would be many more challenges to be faced once I was home, but for now I was just pleased to be leaving hospital. There were so many things that I was still uncertain about, but the one thing I was determined to do was to dedicate myself one hundred per cent to rehabilitating myself and regaining my independence.

Chapter 14

MUM DROVE ME to Westmead for my first day of rehabilitation. It was strange to be going to another hospital, especially one so different from Prince Henry. It was a virtual metropolis and I wondered how anyone ever found their way around the place. It was sterile and impersonal and I was actually glad I had spent my time in Prince Henry, no matter how run-down it was.

I had a letter of introduction and my discharge summary which I was to present to the rehab department when I arrived. It contained all the relevant information about my accident and treatment given, and detailed the progress that I had so far made with my rehabilitation.

I was introduced to the staff in the gym, where my physiotherapist was a young girl named Merrin. She seemed friendly and enthusiastic about taking on my case. Most of the patients who attended rehab at Westmead were older patients who had suffered strokes or other ailments, so she was pleased to have someone who was of a similar age to herself.

Merrin was always happy to see me and was always trying to think of new ways to stimulate various muscles, to get the most out of my session. One day she showed me a contraption I had never seen or heard of before, which she said was called a Tens machine.

'What does it do?' I asked.

'It's an artificial muscle stimulator. Because the transmitters from your brain to your muscles have been damaged, we may be able to stimulate them electronically with it,' she said.

'You mean it'll help me get the use of my legs back?' I asked eagerly.

'That's the idea. We'll use it each session and see if we get any results.'

That was all the motivation I needed. This was the solution I had been waiting for. As my spinal cord had been partially severed and crushed, certain nerves had been damaged beyond repair, which resulted in reduced neurological function in my muscles and loss of sensation in the lower half of my body. In medical terms I was called a partial paraplegic.

However, this didn't worry me too much. Although I had been told that the spinal cord damage was permanent, the doctors had also said that it was possible for other nerves to take over the role of the damaged ones. Because of this, they were unable to say definitely how complete a recovery I could expect to make. But that recovery had to occur within two years, after which I could otherwise expect to make no further improvement. I believed that if I worked hard enough, I could retrain my body to function as it had before.

I knew it was important to get working on them straight-away as I had already suffered extensive muscle atrophy in the lower body. My feet had also wasted and changed in shape, and my toes now closed like claws when I tried to walk. I had lost strength and function in my buttocks and hamstrings which made it even more difficult to walk. Now this little machine seemed to be my answer.

Merrin brought the tiny little box over to the bed I was lying on. She attached some round, black pads to my legs and told me I would feel the electric currents pass through these pads from the machine to my leg muscles. As she increased the strength of the machine I felt my legs tingle.

'OK, now I am going to leave the machine on for about twenty minutes,' she said. 'If you want to turn the strength up a bit just turn this knob here.' She showed me how to increase the current. 'But remember, it isn't meant to hurt— it has to be comfortable.'

The moment she left I turned the machine up to the point where I could just tolerate it. I closed my eyes and tried to visualise the muscles in my legs working. Then before I knew it the machine stopped. My time was up.

'That's all for today, Janine,' Merrin said as she packed it up. 'We'll do some more tomorrow.'

The Tens machine was to become a regular part of my rehab and I used it every day I was in the gym. I measured my legs regularly, looking for some indication of an increase in size. According to Merrin, it was a slow process.

My routine at Westmead was similar to that at Prince Henry. I would spend the first part of the morning practising walking on parallel bars and stairs, and then about half an hour on an exercise bike. They had a few other aids that I used each day, like the balance board. This was a round board with a ball attached underneath. The object was to stand on the board while holding onto the bars and try to balance as it wobbled about on the ball. It took a lot of concentration, but it did wonders for my feet and ankles.

They also had some specialised weight machines called cybex machines. They were particularly useful for rehabilitating muscles which were recovering from an injury, and I found them very useful for regaining the strength in my quadriceps, or thigh muscles.

The weeks passed slowly at Westmead and I soon became bored with the routine of doing the same thing every day. I began to feel that I wasn't being challenged enough and my progress wasn't as fast as I had hoped. One day I overheard one of the physios talking about a pool at the hospital and decided to make it part of my rehab program as soon as I possibly could. I knew I couldn't go swimming at this stage, as I still had my plaster cast on, but when it came off it seemed like a great alternative. I asked Merrin if she would take me to have a look at it and she readily agreed. But she warned me that it was not for lap swimming, but only a hydrotherapy pool and not very large.

She was right. It was very small and being used by mostly older people, who were holding onto the edge and lifting their legs in the water as if they were in an aquaerobics class without the music. According to Merrin, the water was heated to help to soothe the muscles. It also allowed patients to perform exercises in a weightless environment, so there was much less stress on the body.

The thought of being in water was very appealing, particularly as it had been months since I had had a bath or shower. It was something to look forward to as soon as the plaster came off.

The next few months dragged by. I continued with my rehab at the hospital and spent my time at home reading or just lying around. Now that I appeared to be coping well and was no longer in hospital, my visits from friends slackened off to weekends only. They had their own lives to live and I understood this. I became increasingly isolated due to my immobility and I began to experience a range of emotional problems which up till then I had been able to control.

As well as having to cope with learning to walk again and relearning certain physical tasks, I also had to deal with a body that was still unable to function internally either. I had suffered extensive internal injuries, and the neurological damage made it still necessary to rely on the use of a catheter. This left me open to urinary infections and made me extremely tired. It wasn't the sort of thing that I wanted to burden anyone with, being of a personal nature, and I thought it was up to me to cope with it myself.

On top of this, I was expected to submit to questioning by certain rehab doctors at the hospital which was nothing less than humiliating. One day, while attending one of the 'clinics' for spinal patients, I happened to draw the short straw and get the most insensitive doctor on the staff.

He started to talk about my sexuality, which was not only embarrassing but none of his business anyway. He touched on areas which were highly personal, which degraded and upset me greatly. Wasn't anything private any more? How dare this complete stranger who knew nothing about me assume that he could touch on subjects so personal? It was humiliating. Why couldn't they at least have given me a female doctor to talk with? It seemed that I had lost all rights associated with common decency. I was just a patient and my feelings didn't matter any more. They could treat me as they wished.

The fact was that I was a twenty-four-year-old woman and, as if I already didn't have enough to cope with, he had the audacity, in my mind, to question my right to womanhood. I kept a stiff upper lip while I was with him, but away from hospital, in the privacy of my bedroom, I cried myself to sleep.

I didn't seem to make much improvement over the next few months and I began to feel frustrated at plodding along without any real progress. Each day became a boring repetition of the same old thing and it started to affect me. Being able to undertake rehabilitation on my own took care of the physical side of things, but the emotional side of recovery went unattended. When I left hospital, I was told that I might have trouble adapting to the changes in my life, but at no time was I offered any sort of counselling to help me deal with these problems.

I was often on my own, with no way of getting about. Mum had gone back to work a few days a week and I didn't want to bother her any more than I had to. I had great difficulty coming to terms with the fact that my body no longer functioned at the one hundred per cent efficiency, like a well-oiled machine, that I had always prided myself on. I couldn't cope being physically disabled in any way. I wanted to be whole again.

I had always thought I was in control of my life, but now it seemed I was powerless to shape or change my circumstances. I was unable to share my feelings with anyone for fear that they wouldn't want to see me any more. I knew my friends wanted me to be the person they had known before, but now I felt so different that I didn't seem to fit in any more.

My friends would drop in to visit, often on their pushbikes or on their way back from a training session, and talk about what they had been doing, running or riding somewhere, while I sat outwardly smiling but inwardly aching with sadness at not being able to join in with them. I became very lonely and without really noticing it slipped into a deep state of depression.

I would lie in bed in the morning, not wanting to get out and feeling there was nothing to get up for. For the first time since the accident I wished I hadn't fought so hard, because then I wouldn't be in so much pain now. I became deeply unhappy, missing the things I had once treasured, especially the physical stimulation of my sport. I yearned to put on my running shoes and just go out for a run, but I couldn't even do that. There was nothing I could do to overcome the frustration of my injuries, and it grew day by day.

With nothing else to do, I kept brooding about my situation, bringing back painful memories that only depressed me further. I also started to shut Daven out of my life. I felt unable to fulfil my side of the relationship and extremely defensive of my body after the ravages it had suffered. I didn't have the emotional energy to cope with a relationship and needed to be on my own, at least for now, in order to recover.

One day Mum came into my room to find me lying in my bed, staring blankly at the ceiling.

'It's time to get up, darling. What would you like for breakfast today?' she asked.

I looked up at her, tears in my eyes. 'Mum, I don't want to get out of bed today.'

Sensing the sadness in my voice, she sat down on the end of the bed.

'Mum, I don't know what's wrong with me. I can't find any reason to get out of bed any more,' I said, beginning to cry.

Mum knew that things were upsetting me lately and had been doing everything she could to cheer me up, but nothing seemed to be working.

She took my hand. 'I don't know what to say, Janine. It doesn't seem to help to talk to me, maybe we need to see someone else . . . a counsellor.'

'I don't know, Mum, I'm so unhappy.'

'I just think it might help speaking to someone who isn't emotionally involved,' she said. 'We have to try something else. I can't think of any other way.'

I didn't know what was the right thing to do. All I knew

was that I had to do something, not only for my sake but for Mum and Dad also. I went to see my local doctor who gave me the name of a female psychiatrist who was supposed to be very good. I wasn't too keen at first—after all, psychiatrists were for people who had severe mental problems, and that wasn't me. But, I thought I would give it a go. I didn't know who else I should see.

My idea of the typical consulting room was shaken when I turned up for my first appointment. There was no couch in the corner or soft and soothing lights. Instead it looked like the living room of a comfortable home. I was also pleasantly surprised by the doctor herself. She was not wearing a white coat or armed with a clipboard, but nicely dressed and seemed like a warm and friendly person. Maybe I had been watching too much television, I thought. I felt immediately at ease.

I sat opposite her and we just talked. She took a few notes, but mainly listened while I spoke. Strangely, I felt a great sense of relief to be able to talk to someone who hadn't been through the entire accident with me and was able to be objective and understanding.

We talked about my feelings of guilt and my growing bitterness towards the man who had hit me. I told her about the letter he had sent me in hospital and how much it had hurt me. I realised that there were so many emotions that were bottled up inside of me, especially towards this person because of his refusal to accept responsibility for the accident. He made me feel as if it was my fault, and that my parents, family and friends had suffered because of my actions. To make matters worse, his only punishment was a negligent driving charge and an eighty dollar fine. It seemed such a small price to pay for irrevocably altering my life.

We talked about my inability to share my emotions with those close to me. I wanted everyone to think I had the situation under control and everything would be all right. I didn't want anyone to worry about me and didn't think they would understand, anyway. I wanted them to think that the Janine they knew before would be back with them soon.

We talked about all the aspects of my life that had been affected by my accident, which seemed to be just about everything. I did most of the talking and she did most of the listening, giving advice only where it was needed. She was completely non-judgmental, and didn't make me feel as if there was something 'wrong' with me for feeling the way I did. In fact, she assured me that to feel as I did was absolutely normal. I found this very heartening as I had been feeling guilty about some of my attitudes, especially my animosity towards the man that had caused the accident.

Perhaps the most important and reassuring thing she told me was that the periods of depression I was experiencing were also absolutely normal—that in fact it would have been a matter of concern if I weren't depressed. However, normal as they were, she said that these bouts would become less frequent and intense. Although there would always be some degree of hurt to deal with, she added, in time I would be able to handle it more efficiently. After only a few months, I stopped seeing her, feeling better able to cope with things. Mum was right. It had been a help to talk to someone who wasn't emotionally involved and could stand back and look at the 'big picture' objectively. I trusted the doctor's prediction that my 'down' periods would gradually decrease, even though right now there wasn't much sign of that happening. However, it gave me some degree of confidence to face the future and dragged me out of the despair I was in at the time.

At home I kept in contact with the people I had been in hospital with. I rang John and Natalie and they both came to visit me with their families. John was still going to Prince

Henry, which was close to where he lived, for a similar rehab program to mine, while Natalie was attending another hospital. Whereas our main trouble was our legs, she had problems with her arms. She was unable to use her hands in the normal fashion and had difficulty picking things up. Matthew had returned to his home in the mountains and was progressing quite well. He dropped in to see me one day and seemed in good spirits, happy to have escaped serious injury and keen to resume his previous life. I never heard from Matthew after this and can only assume that he recovered fully from his accident.

I kept in touch with Uncle Darryl, who had become a great friend to both myself and my parents, especially Dad. He was a kind and generous person who had a knack of making me laugh and forget where I was. At the hospital, he used to come and see me, even on his days off. One time he came back specially after visiting his mother who lived two hours' drive away. He was like a long-lost uncle.

One day at home, the phone rang and I picked it up to hear Uncle Darryl's familiar voice.

'Hello, little turtle, guess who this is?' I didn't need much prompting, as he was the only one to call me by this nickname he had given me. I really did look like a turtle with my cast on!

'Oh, hi Uncle Darryl, how are you?' I asked, pleased to hear from him.

'Just fine. How's the family? Mum and Dad well?'

'They're fine, thanks. I'm glad you rang. Mum wanted to know if you could make it over for a BBQ next Sunday.'

'That'd be great,' he said.

I was glad that he had rung. He didn't have the phone on at home and the only way to contact him was to ring the hospital, and since he rotated between wards, it was often difficult to reach him. I gave him directions to our house and he said how much he was looking forward to seeing his 'family' again.

However, the day before the BBQ he rang to say he wouldn't be able to make it. He didn't sound his usual self and I thought I could detect a strange note of anxiety in his voice. He said that he had some unexpected family troubles he had to attend to. I was disappointed, but I didn't want to pry into his personal life. He promised he would phone again and come to see us as soon as he could, and we said goodbye.

A few weeks passed and I still hadn't heard from him. I was due to attend a clinic at Prince Henry and thought I'd call in to see him while I was there. I hobbled into the ICU ward, the most likely place to find him, holding onto Mum's arm, and one of the nurses came over to greet us. We chatted for a while and then I asked if Darryl was around.

She paused and looked at me in surprise. 'Oh, you haven't heard, Janine. Darryl died last week.'

The words slammed against my head with such force my legs started to collapse under me. Mum tightened her hold to stop me from falling.

'We're not sure what happened,' the nurse continued. 'He was found dead in his flat. We had a memorial service for him this morning . . . I'm sorry you missed it.'

I looked at Mum and saw that she was crying. I wiped the tears from my own eyes. The nurse gave me a chair to sit down and I was unable to speak. It couldn't be true. My friend, my Uncle Darryl, he couldn't be dead, not Darryl!

Mum helped me out to the car. I was still too upset to speak. I couldn't believe it. It just wasn't fair.

My mind flashed back and I could see him looking down at me as he handed me the ice cubes, sitting by my bed in ICU and reassuring me that everything would be all right, walking around the place in his cute little gown, the ones that he had given me, shaking Dad's hand and talking with us all at my bedside like one of the family. I heard his voice on the telephone calling me 'little turtle'. I remembered how he used to pick up one of my soft teddy bears and pretend to burp it. It looked so funny . . . How I would miss this gentle man . . . my Uncle Darryl.

When we arrived home that night I wondered how to tell Dad the tragic news. I knew how upset he would be. He arrived home just before dinner and as we sat down to eat I told him what had happened. A look of sheer disbelief passed across his face as he tried to take it in. We sat there holding hands crying for the dear friend we had lost.

Next day I rang Uncle Darryl's mother in the country to pass on our condolences. I wanted her to know that her son had been a source of strength for us all, and that his compassion and gentle ways had touched the hearts of so many people. She said that Darryl had told her about his 'little turtle' and that I had held a special place in his heart too. We cried on the phone as we spoke, as she told me about the son that she loved.

Later in the week we suffered an even greater shock. I contacted the hospital to find out more about Darryl's death as I wondered why nobody had rung to inform me of it. They told me that he had shot himself. Even now the full circumstances have not been determined, but it is something I cannot think about without the greatest pain.

Uncle Darryl . . . you will always hold a special place in my heart.

As Christmas approached, I was steadily putting on some of the weight I had lost. Unfortunately, the plaster cast was not as flexible as my body and it began to feel as if I was wearing a straitjacket. After a meal, I often could hardly breathe!

With some embarrassment, I told Dr Stephen about my

difficulties and he arranged for Adrian to cut another piece out of the plaster. However, this brought only temporary relief and after another phone call he said that I could have the old cast removed and a lighter, larger one fitted, made out of fibreglass.

Being fitted for this cast was a lot different from the first time as I was now able to stand up. I had to hold onto a triangle frame while the two girls who were helping Adrian cut the plaster off with a large drill which sounded as if with one slip of their hands I would be sawn in half!

What a strange feeling it was to be standing with no plaster around me. I must have looked a funny sight, in my underpants and the stocking that covered my torso. I had to keep holding on to the triangle frame while the new cast was wrapped around me. It was a lot quicker than the first time and I had the added advantage of being able to expand my chest so that I would have some room to breathe. I was sure the lighter weight would make it easier to get around from now on and it would be a lot less restricting when I put on even more weight.

Mum had left me at the clinic as Adrian had offered to drive me home. He was still keen to take me out, and even though I hadn't taken up the invitation I appreciated his friendship and understanding. However, on the way home he insisted on stopping off for a bite to eat at a little restaurant he knew. Well, I could always rationalise that it would give me a chance to test out the new cast on a full stomach. It passed the test. I could still breathe after I had eaten!

With Christmas fast approaching, I was excited at the prospect of having my cast removed completely. However, it wasn't going to be so easy. Dr Stephen told me that after it was taken off I would have to wear a brace for at least another two months. This was a real let-down for me, and I wondered when or if the whole thing would ever end, but Dr Stephen assured me the brace would be much lighter and not so bulky.

Mum drove me out to the hospital to be fitted for the new brace, which would take a few weeks to make. A technician named Warren took some measurements and showed me what my brace would look like. It was called a Jewett's brace, and was made of lightweight aluminium. It had two soft pads, one at the sternum and the other just above the groin, and opened like a vice to be slipped around the body and then fastened at the side to form a solid piece. The fact that it could be removed was a real bonus as it meant that I could take it off at night, as long as I didn't get out of bed without it on.

At the back of my mind I was thinking about swimming. Surely if I could remove it to sleep, I could also remove it to swim. After all, the water would support my body, so there wouldn't be any chance of damage. I made a note to ask Dr Stephen next time I saw him.

I still had several weeks to wait, but the opportunity of getting the new brace couldn't have come at a better time as I really needed something to perk me up. All my friends had departed for the ski season overseas, including Daven, and I was feeling a bit down at the thought of not being able to join them. Daven had initially decided not to go and stay with me instead. But I told him I didn't want him to miss out on it because of me. Besides I needed time to sort myself out, that was something I had to do alone.

My biggest problem was to work out where I was going. I missed the intense physical exercise that had been such a major part of my life, and I couldn't find anything to take its place. I wanted my independence back; I was sick of feeling like a prisoner trapped inside the house. I wanted to be able to get in my car and drive somewhere—anywhere—but I couldn't. On top of that, my concentration span was very short, which I was told was probably due to the head injuries I had sustained in the accident. Together with the fact that everything was such an effort and I was always extremely tired, I was feeling very frustrated. I needed to find something to take my mind off everything, something to occupy me and challenge me—but what, I didn't know.

I was sitting at the kitchen table chatting with Mum one afternoon, when I heard a plane pass overhead. I don't know whatever put the thought into my head, but at that instant I knew what I had to do.

'Mum, I think I'm going to learn to fly,' I said.

Mum kept on with what she was doing. 'Oh that's nice, dear, but don't you think you should learn how to walk first?' I knew she didn't think I was serious.

'Mum, I'm not kidding. I really *am* going to learn to fly!'

Mum stopped and looked at me. She saw I meant what I said.

'I can't walk properly so I might as well learn how to fly,' I went on. 'Besides, what else have I got to do at the moment? I can't just sit around here forever.'

I didn't know what I was getting myself into, but I was getting more excited by the minute. Flying an aeroplane was the last thing I had ever thought of doing, but now it seemed like the very thing to get me back on my feet, so to speak. I didn't know where to start or who to ask but I was determined to find out.

'Mum, could you hand me the phone book?' Mum reluctantly obliged. She was looking a little worried by now.

I flicked through the yellow pages till I found the words 'Flying Schools'. I was surprised how many there were. I decided to try them alphabetically and dialled the number of the most prominent ad starting with 'A', then waited, going through in my mind what I would say. After a few rings someone answered.

'Um, hello, I'm just inquiring about flying lessons,' I said. 'I'd like some information about learning to fly.'

'Of course,' the voice responded. 'You might be interested in our trial instructional flight, which is a way of letting people see if they really enjoy flying before they commit themselves to learning.'

'What does that involve?' I asked.

'All you have to do is come out to the airport, and we give you a briefing on what to expect, then take you up for about half an hour. The instructor will let you take over for a while so you can see what it's all about.'

'That sounds great,' I said enthusiastically.

'Do you know where Bankstown Airport is?' he asked.

'Not exactly, but I'll find it.'

'I can book you in now if you like. When would you like to come out?'

'Um, well that's a bit of a problem. I'm not exactly sure yet ... You see, I can't drive ... and I sort of can't walk either ... But that's not a problem, is it?'

There was a pause at the other end of the phone.

'But I can get a friend to drive me out. Is that all right if they come on the flight too?'

'Sure, the plane is a four-seater so there'll be plenty of room.'

'Great!'

My mind was ticking over. Chris was coming to visit me for a few days next week, and I knew he'd love to go for a flight. He could drive me out to the airport and come with me. I made a booking for the following Wednesday.

I put the phone down bubbling over with excitement. Crazy as it might have sounded for someone in my situation, I just knew I had to do it. The fact that it was a little crazy was exactly why I wanted to do it—I wanted to do something that was as far removed from my life at present, and past, as I could find, something 'new' and fresh to stimulate and challenge me—and what better than learning to fly?

However, Mum wasn't too keen on the idea. I guess I couldn't blame her, after what she had seen me go through the past seven months. But she knew better than to kill my excitement. So despite her reservations, knowing how depressed I had been of late, she more or less went along with the idea.

When I told Chris what I had arranged he shrugged and said nothing I did ever surprised him. He was as keen about it as I was, as he'd always wanted to fly himself.

The following Wednesday he drove me out to Bankstown Airport. By the time Chris parked the car, I was feeling a bit nervous and anxious. I wondered what my doctors would say if they knew what I was doing. Oh well, too late to worry about it now. Chris helped me out of the car and into the office of the school.

I was wearing a baggy jumpsuit that Mum had bought me when I came home from hospital. It was difficult to find anything that looked reasonable over my plaster cast and I was glad to wear something other than tracksuits. However, even with this outfit on you could still see the cast protruding out of the suit, so that I presented a rather bulging, shapeless figure rather than the sleek lines of a potential pilot.

Chris helped me up the steps into the school and held onto my arm as I waddled over to the counter. A couple of young men behind the desk looked at me strangely, as if they thought I was in the wrong place.

'Hi,' I said. 'I rang last week and booked in for a trial instructional flight. My name is Janine Shepherd.'

There was an embarrassed pause as they politely excused themselves and went out the back to check who was to take me up. I wondered if they were drawing straws to see who would get me!

One of them finally returned. 'Hi, my name is Andrew, and I'll be taking you on your flight today,' he said. He was smartly dressed in dark blue pants and neat white pilot's shirt, and looked as if he could be trusted, I thought.

He took us into a smaller room and sat us down for a briefing, explaining what we would be doing on the flight and especially what I would be doing as a prospective pilot. Then he led us out to the tarmac. The plane was parked a little way away, but too far for me to walk. Chris drove me out in the car as far as we could go, then helped me walk the last few metres.

The plane turned out to be much bigger than I had anticipated—a French aeroplane called a Tobago. It was painted red, white and blue and called JTO, or Juliet Tango Oscar according to the aviation alphabet. There was only slight problem—how to get me inside!

The normal way was to climb up on the wing and step inside, but needless to say that was a bit beyond me. I would have to be lifted up, which wasn't going to be that easy with my plaster cast on. Chris stood on the wing and Andrew at my feet, and somehow they managed to get me up and into the aircraft. It was a bit difficult sitting down in the relatively small cockpit as my cast was very restricting, but I managed to settle myself in.

Chris climbed into the back while Andrew got into the other seat in front and fastened the seatbelt for me as I couldn't reach the straps. I looked around the cockpit and was dazzled by what I saw. There were so many dials and switches I wondered how anyone could ever remember what they were all for. He handed us both a pair of headsets, which we duly put on, and then turned some dials so that I could now hear him talking through them.

We went through a series of checks and started the plane.

'OK, now we're ready to go,' I heard his voice through the headphones. 'This is the control column that we fly the aircraft with. Have a go at moving it and see how it feels.'

I moved it to the left and right as he directed. He then took me through the other controls and showed me how they worked, including of course the throttle. He moved it forward and the plane lurched forward as we taxied towards the runway. Andrew explained some of the other controls.

'We steer the aircraft while it's on the ground with our feet. If you look at the floor you can see two rubber pedals which I am pushing with my feet to keep it on the taxi line. Would you like to have a go?'

I was hoping that he wouldn't ask me that. I knew that there was no way that I would be able to push the pedals. I didn't have the strength in my feet or legs.

'That's a bit hard to reach with my plaster on, Andrew, I might give that a miss,' I said.

'Sure, that's fine.'

We taxied along to what he called the 'run-up' bay, where we stopped next to another plane while he went through numerous procedures to get the engine warm before we took off. I looked around to see Chris sitting smugly in the back; he looked just as excited as I felt. We finished our run-ups and taxied over to the edge to the runway, where we were given instructions from the control tower to line up and wait for clearance.

'Juliet Tango Oscar, clear for take-off,' the controller's voice came through.

'Juliet Tango Oscar,' Andrew responded and moved the throttle forward to send us tearing down the runway. I was busy watching the ground speed up beneath me and everything outside rushing past. Then we lifted off and the runway swiftly disappeared as we soared into a clear blue sky. As we climbed our way upwards, my stomach seemed to sink into the seat, as I looked down at the world below. It was the most fantastic feeling.

We continued to climb until we reached a height of 3,000 feet, which put us in the training area of Bankstown Airport. To the west I could see out to the Blue Mountains and on the other side the city itself, looking so tiny from where we were, with the harbour bridge in the distance. The sky was a dazzling blue and I could see forever. It was magic!

'OK, Janine, now it's your turn,' Andrew said. 'See that mountain? Well all I want you to do is to steer the aircraft towards that. Put your hands on the controls and just try to maintain a straight heading.'

I followed his instructions and held the controls. 'Handing over,' he said as he let go of them. 'Just concentrate on maintaining that heading.'

Now I was actually flying the plane! I couldn't believe it. I felt so free, so in control. It was as if I had power in me, finally. After so many months of having everyone tell me what I could and couldn't do, it was my turn to do something that I wanted to do, something for myself. There was so much that I was unable to do, but at last I had found something that I could do—and it felt great!

We turned back to the airport and Andrew landed the plane. I thanked him for the flight and asked him what I needed to do to get a licence. He told me the first thing would be to pass a pilot's medical. I knew that would be a problem, but I would get around it somehow. Then I would have to pass a few exams, for which there were manuals on sale at the airport shop.

With that we said goodbye and I knew that Andrew thought he would never see me again. I got Chris to stop at the shop and bought a set of manuals on the private pilot's course. I didn't want to waste any time. I would start straightaway and study them until I was fit enough to pass the medical. It was simple.

Chapter 15

I KNEW I HAD a long way to go before I could pass a medical examination as a prerequisite for getting a pilot's certificate, but that didn't matter because it gave me a goal to work for. Until my cast was removed, I knew there wasn't much I could do in terms of preparing for the medical, but at least I could start reading the flying manuals I had bought, so I would be ready when the time came. However, I did resolve to embark upon a strict training program once the cast was off to strengthen my legs and feet as much as possible, and improve my walking.

The day finally arrived when Mum drove me out to Prince Henry to have the cast removed and my brace put on. This time it was Warren who did the sawing, which by now I had become pretty used to. He put the brace in place and showed me how to fasten it. Luckily it was a perfect fit. I had had thoughts of it not fitting and having to go home in the plaster again.

It felt much better than the cumbersome cast. It was a lot lighter and less rigid and the fact that it didn't cover me completely meant that my skin could breathe. My main aim now was to get home and have a shower—my first for seven months! Dr Stephen had said that I could remove the brace to shower myself as long as I kept my back straight.

When we got home, Mum set everything up for me. She put a chair in the shower for me to hold onto or sit on, as I wasn't able to stand long enough on my own, or might slip on the wet floor. I got undressed, which took some time, and then very carefully took my brace off.

I stood holding the chair, naked and very nervous. I looked down at my body. It had been such a long time since I had seen it; I had been covered up for so long. I was so skinny the bones were protruding from my hips and my ribs were standing out like the bars of a cage.

I felt extremely vulnerable. It was the first time I had stood without back support since the accident, and it was very unnerving. What if I fell over? The mere thought of that made me tighten my grip on the chair. I could feel the bones in my back, still weak and unstable, and could imagine them giving way under the strain of supporting my weight, without the help of a cast or brace. But I had to trust Dr Stephen. He wouldn't have allowed it if it wasn't strong enough, surely.

I sat down carefully on the chair and turned the taps on till the water was streaming down my body. Mum had placed the chair right under the taps so that the water ran all over me. I closed my eyes and let it run down my face, revelling in the warmth of it soaking into my body. It was the most wonderful sensation.

'Janine . . . are you all right?'

It was Mum. 'Yes, is there anything wrong?' I asked.

'Well you've been in there for almost half an hour. I was getting a little worried,' she said.

'Oh, I didn't realise, I'll get out now.' I had totally lost track of the time. I really didn't want to get out even though I must have been well and truly waterlogged by now. The thought of getting back into the brace was not exactly inviting.

That night I was to have another 'first'—sleeping without my brace on. If I thought having a shower was a miraculous experience, it was nothing compared with being in bed that night. Words couldn't describe the sheer bliss of sleeping without a hard lump of plaster around me. When I was in hospital I had to lie completely still but now I could actually roll from side to side. It was heaven!

I had already decided that now I had this little bit more independence, I would continue my rehabilitation program on my own. I didn't feel that the hospital could offer me any more help, and I knew enough of training and how my body worked to feel confident of drawing up my own program. The hospital agreed and wished me the best, saying that if there were any problems just to give them a ring. I knew there wouldn't be any. I had a plan.

My day was to start with swimming. Mum drove me to the local RSL club, which had an indoor pool, to begin my program. I chose to go to an indoor rather than an outdoor pool, as it was usually less crowded and I thought I would have less chance of being bumped, a prospect which terrified me.

I had changed into my costume at home and put my brace over it. When we arrived at the pool, Mum helped me get undressed and take my brace off. Then it was time to get into the water. Mum held my hand and walked me over to the edge of the pool. It felt strange and exposed to be walking without any 'protection' and I was worried about slipping on the wet tiles, but Mum had a firm grip and there was no way she was going to let me go. I held on to the rails at the top of the steps that led into the pool, and Mum helped me as I gingerly turned myself around and lowered myself into the water.

There were quite a few people in the pool busily swimming their laps and too involved in what they were doing to notice me. I would have to stay away from them and not bump into anyone. Once in the water, I felt like a normal person, no longer standing out because of the way I walked or the fact that I wore a brace. Nobody could tell there was anything different about me. I looked just like everyone else.

I was excited but still a bit nervous, wondering if it would feel any different swimming now. I walked a few metres in the water, just to get my bearings. Knowing I now had the water supporting my weight I thought I would try to stand on my toes. I tried to raise myself, but couldn't budge. There was no way I could lift my weight, even in the water. Oh well, maybe that would come later.

'I think I'll try a few laps,' I called to Mum, who was waiting anxiously beside the pool.

'Don't you think you should just do some exercises before you try that?' she suggested.

'No, I'll be all right, I'll just go slowly.'

With that I pushed off from the side of the pool. I decided to do freestyle as I wanted to keep my back straight. I moved my arm up and over my head ... It was great ... I could still swim ... It felt just like it used to! My arms felt strong, and though my weak legs floundered behind in my wake, it didn't matter as I still seemed to have an immense amount of power in my body. After a few strokes I knew that I would have to breathe, and suddenly became nervous. I knew my broken neck had by now healed, but I had yet to move it in such a range of movements. I couldn't put it off any longer. I lifted my head to the side and waited in anticipation. Thank goodness, it was all right.

I made it to the edge of the pool and then slowly turned around to swim back to the other side. It was so easy, I was still breathing easily. I hadn't lost that much fitness after all,

I thought. Then I thought I'd try a lap, just to see if I could do it. To my surprise and delight I did, without much effort. At the other end of the pool I decided that I would keep going, wanting to see how long I could last. Up and down I continued to swim until I thought I had better stop. I had swum twenty laps, or half a kilometre, which wasn't too bad for the first day! I reached the end of the pool and looked up to see Mum standing on the edge gazing down at me.

'What do you think you're doing now?' she asked. She saw me press the watch on my arm.

'Oh, I thought I might as well time myself. I wanted to see how much slower I was now.'

'I think you might be overdoing it, don't you think?' she said a bit sternly.

'No, I felt really good, how did I look?'

'You looked great,' she replied. 'Now let's call it a day. You can do more tomorrow. Come on, I'll help you out.'

'OK,' I looked at the time on my watch. I felt like I had been going really fast but that wasn't the case. My time was so slow. Oh well, that can only improve each day, I thought.

Mum helped me out of the pool. I made a mental note of the time that I had swum. Twenty laps, I thought. Tomorrow I'll try for a few more, and I'll try to get my time down.

I put my brace back on over my costume. It would be too fiddly to try to get showered and dressed at the pool. I would wait till I got home, only five minutes away.

I hobbled to the reception area, and said goodbye to the man at the desk. His name was Jules. I already knew him from when I used to come to the gym occasionally to play squash with Dad and some of his friends. He was pleased to see me up and about. Like all of my parents' friends, he had heard about my accident and followed my progress closely. I said he would be seeing a lot of me from now on as I would be at the pool every opportunity I could get.

When I got home, I showered and changed and then sat down to write up my training log. I had always kept one in the past, and this would be no different. I wanted to keep a record of my progress, to see how I was improving and where my strengths and weaknesses were. I would need this to maintain my motivation.

Before filling in a new page in the log I flicked back to the last entry and saw the week of my accident. The columns had been filled in day by day, then there was nothing. It was blank from May 31, the day of the accident. It felt weird looking back on it. I skimmed through the entries ... all that week I had been feeling tired ... the day before the accident was a rest day. I always kept a note of the hours I slept and my resting heart rate, which gave me an indication of how my body was coping with the training. Normally my resting pulse rate was forty beats per minute, which was considered low for the average person, but not for an endurance athlete. And of course I kept a column to record how I was feeling each day, which would now take on a new importance. This was going to be as much a test mentally as it would be physically, and I wanted to keep track of where I was emotionally.

I scribbled in the blank spot ... ACCIDENT! Then I moved on to another page and began afresh. It read: 'Day one with my plaster off ... shower and swim ... 500 metres ... pool crowded, felt fantastic ... day one ... YIPPPEEE!'

Day two ... I woke and immediately took my pulse—58. Normally this would have indicated that I was feeling sick, but now, considering what I had been through, it wasn't too bad at all. At the pool later that morning I managed to swim one kilometre. I was really surprised how easy it was. It felt so natural to be in the water and the fact that I could now exercise was a real boost to my spirits.

Mornings were taken up with swimming and Mum would drop me off at the pool, then pick me up later. My program usually started with a warm-up of about twenty laps, then I would do some exercises specifically aimed at strengthening my legs. I would do what I called 'bunny hops' up and down the shallow end of the pool followed by some striding and running. That was the magic of the water. I couldn't run out of the water, but once I was in I could do anything. I would swim at least twenty laps doing kicking only, to strengthen my feet and ankles. Then I would finish off with some swimming with hand paddles, as I wanted to keep up the strength in my upper body.

After lunch I would spend some time on an exercise bike, which had been provided by one of my lecturers at college, a man named Peter who had come to visit me in hospital when I was doing rehab in the gym. He saw me on the exercise bike and asked if I had one of my own. I said no. Then one day he arrived at home with a bike which he said I was welcome to use as long as I liked. It was a kind and generous thought which I greatly appreciated, as I used the bike every day.

I would dress in proper bike gear, as I felt I would take the session more seriously if I looked the part. The bike was set up in my room, in front of the mirror so that I could watch myself riding. I found the mirror extremely useful as it was another aid for me to improve my technique. I even practised walking in front of it so I could analyse my gait and how I could improve it. I would wear the heart-rate monitor that I had used for training before the accident. This was a device consisting of a belt strapped around the chest which provided signals on my heart rate which I read via a watch on my wrist. I took my training program very seriously and this helped me to feel that I had a purpose, that I was really working towards something.

I decided that at least twice a day I would do some aerobics and weight exercises. I collected the tapes I had used in my aerobics classes and I would sit on the floor and do whatever exercises I could manage. My first attempt was a bit of a letdown, however.

Lying on the floor, I could only lift my leg a few centimetres off the ground and even that was a tremendous effort. I wondered how I would ever get back to normal. It was depressing, but I was determined to keep going. Day after day I lay on the floor, sweat dripping from my brow, as I struggled to perform even the simplest exercise. Gradually, almost imperceptibly, I began to make progress. Even though the improvement was so minute that I could not even notice it, Mum did and commented on how much more easily I was getting around the house and how much better I was looking. It was a great boost.

To practise walking I mastered the trick of moving around the house holding onto the walls for balance, which meant I no longer had to rely on Mum and Dad for assistance. It may not have been the fastest method, but it was effective. Mum used to joke that she had to follow me around the house wiping off the trail of dirty fingerprints I left on the walls behind me.

I then progressed to taking a few steps 'solo' as I negotiated my way between pieces of furniture. It took a bit of planning at first. I would size up the gap and estimate how many steps it would take to get to the other side, then launch myself from my starting place and hurtle across the room, from chair to table and back to the wall again. I didn't look very graceful or coordinated but it worked. Now I was really moving, I thought, and I began to increase the distance metre by metre. Sometimes I would misjudge it and start to teeter, but fortunately there was always another piece of furniture close at hand to catch my fall.

By the end of my first week back in training, my back and neck muscles were sore from the exertion. I also noted in my training log that my legs were extremely weak and my times were too slow. I needed to concentrate more on technique and spend more time stretching. By the end of the second week two significant things had happened. I had got my resting pulse down to 48, and I was sleeping better and longer. I was feeling strong in the pool and had started to introduce intervals into my sessions.

When I wasn't busy swimming or doing weights or practising walking, I had my head down in the manuals for my pilot's licence. I had never been interested in aerodynamics or the intricacies of an engine, but if I was serious about learning to fly, they were subjects I had to get on top of. I had never had any difficulty sitting at a desk studying—in fact I was a master of last-minute cramming, as I always had better things to do, like training and other activities. But now things were different.

I had trouble sitting in one place for very long as my back and neck started to ache and the brace was extremely uncomfortable and constricting. I tired very easily and found that my attention span was limited. But I had a goal, and that was enough to push me further each day.

Normally, most people wanting to obtain a pilot's licence attended a course at a technical college or a flying school. This was impossible for me as I couldn't drive and even if I had been able to get there, I couldn't have sat all day in a classroom like other students. So I had to study the course by myself, which was difficult at times as I didn't have anyone to consult with if I had any problems. But it was good to throw myself into something and it helped to take my mind off all my personal worries.

I was enjoying the brief periods of relief from wearing my brace, when I was swimming, showering and asleep, but I increasingly longed to be able to abandon the ritual of having to put it on again afterwards. I still had a few weeks to go before I could discard it, when I decided to go for my pilot's medical. My walking had improved quite significantly and I felt that I was getting stronger every day. I was still far from what I had set my sights on, but I was making progress. I could now take a few steps on my own, though most of the time I needed to hold onto someone for support.

The flying school had given me the phone number of a doctor who was authorised by the Civil Aviation Authority to examine people who wanted to obtain a pilot's licence— a Dr Henderson, whose surgery was about twenty minutes from our house. When I rang, an answering machine responded, asking me to leave a message. I thought it a bit odd that he didn't have a receptionist, but I gave my name and telephone number and why I wanted to see him. That afternoon he rang back and I made an appointment to see him next day.

Mum drove me to his rooms, in the middle of a small group of shops surrounded by green paddocks dotted with cows and sheep. I hobbled into the waiting room, Mum holding my arm and was again surprised that there was no receptionist. We sat down and waited for what seemed an eternity until at last the surgery door opened and a middle-aged woman and a young boy emerged, followed by a friendly-looking, rather elderly man, with a pair of spectacles perched on his nose, who was evidently Dr Henderson. He ushered the woman and the boy out and turned to me.

'Hello, you must be Janine,' he said. 'Please come inside.'

Well, now came the problem, I thought. I stood up with Mum and she helped me into the surgery, then left us alone. When he saw the way I walked—or waddled—he must have wondered if he had heard me right when I said what I was coming in for.

I looked around the room. It was full of pictures of aeroplanes, none of which I recognised. I wondered if he himself flew.

'Now, you said you were here for a pilot's medical?' he asked.

'Yes, that's right,' I replied hesitantly.

He looked up at me, peering over his glasses, and for the first time noticed the brace poking out of my clothes.

'Are you wearing a brace?' he asked incredulously.

'Yes, I am.'

'Well, you had better tell me what this is all about, then.'

'Well, I've been in an accident, hit by a car while I was riding my pushbike.'

'Goodness me, that's not very nice, is it? What injuries did you sustain?' he asked as he began to make notes on the card in front of him.

'Well, there were quite a few, actually. Let's see, I broke my neck and back, I broke my arm, five ribs . . . ' It took some time to reel them all off and by the time I had finished he had stopped writing and was peering at me in amazement.

'That's quite a lot of injuries,' he said. 'I don't think this is going to be quite as easy as I thought. Maybe we should start at the beginning. Tell me about the accident again.'

So I did. I told him the story that was now so familiar to me. Dr Henderson sat and listened intently. I'm sure he hadn't had anyone with quite my medical history wanting to become a pilot.

When I had finished, he sat looking at me, pondering what to say next.

'Have you been up in an aeroplane before?' he asked at last.

'Oh yes. I went for a trial instructional flight a few months ago, I loved it. I've been spending all my time since then doing rehabilitation so that I'd be strong enough to pass a medical. I really want to fly, I know I'll be able to do it,' I pleaded.

He put down his pen and started talking about his own flying experiences. I could tell that it was one of his great passions. He went on to explain that he could no longer fly as his health wasn't the best, and he missed it greatly. It was a wonderful pastime, he said, and everyone should try it, even me. Thank goodness, he was on my side!

'Well, I guess if we are going to examine you we'd better begin,' he said with a laugh. 'Let's start with the paperwork.' He handed me a form to fill in from the Civil Aviation Authority (CAA) in Canberra, which was responsible for issuing pilots' licences. It was huge. I started answering the lengthy list of questions.

Have you ever had an operation ... Yes.

Was the operation recent? If yes, how long ago? ... Five months.

Have you ever had a head injury? ... Yes.

Have you ever broken any bones? ... Yes.

The list went on and on and on. By the time I'd worked my way through it, it seemed that I had ticked almost everything on it. I felt like a medical freak. How would anyone ever pass me fit to fly a plane?

I handed it back to Dr Henderson and he looked it over.

'Well, Canberra are going to have fun with this one,' he laughed. 'We may as well get on with the rest of the examination.'

It took almost an hour and Mum must have been wondering what on earth the trouble was. After he had finished he explained that I would need a letter from Dr Stephen to say that I was well enough to learn to fly, as the CAA would never okay it unless I had my surgeons' permission. Even then there was a big question mark over my being allowed to undertake the course.

As I was leaving I asked him about his answering machine and why he didn't have a secretary.

'Oh I did have one, but she was too slow,' he said. 'Anyway, I prefer to deal with my patients myself. They all know me so they just give me a ring and line up their own appointments.'

As I left, Dr Henderson wished me luck, saying that he would recommend me for a licence and it was now up to the CAA. He wanted to give me the opportunity to experience this wonderful thing that he could no longer enjoy. Any other doctor would have rejected the whole idea of my wanting to fly as absolutely ridiculous. But Dr Henderson was prepared to give me the chance to prove myself. All I had to do now was get a letter from Dr Stephen and cross my fingers that the CAA in Canberra would be as understanding as Dr Henderson.

I made an appointment with Dr Stephen immediately to convince him that I had recovered sufficiently to learn to fly. Mum drove me over to his office and as I waited to see him, I wondered what his attitude would be. He came out with a broad smile on his face as usual and ushered me inside.

'Well, Janine, so what have you been up to?' he said as he sat down and put his feet up on his desk. 'You look to be walking well.'

'Thanks' I said. 'I've been working out really hard, swimming and doing weights, and I'm feeling much stronger.'

He nodded. 'How is the brace going?'

'Oh, it's much better, the plaster was driving me mad,' I laughed.

We talked for a while as he munched away on a sandwich. It was past lunchtime but the first chance he'd had to eat anything, he said apologetically.

'Well, we'd better have a look at you then,' he said at last.

He came around and helped me over to a bed where he inspected the brace and my back.

'OK,' he said. 'Let's see you walk a bit. Just go over to the door.'

I took a few tentative steps to the door, then turned around and came back.

'That's amazing,' he said.

'Why is that?' I asked.

'Well, the way you've compensated for the muscles you've lost in your legs. I'd like another colleague to have a look.' He went out and called another doctor in the room next door. They watched me closely while I hobbled up and down the hallway outside, which took great concentration on my part just to stay on my feet. I was extremely slow and my feet flopped all over the place, but I did my utmost to make it look as if I wasn't having any trouble as I still hadn't said anything to Dr Stephen about learning to fly. They seemed to be impressed, and back in Dr Stephen's room I decided to take the bull by the horns.

'Doctor Stephen, there's something else I wanted to talk about with you today,' I said.

'Yes, Janine, what is it now?' He said with a wry smile.

'Well, I have decided to learn how to fly. I went for my medical and the doctor said that he would pass me, but the aviation authorities required a letter from you giving me the OK.'

He looked at me and smiled. 'Well, nothing you do would shock me too much, Janine. What on earth put that idea into your head?'

'Well, I just had to find something interesting to do, and I thought flying might be the answer. I really want to do it. I've even been on a trial flight and I love it.'

'I've done a bit of flying myself,' he said. 'What did you go up in?'

'Oh, it was called a Tobago. Have you heard of it? It's a French plane.'

'No, I don't know it. Tell me about it.'

We chatted a bit about the aircraft and I found that he was also a bit of an aviation fan. That was in my favour, I thought.

'The only thing that worries me is how you would use your legs,' he said after a while, 'how you would use the rudder pedals.'

'Oh, that's all right,' I said. 'I'm doing exercises all the time to strengthen them. They'll be fine, believe me, Dr Stephen. Please say it's OK.'

He took a piece of paper from his desk and began writing: 'To whom it may concern . . . ' The letter briefly described my medical history and the operation that he had performed on my back and spine, then said that he saw no reason why I shouldn't be able to hold a pilot's licence.

He handed it to me and wished me the best of luck. I thanked him and said I'd let him know how it went—and maybe one day I'd be able to take him up for a ride. He just smiled.

Next stop—Canberra, and the CAA!

I contacted Andrew, the instructor at the flying school, again and told him I had been for my medical. He informed me that I was allowed to clock up a few hours even before I was issued with a student's licence. That sounded fantastic, and even though I hadn't had any response to my application from the CAA, I took him up on it and booked in for my first official lesson.

I was so excited to be starting off. I still had my brace on, but that didn't worry me, I was itching to go. I still couldn't drive, so my ever-obliging Mum would have to take me out to the airport. As I arrived at the flying school on my first day I felt a little out of place.

There were a few other people standing around inside, most of them dressed in what seemed to be the mandatory airport garb of blue pants and white shirt. I didn't know if they were instructors or students, but they all seemed to be staring at me. I was still very skinny and wearing an extremely colourful outfit that Mum and I had bought, over my brace. Nevertheless, the brace still protruded from my clothes and I looked like a potato sack. Although I was walking on my own now, I wouldn't exactly go unnoticed.

I wouldn't really call it walking—it was more like a limp and shuffle. My feet dragged along, my upper body was very stiff and I looked like I was about to fall over at any moment. I went very slowly, often having to stop and hold on to something, either to rest or just to get my balance. I was a little self-conscious as I slowly made my way over to the counter.

'Janine, how are you?' Andrew greeted me.

'Hi, Andrew,' I said. I could feel the stares around the room.

'Would you like a cup of tea or coffee before we start?' he asked.

'Well, a cup of tea would be nice, thanks.'

'I'll show you where the kitchen is. Please feel free to make yourself a cup whenever you want.'

I followed him towards a doorway across the office. He forgot how slowly I travelled and when he turned around expecting me to be on his heels I was still only a metre or two from the counter. When I finally made it, I found the kitchen was in the corner of a large room with a couple of long tables and a dozen or so chairs around them.

'This is the crew room, for the pilots' use, and over there are the briefing rooms,' he said, pointing to a row of doors along one wall. He made himself a coffee and a tea for me, and then we went into one of the rooms to talk about what we would be doing for the day. It was smaller than the crew room, with a blackboard on the wall covered with diagrams from a previous lesson and several posters of planes pinned up around it. Andrew took out his briefing notes and got down to business.

'Right, today's lesson is your first and it's called Effects of Controls,' he said, writing the heading on the board. I dutifully got a pen and paper out of my handbag and copied it down.

He picked up a model plane and began to explain the primary control surfaces of an aircraft. There were three of these, he said—the ailerons, which caused it to roll and were located on the trailing edge or rear of the mainplane; the rudder, which caused it to yaw, when its nose turned side to side, and was operated on the trailing edge of the tailplane; and the elevator, on the trailing edge on the fuselage, which caused the aeroplane to pitch, moving its nose up and down.

He went on to show me the three main axes that the plane flew around—the longitudinal, the vertical and the lateral. I followed him intently, pleased that I was understanding what he was saying, as I had read it all previously in my training manuals. We covered both the primary and secondary effects of these controls, how they were operated from the cockpit and where they were located, the effects of speed on the controls, some aspects of the ancillary controls and finally some points of elementary airmanship. When we were up in the air, he told me, if he said 'Handing over' this was my indication that it was my turn to fly. When he wanted the controls back he would say 'Taking over'. Thus there would be no mistake as to who had control of the plane.

He also explained that the training area at Bankstown was extremely busy and it was therefore important to keep a good lookout for other aircraft. He then went on to talk about the clock code, which was a means of identifying the location of other aircraft in relation to our own, by using the hands of a clock as a reference—eg, aircraft at eleven o'clock high and so on. Finally we discussed the procedures involved in taxiing around the aerodrome, and he gave me some notes on the plane we would be flying, a Tampico, which he said we would discuss later.

All in all, the briefing took about forty-five minutes, and I had taken in quite a lot of information. I was reaching my limit of sitting in one place for such a long time and was relieved when he said we were now going up. I followed him out to the front desk where he showed me how to sign on each time I went for a flight and gave me some headsets to use. Then I trailed across the tarmac with him to the aircraft. It was such a long way for me to walk, but I didn't want to let Andrew know that I was having any trouble.

Juliet Tango Lima, or JTL, was our plane for our first flight, a brown and white machine that looked badly in need of repainting, but as long as it was airworthy, it didn't really matter. It was still going to be tricky getting into the plane and I was a little embarrassed that I had to ask Andrew to help me up again. It was a real knock to my pride to admit that I couldn't manage something on my own, but I had no choice. If I wanted to fly, I had to have some help, and Andrew was there to give it.

When I was safely inside, Andrew went about the pre-flight, starting from my side and making his way around the plane. I couldn't see exactly what he was doing as he disappeared out of sight behind one of the wings, but by the time he reappeared, I gathered that he had done whatever was necessary to make it fit to fly ... I hoped!

After helping to strap me in he went through a list of all the things that had to be checked prior to take-off, pointing to the particular switch or lever and directing me to carry out the appropriate procedure with each. There was so much to do, I wondered how anyone could ever remember it all.

Then he yelled out the window, 'Clear prop' and turned the ignition key. With a cough and splutter the propeller started to rotate until it was spinning at full force. We put our headsets on, which reduced the noise, and then carried out some more checks. Andrew dialled a radio frequency called the ATIS, which gave recorded information about our flight, such as wind direction, runway direction and the like. He then called up another frequency to air traffic control and told them we were leaving for the training area. 'Juliet Tango Lima,' they responded, and at last we were off.

Andrew moved the throttle forward, then pressed his feet on the floor pedals and swung the plane around to the right as we set off down the taxiway towards the runway. He asked me if I was ready to try my hand at taxiing, but I told him that I still needed to strengthen my feet and legs a bit more.

We arrived at the run-up bays and parked close to the runway to wait until a number of planes ahead of us took off. Andrew went through some more checks, making sure that the engine was running properly before we left the ground. Satisfied that it was all OK, we made our way to the line-up point on the runway.

Andrew called up the man in the control tower again, who told us that we were clear to line up and wait for a clearance to take off. It was another few minutes before it came.

'Juliet Tango Lima—clear for take-off,' the voice said at last.

'Juliet Tango Lima,' Andrew replied.

He told me to put my hands on the control column in front of me, which resembled the steering wheel of a car, then to put my hand on the throttle and gradually move it forward. The aeroplane picked up speed and we roared along the runway. I had my eyes fixed on the runway in front of me, not daring to look to the side, everything seemed to be happening so quickly.

'OK, start pulling back on the control column,' Andrew said. I did. The aeroplane lifted off the ground. We had taken off ... *I* had taken off! The land disappeared beneath us and the windscreen was filled by blue sky. I kept my eyes firmly ahead, remembering what Andrew had said about other aircraft and determined to keep a good lookout.

'Taking over,' Andrew said, and I released my grip on the control column. 'Now let's look at some of the primary controls that we talked about.'

He went over the various points we had discussed in the classroom, demonstrating them to me one by one and then saying 'Handing over' for me to have a go at them. It all flowed logically and I finally got to 'see' all the things I had been reading about for the past few months.

I couldn't help but feel excited. There I was, sitting in my brace with my weak little legs that didn't work properly ... but I was flying! How I wished my doctors could see me now. Maybe there were things that I couldn't do for now anyway, but I could fly and not even a broken body could stop me.

The flight passed much too quickly and before I knew it we had landed JTL and taxied back to the flying school. Next stop was back into the classroom for what Andrew called a 'debrief' to talk about how the flight had progressed, over another cup of tea.

Mum arrived to pick me up and with my head bursting with all the knowledge I had absorbed during the day, I said goodbye to Andrew, having made a booking for my next lesson in a few weeks' time. I wanted to get as many lessons under my belt as I could before the decision was made about my licence as I was still unsure if I would be allowed to hold one.

I got Mum to stop off at the airport bookshop, where I bought a log book to write up each of my flights. In the weeks before my next lesson, I would do as much reading as I could manage and be thoroughly prepared for it.

In the interim, I would keep up with all my exercises and training, I needed to get the strength back in my feet and legs so that I would be able to taxi the plane. I really had something concrete to work for now, and that in itself was all the incentive I needed to push myself even harder.

Chapter 16

THE WHOLE ORDEAL of my accident was starting to take its toll on Mum and Dad. Ever since it happened they had devoted themselves to me and my recovery, without a minute to themselves. They needed a rest, a break from constantly looking after me, and after a family discussion we all decided that it would do everyone good if they got away and had a holiday.

Mum was reluctant at first, as they couldn't leave me on my own at home. However, my eldest sister Kim, who was living in Adelaide at the time, said she would be happy to come and stay for a week or so to look after me. I hadn't seen Kim since just after the accident, nor had we seen much of each other before that as she had been living interstate with her husband Lenny for the past few years, so there was a lot to catch up on. Dad made a booking for a week in Tasmania and he and Mum began preparing for the trip.

Kim arrived a few days before they left and quickly settled in. After they had gone I asked Kim if she would take me shopping to buy some new clothes. Kim was what could be called a 'professional' shopper and didn't need much persuasion.

She drove me to the local shopping centre to see what we could find in terms of a bargain, and I wanted to find some decent gear that would fit over my brace. I was sick and tired of looking like a sack, and wanted something that was at least a bit fashionable.

We looked around and I found a rather large top in black and white stripes that came down to just above my knees with a zipper up the front. I loved it! I tried it on over my tracksuit and brace and it covered the brace entirely. Fortunately, big clothes seemed to be 'in' that year so I had a bit of luck. Kim agreed that it was perfect for me so I bought it and wore it straightaway.

It made a difference to the way I felt. Feeling so unattractive inside it was important for me to feel I still looked good on the outside and the best way to do that was to find some decent clothes that I felt comfortable and attractive in. It made me feel less conspicuous and that I blended in with everyone else. After some more shopping we decided to head off and have some lunch.

Kim has always been a large build, and as long as I could remember she had always been on a diet of some sort. I was the exact opposite when it came to body shape. I was always thin and could eat and eat and not put on any weight, which was exactly what I did, much to the horror of both my sisters who were not so lucky. Today wasn't any different. Kim was on yet another diet. The funny thing was that I was on a diet too, but mine was to put on weight, not to lose it! A recipe for trouble, no doubt.

We sat in the restaurant and I decided to order something with the most calories possible in it—a double helping of pancakes with the lot, ice-cream, cream and every imaginable kind of syrup, and a banana milkshake. Then it was Kim's turn to order—a wheatbread cracker with a small salad and a cup of black coffee.

The waitress arrived with our orders and put them in front of us. My plate was piled so high with ice-cream and cream I could barely see over it. Kim's on the other hand looked like an ad for a weight watchers' clinic. We looked at each other, and in my mind I knew what she was thinking. 'You'd better eat every bite on your plate—if you leave one tiny bit I'll kill you!'

We both dug in, she crunching away on her cracker bread and I wolfing down my pancakes as quickly as possible. Before long, however, I was full to the brim. My eyes were still larger than my stomach and I couldn't face another bite. And half the pancakes were still left on my plate.

'Oh, Kim,' I said. 'I'm so sorry, but I can't fit in any more.'

She looked at me in despair. I knew it would be some time before she took me out to lunch again!

When Mum and Dad returned from their holiday, they were in for a big surprise. While they were away, Adrian had called in to say he had a special present for me—a puppy. One of the nurses at the hospital had a dog which had just had a litter and Adrian thought it would be good company for me to have one of them.

Kim and I arranged to go and have a look at them. A bunch of cute little puppies all begging to be taken home jumped all over us. I finally settled on the one that looked a bit different from the rest.

It was a female covered in black and white spots and she was gorgeous. All she needed was a name, which I couldn't think of for the moment. On top of this Kim had acquired a kitten, so Mum and Dad were going to be in for quite a shock, I thought. I was right. Mum wasn't exactly ecstatic about her new boarders, but after seeing how much fun I had with the puppy she was hardly going to put it out on the street.

However, she indirectly got her revenge on Adrian the next time he came around. He was dressed immaculately as ever and had on a very expensive-looking pair of shoes, Italian, no doubt. As he was standing by the door, the still-unnamed puppy came to say hello and politely sat on his foot and did the biggest pee I'd ever seen! Mum and Dad had their revenge after all!

My next flying lesson proceeded like the first—the cup of tea, the briefing, notes, and of course the long, slow walk down to the aeroplane. Because of my brace I was still unable to bend down to do all the checks on the aircraft, and even without it I wouldn't have been able to get down that far anyway. Andrew excused me from the pre-flights, knowing there was time for that later. I just watched what he was doing as he explained it all to me.

It was a straightforward practical session. I learned about the various speeds the aircraft could hold and the different configurations in which it could fly while still maintaining a straight course and level attitude. It was all very new and exciting to me, and I made every effort to perform as well as I could.

When I got home that day, there was a letter waiting for me. I looked at the envelope and saw that it was from the CAA. This was what I had been waiting for, the reply to my application for a licence. I nervously opened it. What if they had rejected me? My heart jumped as I read ' . . . Student pilot licence . . . approved'. I couldn't believe it—I had passed!

The date was December 22, only three days before Christmas, and I couldn't have wished for a better present! I rang the flying school straightaway to tell them the good news and made a booking for another lesson on Christmas Eve. Most people would have been out celebrating the festive season, but all I could think about was getting back into the cockpit for my next lesson.

The flying school was closing over Christmas so I would have to wait another few weeks before I took to the air again. Christmas that year was filled with mixed feelings. Although happy to be home with my family, I was saddened by the thought of not being overseas skiing with the team. I couldn't help thinking if it hadn't been for the accident, I would be away preparing for the Olympics.

My birthday fell a fortnight after Christmas and Mum decided to throw a big party for me, thinking that a celebration was just what I needed. I had an appointment with Dr Stephen the week before my birthday and I pleaded with him to let me take my brace off for good in time for the party. I wasn't due to have it removed for another few weeks, but Dr Stephen must have been having a good day, because he agreed.

As soon as I got home, I took the wretched thing off. Free at last! And what a feeling it was to know that I didn't have to put it on ever again. It had been almost eight months since the accident and finally things seemed to be coming to an end.

I walked around savouring my new-found freedom. I felt vulnerable and unprotected, but it felt good nevertheless. The first thing I wanted to do was to have a bath, something I had dreamed about for ages. Mum filled the tub for me, and in I stepped. To my surprise, although the water was hot, the lack of sensation in my legs meant that I couldn't feel it until I was actually sitting down. I hadn't realised how much of my body was still numb.

I sat upright in the bath, hesitant to lie down because it had been so long since I had bent my back. But what was a bath if you couldn't lie down? I lowered myself cautiously into it holding onto the sides. I felt the water level rise around my neck, closed my eyes and sank back in absolute bliss.

My birthday arrived and quite a crowd turned up for the party, despite most of my skiing friends being overseas. Daven was away with them too, but his parents and the rest of the family came. The weather was hot and I enjoyed being able to wear 'normal' clothes like everyone else instead of the baggy outfits that made me look like a sack.

Mum had cooked a veritable feast, crowned by a huge birthday cake inscribed with 'Happy 25th birthday Janine' in big icing letters and everyone gathered around the table to blow out the candles and sing 'Happy Birthday'. Then Dad said a few words.

As he thanked everyone for coming and for the support that they had given me and our family since the accident, he became quite emotional and had to stop in mid-speech. There wasn't a dry eye in the room. As I looked around the crowd of faces, I realised again how fortunate I was to be here celebrating at all. I had been given a second chance at life and that made this birthday even more special.

Now that my brace was off, there were a million things I wanted to do, one of which was get back behind the wheel of my car. I was fed up with having to ask people to drive me around everywhere, much as I appreciated it. However, I just wanted some independence back.

My little car was a manual, which meant that I had to be able to put my foot on the clutch to change gears. My legs were still very weak and I didn't know if I would be able to manage it yet. But I would never know until I gave it a try. I knew that Mum wouldn't be too keen to have me back on the road, so I waited until she was out at work one day and

I went out to the car, put the keys in the ignition and started the engine.

It seemed ages since I had driven a car and I was feeling a bit nervous. I put my left foot on the clutch pedal and tried to push it in. It worked! I couldn't get it all the way down, but far enough to force the gear stick through. I put the car into first and away I went, up the driveway and back, then up and back again. I managed to kangaroo-jump all the way up the drive till I was just about on the road. It wasn't the most efficient way to travel but it got me from A to B. Now I just had to get the timing right.

Next step was onto the road. I looked around and saw the coast was clear. Luckily we lived in a quiet street and there wasn't much traffic during the day. Perfect for learning how to drive again. I put my foot on the accelerator once more and off I went. Watch out, world, here I come! I hopped my way up the street in first gear, not too good for the old engine. It was too risky trying to change into second, so this would have to do for now. At the end of the street I decided to go the whole way around the block. As I made my way along the next street I was really getting the hang of things and took the plunge into second. Now I was really moving!

I went around again and then a third time until I could manage to change the gears smoothly. The trouble was I had so little strength and feeling in my feet that it was difficult to tell what they were doing, I had to look down to check that they were obeying their orders.

I managed to get the car back into the garage before Mum got home. I thought I had better break the news gently to her. When she came in I was sitting at the kitchen table, looking just a tad guilty, I suspect.

'Hi Mum, how was your day?' I asked. She started to put away the groceries she was carrying.

'Oh, pretty busy,' she replied. 'How was your day, have you been doing your exercises?'

'Yes, and guess what else I did?'

She looked suspicious. 'I'm afraid to ask.'

'I went for a drive in my car.'

'You didn't!' she said.

'I did, and I was fine.'

'That was a silly thing to do,' she sighed, 'you could have been hurt.'

'No, it was OK, really, I had to know if I could do it. Come on, I'll show you. I'll take you around the block.'

Mum reluctantly agreed. She knew that she couldn't stop me even if she had wanted to, so she was anxious at least to make sure that I was safe. I drove around the block a few times until she was satisfied that I wouldn't do any harm to myself or anyone else.

Getting my wheels back was a real stepping stone for me. I no longer had to rely on others, especially Mum, and most importantly I could now drive myself out to the airport, which meant that I could go out there more often.

My lessons now continued at a rapid rate. Sometimes I even managed to get in two flights a day. Now that I could drive my car I found I could also manage the rudder pedals in the plane. It took a great deal of concentration and all of my strength, but I was able to keep the plane on the taxiway quite successfully. The only thing was that I didn't work the pedals the normal way, as Andrew soon commented.

'No, Janine, don't do it like that,' he said sharply. 'Leave your heels on the floor and use the top part of your feet to depress the pedals.'

'I can't, Andrew, this is the only way I can do it,' I answered.

I had to slide my feet right up the pedals so that I was pushing with my heels, so that the strength came from my upper legs, or quadriceps, and I was able to have some control. This was the only way in which I could compensate for the lack of strength in my feet.

I came to a point in my training called 'circuits', which involved flying continually around the airport using all the necessary skills that had to be mastered before being allowed to go 'solo', from taking off to landing.

Circuits were very demanding as the workload was so high. You had to think all the time, working the controls, doing checks, calling traffic control on the radio for instructions and of course watching out for the numerous other aircraft also in the area.

One day I took my friend Pauline out to the airport with me, as it was her birthday and I had given her a flight for a present. Andrew was going to take her up so I was booked in with another instructor named Bill.

Bill and I went out for a session of circuits. It was a beautiful day and there was not much traffic in the circuit area. I was concentrating hard and everything seemed to be going well. After a couple of landings we started to taxi off the runway again when Bill called up the tower and told them he had a student going solo for the first time. I was surprised but very excited. I was really going to fly this thing all by myself.

'All right, Janine, I think you are ready to do this one on your own,' he said. 'I'd like you to do just one circuit then come back and pick me up. How do you feel about that?'

'Oh, I feel great,' I said.

'Take your time and relax, just like you've been doing and you'll be fine, but most of all, have fun.' With that he climbed out and I was on my own.

I looked around the cabin, not wanting to forget anything.

With the checklist in my hand I ran through what I had to do. Trim ... set for take-off. Flaps ... take-off position. Fuel ... selection and contents. Fuel pump ... on. Carby heat ... off. Mixture ... rich. Flight instruments ... checked. Avionics ... set. Magnetos ... both. Seatbelts ... fastened. Doors ... secure. Controls ... full and free movement. I was ready.

I taxied along the taxiway and over to the runway holding point. Here I go, ready or never. I depressed the transceiver button.

'Juliet Tango Lima, ready runway left,' I said.

'Juliet Tango Lima, line up,' my instructions came back.

I had one more look to see that there was no traffic on final approach to my runway, just as I had been taught. Nothing. All clear. I taxied over to the centre of the runway, and made sure that I had lined up straight. I looked over to the windsock to check the wind direction. It was moving around just a little, the wind was light and variable.

I looked at my instruments. Everything seemed OK. I sat nervously, waiting for my final instructions from the tower.

'Juliet Tango Lima, clear for take-off.' That was my cue.

Here goes ... I moved my hand forward, advancing the throttle. I was on my way. JTL picked up speed and began to roll down the runway. I looked at my airspeed ... thirty knots, forty knots, fifty knots, sixty knots ... I pulled back on the control column and lifted off the runway. There was no turning back now, I was on my own.

Eyes straight ahead, I had to concentrate. Climb, eighty knots ... Three hundred feet checks ... Flaps up, fuel pump off ... Check temperatures and pressures, maintain runway heading. Five hundred feet, I began to turn to my left onto the crosswind leg. Eight hundred feet, level off and reduce power to circuit power. I looked to my left to make sure that I was maintaining a neat circuit. It looked good.

I turned left onto the downwind leg and began my downwind checks. When I got to the hatches and harness check instinctively I looked over to the seat normally occupied by my instructor. It was empty. I let out the biggest yell of my life in sheer excitement. I looked down at the airport spread out below me, then away to the city in the distance. It was absolutely exhilarating.

Back to work. Concentrate. I still had to get this thing down. The runway was coming up fast to meet me and I checked my airspeed. Everything was OK. I flew to the runway threshold and brought the power back as I raised the attitude to straight and level. I felt the mainwheels gently settle on the ground, then held the nose wheel off for a little longer. Down it went. I slid my feet up the rudder pedals and used all the strength I had to apply the brakes. The plane began to slow down. Then I pushed the left pedal as hard as I could and the aircraft swung left onto the taxiway.

I was on the ground. I had done it!

I taxied back to where Bill was waiting for me and called the tower. A controller responded, 'Congratulations, Juliet Tango Lima.'

I parked the plane and Bill jumped in. 'Well done, that was a nice landing,' he said as he held out his hand for me to shake.

'Thanks, it was easier than I thought,' I said.

We went back to the flying school where I looked for Pauline to tell her all about it. She and Andrew had seen my aircraft in the circuit area and when they saw Bill waiting on the ground they knew I was on my own.

Everyone congratulated me on my first solo and they even stamped my log book for me. I was on a real high, and couldn't wait to get home to tell Mum and Dad. I knew they would be proud of what I had done. I was over the moon— this was one day I would *never* forget!

Having completed my first solo, I felt as if I was really on my way. Now it was back out to the training area to complete other exercises in forced landings—I hoped I would never have to do one for real—basic instrument flying and precautionary search and landing procedures, and then I was sent out on my own. To fly around the circuit area solo was fantastic, but help was always close by if something went wrong. Once I was out in the training area, away from the security of the airport, however, it was a different matter.

I took my flying very seriously. I felt as if I had something to prove, not just to myself but to everyone else. Because of the way I walked, people were always staring at me. I knew they had no idea what I had been through, but it was still very demoralising. On top of that my body was still recovering from the trauma of the accident. I still suffered quite a lot of discomfort and pain, and the sheer effort of getting around tired me out terribly. But I pushed myself despite this and it gave me a great sense of achievement which made it all worthwhile.

After months of lessons and actually flying, the time finally came for me to do my test for a private pilot's licence, under the chief instructor at the school, whose name was Neville. He had shown great interest in me since I first began and always offered me encouragement.

As the day of my test approached it just so happened that the planes I had been flying were out of service. They were all fixed-pitch aircraft and the only others available were of a different type called constant speed. It was all related to the type of propeller they had and each type required different systems knowledge to fly them.

I was naturally eager to take the test, no matter what, so Neville suggested I learn to fly one of the constant-speed planes the school had on line. I agreed and spent a few hours with one of the other instructors learning the different system involved. There was an extra power lever to worry about, so I had to go through a whole new set of speed and power settings, and then become familiar with the plane itself.

At last, I was ready. I went out to the plane and did my pre-flight inspection, while Neville watched to see that I was doing everything correctly. He then asked me questions about the different parts of the plane, to make sure that I had a good understanding of it. Then I had to take it up into the training area for the most important part of the test, with Neville sitting beside me hardly saying a word. I was a little nervous, but told myself I just had to do everything as I was taught and I would be OK.

I made it out to the training area without any mishap, and then it was down to business. As if working through a checklist, Neville asked me to demonstrate all the things that I had covered in my training. I had to stall the aircraft, put it through steep turns, and fly it in different configurations. Then, out of the blue, he suddenly pulled the power back to idle to simulate an engine failure, to which I had to respond immediately by finding a suitable open space like a paddock to land in and then go through the entire scenario as if it was really happening. I flew as low as possible over a large open field until Neville said, 'OK, go around.' I added power and raised the nose to the climbing attitude, hoping the poor farmer in the house below wasn't too perturbed!

On our way back to the airport, Neville put me through the same routine again, except that this time we were over a built-up area and there were no paddocks to land in. I lowered the nose and fortunately spotted a small sports field just off to my left. 'I'm going down there,' I said and started to go through my drills. 'OK, that's fine,' Neville said. 'Go around.' So off we headed back to the airport.

The landing went well and when we taxied back to the

flying school I was feeling confident that I had passed. But Neville hadn't said a word. I stopped the plane and looked at him. He grinned at me.

'Congratulations, young lady, you are now the holder of a private pilot's licence,' he said, and shook me heartily by the hand.

I could feel a smile spreading across my face from ear to ear. I had actually got my licence. I was a real fair dinkum pilot!

Back at the flying school, Andrew was waiting for me on the edge of the tarmac. One glimpse of my happy smile was enough for him to know how I had gone.

'Congratulations, I guess you passed,' he said, beaming like a proud parent.

'Yes,' I laughed, 'how can you tell?'

'How about a cup of tea?' Neville asked, putting his arm around my shoulder.

'That sounds great, I really need one now.'

After my cup of tea, I did what any new pilot would do— I made a booking for my first fully qualified flight, in two days' time. They didn't know it yet, but my first passengers would of course be Mum and Dad.

Mum and Dad were delighted to hear of my success. But Mum wasn't exactly thrilled by my little surprise. Going up in a light aircraft was about the last thing she ever wanted to do. However, my powers of persuasion got the better of her, especially when I told her that all new pilots took their parents up as their first passengers. So she reluctantly agreed, mainly not to disappoint me, I think. Dad on the other hand was excited at the prospect.

We arrived at the airport bright and early for our big flight. The weather was perfect, clear and sunny, which made Mum feel a little better. We were booked in to fly Juliet Tango

Oscar, a Tobago, and after I had completed all the paperwork I took my passengers out to the aircraft to prepare for the flight.

I took the whole thing very seriously and tried to be as professional as possible, to make Mum feel a bit more at ease. After Mum and Dad were inside and I had finished my pre-flight inspection, I gave them a briefing on the standard emergency procedures should something go wrong. Mum wasn't thrilled to hear the word 'emergency', but I told her it was just a precaution.

I taxied down to the run-up bay, did my run-ups and lined up on the runway. As soon as we had taken off Mum, who was sitting in the back, leant forward and tapped me on the shoulder.

'Janine, what's that on the wing?' she asked nervously.

I looked out to the left and saw fuel spilling out of the wing tank.

'Oh, that's normal, don't worry about it,' I said reassuringly. But to be honest I didn't have a clue what was wrong. However, there was no point in panicking, I thought.

I continued as normal out to the training area, keeping my eye on the wing. To my dismay the fuel was still spilling out, and not knowing what the problem was I thought I had better go back and get it attended to. I calmly told the control tower what I was doing and when I landed and taxied back to the flying school, one of the instructors came out to see what was wrong.

It turned out that someone had overfilled the tank. But it hadn't been leaking, as I secretly feared. Instead, the excess fuel was simply venting itself out of the tank, which was completely normal in such circumstances. I had never heard of this before and I was relieved to know it was nothing serious after all. So we got back in the plane and took off again.

Once we were out in the training area I flew around and showed them the sights. Dad loved it, and I had a sneaking suspicion that Mum was enjoying herself too. I pointed out Warragamba Dam and the Nepean River and Wollongong over in the distance. On our way back I thought I'd show Dad some of the tricks I'd learned and brought the power back to idle to demonstrate a glide descent. Mum immediately began to panic, tapping me on the shoulder again.

'Don't you practise one of your stalls on me!' she said.

'Don't worry, Mum, I'm just descending to go back to the airport,' I assured her, but I made sure I did a smooth landing, so as not to upset her any further.

Back at the flying school, Mum got talking to one of the instructors.

'You're brave,' he said. 'My parents still won't go up with me!'

'What do you mean?' said Mum. 'Janine said you all took your parents up on your first flight.'

'Not my parents! They were too scared, they would never have come!'

Mum just looked at me. 'That's not what Janine told us.'

Oops, I was found out! Oh well, I think Mum actually did enjoy the flight, despite the fact that she thought it would be her last. Anyway, she was proud of me and what I had achieved, and so was Dad.

And I was just as proud of Mum for coming along.

Chapter 17

MY FRIENDS AT college had stayed in regular contact with me since I came home from hospital. They were all keen to have me back with them in class and kept encouraging me to finish my studies. When I was still in my plaster cast, my friend Pauline had driven me into campus to visit everyone. I hadn't told anyone that I was coming, but from checking the timetable I knew they would all be in the sports lab for a class on human performance.

I walked into the room, with Pauline holding my arm. I guess I was the last person they expected at the time. They all looked astonished, then gave me a great cheer and began to clap. It was a very moving experience and I realised how much I missed them all. My lecturer, Warwick, was just as surprised as everyone else and he abandoned the lesson so they could all sit around and talk to me.

They had all been wonderful during the whole ordeal of the accident, and I always had a regular stream of visitors, both students and lecturers, while I was in hospital. They had even taken up a collection and bought me a sheepskin bed rest and sent me a get-well card signed by just about everyone at college, even people I didn't know.

Their encouragement persuaded me to give college another try, even though trying to finish a degree in physical education seemed a little far-fetched at the time, considering my injuries. However, they all believed I could do it—and so did I. I only had six months' courses to do before I graduated and I believed it wouldn't be that difficult.

My lecturers did everything they could to help me. As I wasn't able to undertake the physical lessons at present, they arranged for me to enrol only in theory subjects until I could manage the practical side. Nonetheless, I found it harder to readjust than I had at first anticipated. It wasn't just that I was physically impaired, but I no longer saw myself as an athlete and, much as I tried, I just didn't know where I fitted in.

The first day back I had to go to the medical centre to pick up a disabled driver's pass so I could park close to where I had to attend class. The fact that I needed a 'disabled' pass was a real blow to me. It seemed like some sort of label, but no matter how much I disliked it, I needed it. No matter how hard I tried to forget that I had had an accident and tried to 'fit in' with all my friends, I couldn't, and this caused me a great amount of torment.

I wasn't able to join in things the way I used to. At lunchtime, for instance, we would all be sitting together talking and laughing, and someone would organise a game of basketball or softball and everyone would head to the gym or down to the oval. It upset me greatly that I wasn't able to take part. I felt like an outsider.

So after only a few weeks at college, I began to get quite depressed. I missed my sport so much, but no matter how hard I tried I couldn't get my old life back. I hated the way I saw myself physically, and being at college was just rubbing salt into the wound.

One day Mum came into my room and found me crying. She sensed that my return to college was upsetting me but she had been hoping I'd be able to cope. We both sat on my bed together, crying. I thought I was getting on top of everything but this had brought me down again. Sport was my entire life, even my vocation. If I didn't have that, what did I have?

I knew at the back of my mind I had to leave college. It was starting to destroy me and making it impossible for me to function properly. I had no idea what else I would do, but I had to get away and give myself a chance to think. It was a big decision for me, because I had always planned my life to a tee.

After the 1988 Olympics I had intended to return to college and qualify as an exercise physiologist. A few weeks before my accident, when I was attending a camp for the ski team at the Australian Institute of Sport, I made some inquiries about the courses available in this field and the job prospects available. This was where my real interests lay. I loved the study of physiology, learning what made the body tick and how we could exploit our abilities to get the maximum from ourselves. It was a natural choice of career for me and I found that my knowledge in the area aided my own training and performance.

Flying was a saving grace. Although it was only a hobby, it gave me a real sense of satisfaction and achievement. When I was up in a plane, I was just like everyone else and nobody could tell that there was anything different about me, or that I walked 'funny', and that was important, whereas at college I felt self-conscious and inadequate.

So I did the only thing I could do at the time—I continued to fly. I went on joy flights in the training area to keep my hand in and I read whatever I could on the subject. But most importantly I decided to try for an unrestricted private licence, or UPPL, which would allow me to fly anywhere I liked on my own. It entailed sitting for more exams on the fundamentals of navigation, meteorology, and flight rules and procedures. I was unable to attend classes on the course, as travelling into the city was too much for me, so I studied at home on my own. After a few weeks I sat for the exams and passed. Now I was ready to tackle the practical side of things and in an aircraft.

There was a lot more involved than for the restricted licence and there was a great deal of preparation before each flight. First I'd have to call in at the briefing office at the airport to get weather details for the day and a special bulletin called NOTAM, or Notice to Airmen, setting out any special requirements or procedures in the area where I intended to fly, which had to be carefully scrutinised. The people behind the counter would answer any questions I had regarding the flight and accept my flight plan to submit it to flight service. Then I'd go back to the flying school to discuss the practical problems of the flight with my instructor.

My first trip out of the training area was to be up to Cessnock and back to Bankstown. I was to be flying under Visual Flight Rules, or VFR, which meant navigating by map without the use of instruments and finding my way to Cessnock by coordinating what I observed of the countryside below with points on the map.

I would also be using Dead Reckoning Procedures, which meant estimating my whereabouts and making any necessary corrections to the track I was on. In addition to this, I had to maintain contact with flight service, fill in my flight plan, plan climbs and descents, and of course actually fly the plane.

Using a number of maps, I planned the trip and filled out my flight plan accordingly, giving the track I would fly, the forecast wind and the heading I should take, as well as my estimated time of arrival (ETA) at Cessnock and time segments for each of the legs I would be flying. I then went back to the briefing office with Andrew, who would be accompanying me, to lodge the plan. It was checked and stamped, meaning that it was officially approved, and we returned to the flying school to depart.

I set myself up in the plane as Andrew instructed me, with a clipboard on my lap and my flight plan in easy reach. We were to head north from Bankstown along the light aircraft lane, a designated departure lane for light aircraft to keep them away from the large jets coming in from the north. To deviate from this lane, either laterally or vertically, would put us in the path of an approaching airliner and in clear view to the radar controllers in Sydney.

We took off and headed up the light aircraft lane. Instead of letting me take things one at a time, for some reason Andrew lumped everything on me at once and I got a bit flustered. Andrew started to bully me and raised his voice to hurry me up, which only upset me more, although I didn't let on to him. It was the first time I had seen him like this, although I later learnt it was part of his teaching style. It may have been alright with anyone else but, with my confidence at an all-time low, it really upset me. I needed all the encouragement I could get.

Once we were out of the Bankstown control zone, I calmed down somewhat and was able to enjoy the scenery en route. As we neared Cessnock, I listened in on flight service frequency to find out which runway other planes were using and joined the circuit pattern to land. The airfield was full of other aircraft as there was quite a large flying school at Cessnock operating from the strip.

We stayed on the ground long enough to get out and stretch our legs, and then climbed back in for our return journey. I made it back to Bankstown without any problems, relieved that I didn't get us lost even once! I managed to enjoy most of the flight, or at least the scenery, despite Andrew's continuing 'aggressive' teaching style.

Back at the school, Andrew started to debrief me on the flight. He managed to tell me everything I had failed to do, omitting to praise me for anything I had done right. So much for positive reinforcement, I thought. I was getting pretty upset and could feel tears welling up, which was the last thing I wanted to happen. I didn't want him to think I was 'weak' or that I couldn't take it, and I certainly didn't want any special treatment.

Andrew knew about my accident, but had no idea of the sort of adjustments that I had had to make to my life as a result. Nor did I want him to know. My personal problems were my own business and I didn't want to bring them to the school with me.

Fearing that the rest of our flights would follow the same pattern, I decided to pipe up so that he would pipe down. I said I had a few problems at home, and that in view of the way things were going maybe we should consider changing instructors for the rest of my training, maybe that would work out better.

Andrew stared at me. I could tell my suggestion had taken him completely by surprise. He had no idea that he had upset me and he apologised for anything he may have said that had done so. We talked about it and managed to work a few things out. Andrew was a junior instructor and still feeling his way, so it was a learning experience for him too. We agreed to continue lessons together and Andrew softened his approach somewhat.

I finished the course in just under a month. I managed to fly around the country, from Scone to Goulburn to Mudgee, without getting lost once, which I was pretty pleased about! The day finally arrived for me to undertake my flight test, which I was to do with Neville again. We were to fly up to

Cessnock, just like my first 'Nav', except that on the way home we landed at Mascot airport. This was actually the second time I had flown into Sydney's major airport and I still found it exciting, although I did feel like a speck on the ground next to all the big jets.

The test took two-and-a-half hours and Neville really made me work. He threw everything in the book at me and by the time I got back to Bankstown, I was exhausted. The flight had gone as well as I could have expected and I was pretty sure I had passed—and I was right!

I was now a fully-fledged private pilot, able to fly anywhere in the country on my own. It was a wonderful feeling, not to mention a great boost for my morale. I had kept on and done something many people doubted was possible, and more importantly I had proved something to myself.

I remembered that it was only eleven months earlier that I had taken my first non-commercial flight—in the Westpac helicopter on the way to hospital ... and what a long way I had come since then!

Chapter 18

WHILE I HAD been pursuing my flying over the past few months, Daven was overseas with the ski team following the circuit I would have been on. When he came back, he told me a lot of people had been asking after me and sent their best wishes. He or Chris had told the Canadians of my accident and while they were away I received a letter from Marty Hall, the coach, to say how sorry they were to hear of it. He said that they had all enjoyed having me with them the year before and that he hoped to see me again soon. This meant a lot to me, and made me even more determined to get back on the snow.

It had been months since I had seen Daven, but in the meantime I had seen a lot of Adrian. He was still obviously keen on pursuing our relationship and although I kept insisting that I was spoken for, I enjoyed his company a lot.

When Adrian first rang to ask me out after I got home from hospital, I still had my doubts about it. I enjoyed being with him, but didn't think it would be fair to Daven. But I felt a special link with Adrian. He knew the other side of me, the patient persona, and understood what I had been through as no-one else could. The other problem of course was that, although he was only Dr Stephen's registrar, he was still in a sense my doctor. It just didn't seem right.

His first invitation was to see the Sydney Dance Company at the Opera House. I was still in my plaster cast and didn't think I could handle such an occasion. I thanked him for the offer but declined. That was when Mum and Dad were away and Kim was looking after me. She loved ballet and modern dance and couldn't believe I had turned Adrian down.

'What, you said no!' she exclaimed. 'If you won't go, tell him I will.' Kim was never backwards in coming forward.

I had the perfect solution. I rang Adrian back and told him I would go if my sister Kim could come, as a sort of chaperone. This way I convinced myself that it wasn't really a 'proper' date, just three friends going out together. Adrian agreed and we set a date and time.

Adrian picked us up and drove us to the show and home again, despite the fact that it was a long way from where he lived. He was always the perfect gentleman, the sort who would open the car door for you, which I wasn't used to. I really enjoyed myself that night and knew that it probably wouldn't be the last.

Adrian and I began to see quite a lot of each other. He showered me with affection and gifts and the attention did wonders for me. He was a very handsome and eligible young doctor and I was very flattered. He sent me flowers, rang me constantly and when he was away on holidays he always wrote to me. I even received an overseas cable from him at one time.

Our relationship was starting to get more serious and although part of me wanted to stop it going any further, it seemed to be just what the 'doctor' ordered for me. Perhaps it was just a matter of bad timing, but our 'romance' was destined to be short-lived and our relationship became one of solid friendship. I was carrying too much emotional baggage and getting involved in another relationship was too much for me to deal with at the time. I had to sort myself out with Daven, and get my life back into some degree of order. I was far too vulnerable to deal with other people's emotions on top of my own.

One night I was sitting on the couch playing with 'Buddy', as I had finally named the puppy Adrian had given me, when the doorbell rang.

'I'll get it,' I said to Mum, who was busy in her chair knitting.

I opened the door to find myself staring at the biggest bunch of flowers I had ever seen in my life. From beneath them poked a pair of legs. 'Hello,' I said.

The flowers lowered to reveal Daven hiding behind them.

'Surprise,' he said as he lifted me up in his arms and gave me a tight hug.

'Dav, what are you doing here?' I exclaimed. 'You're not supposed to be home for another week.'

'I know, but I missed you, so I thought I'd catch an early flight and surprise you.'

That's exactly what he did do—surprise me. He came in and Mum got him a drink while he brought us up to date on his time away and I told him about my flying achievements.

After he left I couldn't help thinking of the irony of the situation. Although flying had given me a new direction in life, I knew inside that it was actually taking us further away from each other. The awkwardness I felt among my sporting friends was offset by the satisfaction I got from flying. It wasn't that I didn't want to be near my friends—it was just that it hurt too much.

Daven had thought after the accident that we could still make a go of it, and so had I. He wanted things to be as they were before—he wanted me back, the old Janine, doing all the things we had done before. Sure I couldn't do them now, but it would get better and all work out eventually. But that night I realised he was wrong. It couldn't be the same as it was before. I had changed too much for that.

There was too much happening in my life now that I was unsure of. I didn't feel capable of giving Daven the sort of relationship that he wanted, and I didn't think it was fair on him to continue this way. Perhaps the accident was only the catalyst of something that would have happened anyway, I wasn't sure. I had been uncertain about things long before the accident, even before I went overseas, and I didn't want to continue with the relationship just because I needed someone to lean on. I had to sort myself out alone.

It was almost a year after the accident when I ended the relationship with Daven. Although I knew it was best in the long run, it was a painful and difficult decision to make. We had been together for such a long time and were such great friends, but the time had come to part ways. And so for the first time in six years, I was now truly on my own.

Now that I had an unrestricted licence I didn't think there was much further I could go. The next qualification I could get was a commercial pilot's licence or CPL, but there didn't seem much point in trying for it as the medical standards were even higher than for a private licence. Besides, it was only necessary if you were thinking of pursuing a career in aviation and this was the furthest thing from my mind. I couldn't even walk properly—who in their right mind would hire me to fly passengers around? And who would get in an aeroplane with a pilot who limped down to the aircraft? I'm sure they would have thought I was a liability. No, this was not even a consideration for me.

Instead, I decided to get my licence endorsed for another plane in the fleet at the flying school, the Trinidad. It was also a constant-speed aircraft, but as well as a more powerful engine, it also had a retractable undercarriage. This meant learning how to bring the wheels up after take-off and even more importantly, of course, lowering them before landing.

Neville took me through the check ride for the endorsement and afterwards we sat down for a chat and a cup of tea.

'Sheppo,' he said, as he used to call me, 'now that you've got your PPL, why don't you think about getting your commercial?'

'My commercial? Neville, are you kidding?'

'What do you mean?' he asked.

'Well, who would ever give me a job?'

'I would,' he said bluntly. I looked at him. He wasn't joking.

'What sort of job?' I pressed him.

'Well why don't you think about getting a commercial licence, then your instructor's rating, and I'd give you a job as an instructor.'

'Are you serious, Neville, you'd really give me a job?' I asked incredulously.

'You bet. Why don't you think about it?'

'Yeah, I'll do that,' I said, still a bit flabbergasted.

The thought seemed quite daunting. Not just a qualified commercial pilot, but an instructor to boot! Who would have believed it! Imagine my students seeing me limp down to the aircraft to teach them how to fly. What would I say?

'Oh, don't worry, I was in a serious accident, that's all. I'm a partial paraplegic ... But don't worry, you're in safe hands with me—lightning doesn't strike twice, you know!' It just seemed all too unreal.

And of course it all depended on whether I could pass a strict medical examination. Oh well, I thought. I certainly had nothing to lose and even if I didn't pass it was no skin off my nose. So despite many reservations I made up my mind to try for my commercial licence. The very next day I got on the phone and made another appointment to see Dr Henderson.

He was really pleased to see me so much more active than the last time I'd been there, and even more so when I told him that I was now a fully fledged private pilot. But when I told him that I had decided to go for my commercial licence so that I could get an instructor's rating he just stared at me. Then he took off his glasses, wiped them on his shirt and replaced them on his nose.

'Janine,' he said, in his wavering voice, 'I think it's fantastic that you've decided to do this. I really want you to get your commercial, but there's one problem—I don't want you to kill anybody.' He paused for a moment. 'This is something entirely different from just flying for pleasure. It's a huge responsibility. We're talking about other people's lives.'

My heart fell. I thought he was going to tell me he wouldn't be able to pass me.

'You see, with your medical history . . . I don't think this has ever happened before, and we have to make sure you're really one hundred per cent fit and up to it before we pass you. The CAA will go through your application with a fine tooth comb so we have to make sure we do a good job.'

So he was going to give me a chance after all. I knew why he was taking it so seriously. It was an enormous responsibility he would be taking if he recommended me as suitable to hold a commercial licence and something subsequently went wrong. But despite this I knew that he would do everything possible to pass me. I knew he wanted to help me, he believed I could do it if I was given the opportunity.

So we got started. The examination took a lot longer than the previous one as there were many things he had to check up on. After he had finished and filled out the lengthy form, I was still unsure if he would be able to pass me.

Some of my reflexes were still missing altogether, I had considerable weakness in both legs and feet, I couldn't stand on my toes, I still walked slowly and with a significant limp, my balance wasn't too good, I couldn't run, half my body was numb, I was covered in scars, my back was held together by a rib taken from my left side—the list of injuries went on and on. Not exactly the ideal candidate for a commercial pilot!

But Doctor Henderson wasn't about to let me down. He told me he was going to recommend me for the licence and wished me the best of luck in my new career. I still had to get the go-ahead from the CAA, but that didn't worry me too much. I was already on my way. There was no stopping me now.

It was some time later that I heard that Doctor Henderson had passed away. He was a fair age and I'm sure he had lived a full and rich life. I will always be grateful for the fact that he believed in me, and never thought my flying ambitions were silly or impossible. If he had, I might have given the idea away. Instead he gave me something really precious—the chance to prove that anything was possible.

The big problem now was how to pay for the licence, which I knew would be very costly. I had used up all my savings on my pilot's licence and Mum and Dad had helped me out with some of the additional expenses. I decided to apply for a bank loan. Being the victim of a road accident, I had taken legal action for damages against the driver who hit me, so I was hoping the bank would accept this as a guarantee against a loan.

The bank manager knew Mum and Dad and was well aware of my accident. He said all that was needed was some documentation from my solicitors and he could approve a deferred repayment loan for me, meaning that I wouldn't have to start repaying it until the court case was settled, which could take a couple of years at least.

I had no idea just how much the court case would affect me and my life. The whole protracted procedure meant that I had to relive the very thing that I was trying so hard to forget. In the end I just wanted to accept whatever was offered to me so that I could forget the entire business and get on with my life. On top of this, I had to live with the inane comments of some people when they heard I would be getting some compensation for my injuries—'Oh boy, aren't you lucky!'

What could I say? 'Oh well, you can have one too. Why don't you go out and get yourself run over—it really is worth it!' I couldn't believe that anyone could actually see things like that.

The entire experience of the court case was traumatic and humiliating. I was scrutinised by so many doctors, I never wanted to see another one again. The fact that I was an innocent victim was immaterial to them. They gave me a hard time irrespective of whether they believed I was in the right or wrong.

The main reason for this was the number of bogus claims which were being made. This caused doctors to suspect even the most innocent of victims, which only magnified the suffering they already had to go through.

I had the fortune, or misfortune, to meet one such person. One day when I was swimming at the club while I was still wearing my brace, I noticed another swimmer wearing a strange kind of brace I hadn't seen before. I was keen to talk to him, thinking he must have also been in an accident.

When he stopped I said hello and asked him what had happened to his back. He had broken it, he replied.

'I broke mine too. How did you do yours?' I thought it was quite a coincidence and that we had something to share.

'I fell off a house I was building,' he said.

'That's terrible. What hospital were you in?'

'I wasn't in hospital.'

'You weren't in hospital?'

'No, I just had to rest for two weeks at home.'

'You're kidding, I was in hospital for four months.' I couldn't believe it. How could someone break his back and not go to hospital? Something didn't seem right here. He had a very sheepish look about him.

'So when do you think you'll be able to return to work?' I queried.

'I can't work any more, there's too much damage to my back.'

The penny dropped. He was taking someone for a ride. Broken back, no hospital, no operation, no more work ... I'd bet my bottom dollar he was making a phoney claim for compo.

He got out of the pool, obviously sensing that I was suspicious, and headed towards the dressing room with what seemed to me an exaggerated limp, making sure that I could see him. Maybe I was wrong, but he just didn't ring true to me.

It wasn't long before I found out I was right. Some weeks later Mum picked me up from the pool and helped me to the car out in the disabled parking area at the front of the club when this same man came out the door waving goodbye to his mates.

He bounded down the steps to the car park, his bag slung

over his shoulder and a cigarette hanging out of his mouth and jogged over to his car, which was also parked in the disabled spot next to ours. He caught sight of me and knew he had been caught out. Without a word he threw his bag into the car and sped off. He was a phoney!

It was because of people like this that I was subjected to the most painful ordeal when I had to be examined by doctors acting for the driver I was suing. One particular doctor had me close to tears one day when he continued to grill me in the most cruel manner.

'So tell me what happened,' he said. He had already read the notes and knew the details, but he made me go through it all again.

'I was hit by a car while I was riding my bicycle.'

'Did you hit your head?' he asked, looking at the notes in front of him.

'Yes, I did.'

'Did you have head injuries?'

'Yes, I did. My head was cut open across the front and the back.'

'So you were not wearing a helmet?'

'Yes, I always wore a helmet.'

'So you didn't receive any head injuries then?'

'I'm sorry, doctor, but I did.'

'But then you couldn't have been wearing a helmet.'

'I was, but it came off in the accident.'

'It mustn't have been a very good helmet,' he sneered.

What comeback did I have to that? But there was more to come.

'Then what happened?' he asked.

'They flew some blood up to Katoomba for a transfusion.'

'How did they know what blood group you were?' What a

stupid question, I thought. He was the doctor!

'I guess they took a sample. I don't know, I was unconscious.'

'Then what?'

'Then they flew me to Prince Henry hospital by helicopter.'

'The notes say they were going to stop at Westmead.'

'Yes, but apparently they decided to go straight to Prince Henry.'

'Oh, it couldn't have been that serious then.'

What could I say? He was a pig.

'So what operation did they perform on you?' he went on.

'An anterior decompression laminectomy.'

'Anterior? They went in through your stomach?'

'No, they went in through my side.'

'Oh, then it wasn't anterior?'

'Yes, it was anterior, but they went in through my side.'

'Well, it wasn't anterior then.'

And so on, until he almost made me feel as if I hadn't really been injured at all.

'Get undressed and lie on the couch,' he said curtly, and proceeded to examine my legs.

'Push down with your feet,' he ordered, I tried. I could barely move his hand, which he had against my foot.

'Oh, that's not too bad. Now the other one.'

This went on for almost an hour. I was so humiliated and hurt. Why did I have to put up with this? I was the innocent one. It was the man who hit me who should have been going through this, not me! I wanted to cry, but I wasn't about to give him the pleasure of seeing that.

So these inquisitions continued. Just when I thought I had put everything behind me, I had to go through this sort of thing and bring it all to the fore again. It was cruel. Until it was settled, I doubted if I would be able to get on with my life.

But life had to go on and I tried as much as possible to put the accident out of my mind. I continued with my goal of gaining a commercial licence and after months of study and innumerable tests I passed all the theory subjects needed to obtain it. Now all I had to worry about was the practical side.

I needed to log quite a few hours on my own, or 'in command', to be able to qualify. So I decided to make a trip to central Australia, to make up the hours, taking a few of my friends as passengers. I didn't have to hunt too hard to find some. The idea of flying halfway across the continent for a holiday sounded rather exciting.

Two of my girlfriends decided to come—Meredith, a red-headed former schoolmate who was now a solicitor, and Linda, an air hostess, who was also able to take time off. The other passenger was an American holidaying in Australia whom I had met at my old family friend Hap's house. Everyone called him 'Dude', as he had the unfortunate habit of calling everyone else by that name. So it was just the four of us ... dudes!

We were booked to take Juliet Tango Yankee, a very slick-looking Trinidad. I spent hours planning the flight and making other arrangements. We were going to fly to Ayers Rock via Broken Hill, and then back across Queensland and down to Dubbo. I packed a lot of maps and other items, including a first-aid kit and water, in case we got stranded, as we would be flying over some very barren country, much of it desert.

We met at the airport on the morning of the flight and after I'd gone through the ritual of getting the weather details, putting in my flight plan and doing a pre-flight check of the plane we set off. My passengers were all pretty excited, especially the Dude, who thought he was out to have the outback adventure of his life! Our first stop was Forbes to refuel before going on to Broken Hill, where we took on more fuel and headed into town to get some lunch. Then it was off to the tiny settlement of Leigh Creek, some 250 kilometres across the border in South Australia, where we stayed overnight and by chance I met up with one of the students that I had met at the flying school some months earlier.

At dawn next day we headed north for a bumpy ride across the desert due to the intense heat. It was so hot the perspiration poured down my forehead, making it almost impossible to keep my headsets on. For hours there was nothing to see but sand, sand and more sand, and I had to concentrate on holding to my heading until I could positively fix my position, otherwise we could have got awfully lost.

We stopped at Oodnadatta for more fuel and then set off on the final leg of our journey. We had been in the air for over five hours and I was feeling exhausted from the heat. At last, with sweat dripping in my eyes and the aircraft bumping all over the place, I saw the majestic shape of Ayers Rock rise out of the desert ahead. It was magnificent.

The heat made for a very bumpy landing, and it was with much relief but immense satisfaction that I brought the aircraft safely down at Yulara, the resort centre some twenty kilometres from the Rock itself. I had flown all the way from Sydney to the very heart of Australia with nobody to assist me. Now it was time to relax and enjoy things. I parked the plane and we made our way to the motel we had booked into.

We spent an exciting few days exploring the Rock and its surroundings. Of course we all planned to climb it, me included, although I didn't know how I would manage it. We set out to make our assault early next morning, as it would have been impossible in the full heat of the day. When we got out to the Rock I was amazed to see that the start of the climb was almost vertical. Fortunately there was a rope along the path to pull yourself up on.

We all set off on the climb. I discovered that I could climb very quickly if I went on all fours. It may have looked funny, but it worked. Somehow I clawed my way to the top and we sat down and enjoyed a glass of champagne the Dude had lugged up in his backpack. Unfortunately it was a bit warm by now but it still tasted great. And the climb was worth every ounce of effort it required, for the view from the top was nothing short of breathtaking. We stayed until the heat threatened to overpower us, then we made our way back down to the bottom.

With our stay in Yulara over, we set off on our return journey, heading over to Charleville, in central Queensland. There were only three of us left now, as Linda had been recalled to work and taken a commercial flight from Yulara back to Sydney.

The day was getting late when flight service called me up to tell me that there were thunderstorms expected at Charleville very shortly. They suggested that I make alternative arrangements to find somewhere else to spend the night. I took out my maps and looked for a suitable place. We had been flying for hours over desert and there hadn't been anything in particular to fix my position on for quite a while. I looked around for a small airstrip that should have been around our location, but for the life of me I couldn't see anything remotely resembling one in the endless expanse of sand and rock.

I didn't want to spend hours looking for a strip that might not even exist any more, so I took my map out again and began to search for the nearest place that had an instrument aid, called an NDB. This way I could tune the aircraft's instruments into the aid and positively identify it.

I found a place I had never heard of, called Windorah. It was in the middle of nowhere, about 400 kilometres north-west of Charleville.

I tuned up my instrument aid and got a positive fix, then

called up flight service and told them we intended to head for Windorah and spend the night there.

By the time we reached the strip it was getting late and I turned my landing lights on. I was getting a little anxious by now as we had already been in the aircraft for well over five hours, and I knew our fuel wouldn't last forever. Meredith was in the back and totally unaware of what was happening, but the Dude was kept informed as he had headsets on and heard all the conversations I was having. In fact, he was a pretty good hand to have along. He had done quite a bit of sailing in his time and was familiar with navigation techniques, so he was busy with the maps on his lap helping me to spot anything along the way.

I was relieved to finally catch sight of the strip, as I still wasn't certified to fly at night and wanted to land as quickly as possible. I circled the strip and prepared to land. By the time I touched down, there was already a truck waiting to refuel for us. This was a common occurrence on outback strips. When they heard a 'lightie' overhead they always headed out to meet it.

As soon as I parked the aircraft, the Dude jumped straight out and when I looked down, much to my amazement, he was kissing the ground.

'God, it's good to be here,' he said in his characteristic drawl.

I knew what he meant. I was glad to be on terra firma myself. Meredith on the other hand just stood there, wondering what all the fuss was about.

I looked up to see a large figure approaching the aircraft. It looked very masculine in shape, but to my surprise, when it got closer it turned out to be a woman and a very big one at that.

'G'day,' she said in a voice deep enough for any man. 'Guess youse'd be wantin' some fuel?'

'Yes, that's right,' I said timidly. She didn't look the sort of woman I wanted to get on the wrong side of.

'What sort of plane is this anyway?' she growled.

'Oh, it's called a Trinidad,' I answered.

'I'll just call it shit for short,' she almost bellowed. I just nodded. Whatever she said was OK with me.

I stood back and watched in awe as she refuelled my little aircraft. Then we followed her like sheep to a tiny shed tucked away at the side of the strip.

I looked up on the sign on the wall outside. It said in large letters, 'WINDORAH', except that the 'D' was backwards. I wondered if this was any reflection on the sort of town we were about to spend the night in.

'Guess youse'd be wantin' some dinner?' the woman said as she handed me a docket for the fuel.

'Yes, that would be great,' I said. 'And somewhere to spend the night.'

She got on the phone, one of the wind-up sort that was hanging on the wall, and turned it so hard I thought she'd pull it off.

'Yeah, that's right, I got 'em, they'll be coming in for dinner,' she said to the person on the other end. I didn't quite know what she meant by 'got 'em', but I hoped it was meant as a friendly gesture.

I thought I had better introduce ourselves to this stranger who was now responsible for our fate. 'Anyway, my name is Janine, and this is Meredith and this is the Dude,' I said, holding my hand out.

She almost crushed my hand, then looked at the Dude. 'You can call me Bub, and I'll just call you Shithead,' she said and roared with laughter at the joke.

Now I was really worried. Was this for real? I looked at Meredith and saw that she was as surprised as I was, but when I turned to the Dude, he was grinning madly. 'This is fantastic, she's great,' he said. He had never met anyone like this in his life—nor had I for that matter—and he thought he was about to have the adventure of his life.

Bub pointed to a truck out on the road beyond the strip, which was evidently our transport into town. Meredith and the Dude walked around the back of the shed and I followed Bub over a low barbed-wire fence, to lessen the distance I had to walk. The only problem was that I got my jeans caught on the wire on the way over and fell flat on my face. When I looked up I saw Bub standing over me laughing heartily. 'Hey, that was a good one!' she guffawed. I got up and put myself, and my pride, in the front of the truck.

She drove into town at warp speed and we arrived at the pub to find the entire town there—all six of them! There were only a few buildings in Windorah and the pub was without doubt the busiest. We trailed in after Bub, now our protector, and the men at the bar turned around and looked at us. Bub immediately brandished a ham of a fist at them and snarled, 'I got 'em, they're mine!' I had no idea what she meant by this but wondered what they might have had in mind for us.

Looking around the pub I noticed that everyone had something in common—they were covered in mud and dirt from head to toe! In fact I had never seen such dirty people in my life before. The only exception was the barman, which was just as well as he was the one responsible for getting us a meal. We were all starving and it was a relief to find it was a real home-cooked baked dinner, and we devoured every scrap.

When we had finished I looked up to see one of the barflies, quite an elderly man, approaching us unsteadily.

'G'day,' he said in a drunken slur. 'Where's the pilot?' He had to hold onto the bar to stop himself from falling over.

'Me, I'm the pilot,' I replied.

'Go on,' he hiccupped. 'I always wanted to fly, can you teach me?'

Well, I was sure he was about to be sick in my lap any minute. I didn't quite know how to respond, but I didn't want to offend him and tried to fob him off as politely as possible. But he kept on pestering me and I couldn't get rid of him until one of his mates, who'd evidently decided enough was enough, came over to rescue me.

'Don't take any notice of him,' he said. 'His name is Sandy Kidd and he has more flying hours under his belt than you can poke a stick at—about twenty thousand I think at the last count.'

Well, didn't I feel like a fool! He'd been pulling my leg the whole time. I thought he didn't look capable of walking, let alone flying a plane. And here I was with all of a hundred hours to my name.

I looked over at the Dude to see him speaking to an elderly woman, who seemed just as drunk as the men. She had him cornered.

'G'day, me name's Margy,' she was saying. 'Hey, do you know any songs?' She took another swig from her beer, half of it ending on the floor.

'I know a few,' said the Dude.

'What about Ringo the Dingo?' Margy yelled at the top of her voice, dissolving into laughter.

The Dude glanced at me with an 'I can't believe this place' look on his face. We spent the rest of the night talking to the locals, and playing darts with them. I just made sure I was standing well clear of the flight path when it was their turn to have a go. It was turning out to be quite a night.

As the night progressed Sandy sobered up a little and tried to impress me by telling me about the decorations he claimed to have from the Queen. As it happened, he was an absolute nut when it came to flying—he loved it. And there was only

one thing that he loved more than another pilot—and that
was a female pilot.

It turned out he had a son named Tom and all he wanted
in life was to find a wife for him who could actually fly an
aeroplane. Tom was in the pub as well, and Sandy called him
over and introduced him. He looked no more than about
eighteen years old, and he was just as dirty and just as drunk
as his dad. But underneath the dirt I could see that he had
lovely blue eyes and after a good wash he probably scrubbed
up quite well.

Sandy invited us back to his house to meet his wife. The
Dude wanted to see a 'real' outback property and jumped at
the opportunity, so despite being on the point of exhaustion,
I agreed so as not to disappoint him. We all piled into Sandy's
ute, me in the front with Sandy, and Meredith, the Dude and
Tom in the back—with a whole pack of dogs!

It was quite a trip back to the property. Sandy drove like
he talked, all over the place, and I was sure he couldn't see a
thing in front of him. Luckily, there wasn't anything to hit
had we run off the road, and we finally made it in one piece.

We spent the next few hours talking to his wife and looking
at videos of the ABC TV show *A Big Country*. They had done
a story on Sandy and his family and I was surprised to learn
that everything he had told me was absolutely true. As it
turned out Sandy did have a medal from the Queen, having
been decorated for being the first aerial crop-sprayer in the
country. He even got it out to show us and we were all
suitably impressed.

It was getting late and we thought we had better get back
to the pub to get some sleep. We thanked Sandy's wife for
having us and Tom drove us back into town. Fortunately he
had had a bit of time to sober up before he got behind the
wheel. Before I left, Sandy offered me a job flying his crop-
dusters. I thanked him very much but declined as graciously

as I could. I figured there might be a few strings attached!

When we headed off next morning, I flew over Sandy's property, being curious to have a look at it. I was surprised to see a large airstrip in perfect condition, and a couple of large hangars as well.

When we stopped off at Charleville later in the day, I happened to mention our stay in Windorah to the blokes in the briefing office.

'Oh, so you went out to Little Dell—that's Sandy Kidd's property' one of them remarked.

'Yes,' I said, rather surprised.

It turned out Sandy was a bit of a legend in these parts and had quite a reputation when it came to flying. Whenever anything went wrong, it was always Sandy to the rescue, helping out in whatever way he could. He was one of the most experienced pilots in the country. In fact, he was held in such high regard, they told me, that whenever he flew to Brisbane he didn't bother to get a clearance like everyone else. He just had to call up flight service and say, 'It's Sandy Kidd,' and they moved everyone aside to make way for him.

We got back to Bankstown just over a week after we left. We had travelled around the country without any major problems, I had gained a lot of valuable experience and we had all had a great time. We had some great memories but we would always remember our stay in Windorah as the highlight of the trip.

With Ros Kelly at the Air Show.

*Being interviewed at the Air Show about my forthcoming ride
in the FA-18.*

Publicity shots for the FA-18 flight taken at the Air Show.

Packing away my racing skis. I wouldn't be needing them any more.

Learning to fly. I had to have a pillow behind my back so I could reach the pedals!

Accepting a cheque from Westpac on behalf of the Surf Lifesaving Association of Australia.

Me in the FA-18 simulator at the RAAF base Williamtown.

Setting off for Ayers Rock in Juliet Tango Yankee.

*We made it! From left: Linda, me, the Dude and Meredith on
top of the Rock.*

About to head off to Coolangatta on the Instructors' Course with Jeremy (left) and Herc.

Flying the Robin Aerobatic aircraft with the Sydney Aerobatic School.

Getting suited up before the FA-18 flight with Squadron Leader John O'Halloran.

Just taking her out for a spin!

Having the ride of my life in the FA-18! They'd even gone to the trouble of putting my name on a helmet.

Tim and me on our trip to Cooma in the Skybolt.

I eventually returned to my studies and received my degree in Human Movement Studies (a little ironic!). Me with my friend Debbie.

I've got my man! Tim and I announce our engagement.

Me and my family. (From left) Lenny, Kelley, Mum, me, Dad, Kim.

Our wedding day in the grounds of Ranelagh House.

Home from the honeymoon.

Annabel's christening. From left: Hap, Kelley, me, Tim, Debbie.

Brian 'Hap' Hannan, Annabel's godfather and a great friend.

The aerobatic aeroplane Tim and I owned for a while. I named it Mike Uniform Mike, or MUM – I thought that was appropriate.

Annabel making a mess as usual!

Annabel in Tim's hat. When he wears it she calls him Postman Pat.

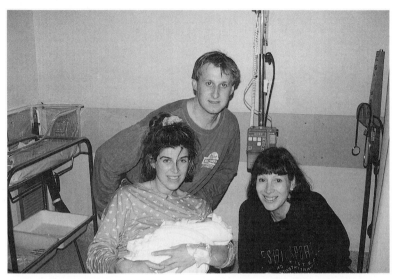

Minutes after giving birth a second time, with Tim, new baby Charlotte Rose, and my obstetrician, Sue Fleming.

A proud Annabel with her new baby sister.

Chapter 19

FLYING HAD FILLED a void in my life, one that was created by the loss of my sport. But I still missed my life as an athlete as much as ever. I still hoped and believed that one day I would be able to ski again and reclaim the things in my life I had lost.

About eighteen months after my accident Chris invited me to spend a holiday with his family, who managed a ski lodge at Falls Creek in Victoria. I jumped at the chance to get away for a week in the snowfields. But it wasn't the only reason I wanted to go.

My walking had come a long way since the accident although I still had a significant limp and couldn't go very far. Despite this, I was convinced that once I was on skis I'd be able to get around just as I had before. I was sure that once I got them on my feet everything would come back to me.

I got my ski bag out and decided to take two pairs of racing skis, leaving my other four pairs behind. Then I tried on my ski boots and walked around in them for a while to get used to them again.

The week I was going away happened to coincide with some championship races and a clinic for junior skiers. It would give me a chance to catch up with people I hadn't seen for some time and thank them for their support and all the letters that they had sent while I was in hospital.

On arriving at Falls Creek I got out on the snow straight-away. The thought of skiing again was irresistible—it was what I had been working so hard towards in all my rehab sessions. Chris helped me up the mountain to where the cross-country clinic was being held. Now I was about to find out if I would ever be able to ski again. It was fantastic being on the snow again, and when I saw everyone skiing around, it looked so easy, I was sure that it would come back in an instant. I couldn't wait to give it a go.

Chris helped me put my skis on. For the first time, they seemed so thin and flimsy. I tried to take a small step forward and fell flat on my backside. I hauled myself back on my feet, and down I went a second time. I couldn't believe it. I couldn't even keep my balance when I was standing still. What was wrong?

I tried again and again, but each time it was the same. I couldn't even stand up on the wretched things.

I looked up to see everyone watching me. I know they wanted me to do it as much as I did. Right now, however, I didn't want anyone to see me like this—a once-competent athlete grovelling in the snow. It was so humiliating. I could feel the frustration building up inside me.

As much as I wanted to go away, to never be seen again, I did go back. Day after day I tortured myself on the mountain till I could barely walk. Eventually I managed to stand and take a few steps before I crashed over, but the continual falls left me black and blue with bruises. My legs and side were so swollen that Chris's mum had to pad my ski suit with towels before I went out each day. I was aching all over, inside and out.

I returned home with not just a battered body but the realisation that my dreams of skiing again were over. The pain this caused me was immense, like an intense physical ache that came from deep inside. The sense of loss was a terrible burden to carry. Before the accident, when I had a problem I would simply put on my runners and head out the door. I would run as hard as I could, pushing myself up hill after hill, till my legs ached and my heart could pump no harder. That was my way of coping. That was what I wanted to do now, just one more time at least . . . but I couldn't. That part of my life was gone . . . forever.

The two-year deadline the doctors had given me for my body to repair itself was approaching, and the reality was that I hadn't had the nerve growth that I had anticipated. I had to face the fact that my injuries were permanent.

As painful as this was to accept, I knew I had to get on with my life. I had spent so much time in the past year hoping against hope for my condition to improve that I hadn't been able to come to terms with what was now inevitable. But I was too proud and too stubborn to settle for anything less than total happiness. I had as much right to that as anyone else, and although I might not like the way things had turned out, I still wanted to succeed at what I was doing. I didn't want to throw the towel in—I wasn't going to let this accident control my life. I was going to beat it.

With that resolve behind me, I threw myself into my flying with a vengeance. The time had come to let go. Circumstances had changed—and so had I.

As much as I wanted to get on with my life, it wasn't easy. What I wanted most of all was to feel 'normal' again and fit in with the crowd. But my life was governed by circumstances that constantly reminded me of the accident. I resented the fact that I had to attend clinics, see doctors, have my progress monitored, and most of all be on medication all the time.

I particularly disliked going back to hospital for spinal clinics. Everyone had to live with a label of some sort—'para' or 'quad' or suchlike. Mine was 'partial paraplegic'. I hated it.

Tests, tests and more tests—that seemed to be my life. I was sick of being a patient, and I didn't want to see any more doctors. But I had injuries that needed to be checked regularly, not just for the short term but for the rest of my life. I had to have tests done on my kidneys to make sure that they were functioning normally. As I was constantly plagued with urinary tract infections there would always be the risk of some damage to them in the future. The infections made me terribly tired, and I was forever on antibiotics to clear my body of them. Blisters and ulcers were another incessant problem I faced, developing so insidiously that I was often not aware of them until it was too late.

On one occasion I was down at the club for a swim, and when I got out I inadvertently scraped my leg on the side of the pool. Weeks passed and I developed a large ulcer on the back of the leg which filled with pus. There was a real danger that it would become systemic, so it had to be treated urgently.

I rang Adrian and went in to the hospital so that he could have a look at it. He dressed it with a special cream and gave me some more cream and bandages to treat it with at home. It was impossible for me to reach it, so Mum had to do all the dressings for me. It took weeks to heal, and when it did I was left with a large scar on the back of my leg—just another to add to the list! The lesson I learnt was that I had to check myself regularly as my permanent loss of sensation meant I would always be prone to this sort of thing.

I continued to see Dr Stephen on a regular basis to check

up on my progress. One day when he was assessing the loss of strength I had suffered in my feet and legs he came up with a suggestion.

'You know, I might be able to do something about this,' he said as he leant back in his chair.

'What do you mean?' I asked.

'Well, I was just thinking . . .' He paused. 'I may be able to transfer some of the tendons from around your leg and insert them in the back of your ankles.'

'What would that do?'

'Well, we might be able to get some strength back in your lower legs. That would help you to walk better.'

The nerve damage was so great below the knees that my legs had wasted away quite considerably. I didn't have much muscle left covering my feet, which meant that they were now causing me a lot of pain and discomfort. The operation was a glimmer of hope for me. If I could get the use back in my lower legs, perhaps I could even run again—and maybe even ski, who knew? Anyway, I had nothing to lose.

We discussed the details of the operation and decided I should have one leg done at a time. I would have preferred them both to be done in one go, but Dr Stephen said that would mean I wouldn't be able to get around as they would be in plaster for at least eight weeks. Besides, he couldn't guarantee that it would work, so it was better to do one leg first and see how it went.

I was booked into a private hospital at Mosman, which was a lot more comfortable than Prince Henry, with a room to myself and *en suite* bathroom attached. Dr Stephen came to see me the day before the operation with his anaesthetist, Dr Henessy. Then next morning I was given a pre-med injection which made me feel extremely sick and by the time they came to take me down to the theatre, I was feeling anxious and beginning to shake.

I had been warned to expect some painful after-effects. I had no idea how severe they would turn out to be. When I finally woke after the operation, my right leg was throbbing with the most excruciating pain. I looked down to see it propped up by pillows and encased in a huge slab of plaster.

When Dr Stephen came to see how I was, I told him in no uncertain terms that my leg was absolutely killing me. Apparently it had swollen up a lot more than he had anticipated and the plaster was now far too tight. He immediately arranged for the physiotherapist to come and put on a new and even bigger cast.

This alleviated the pain somewhat, but it was still far too sore for me to get out of bed for another three days. I spent most of the time sleeping, dosed with pain-killers. The operation hadn't been the simple routine I had thought it would be. It had required quite lengthy and delicate surgical procedures, with Dr Stephen having to make no less than three different insertions to remove and transfer the tendons, which had traumatised the leg and explained why it was so painful.

It was almost a week before I left hospital, unable to walk without the aid of crutches. It was still very painful and I was told to spend the next few weeks at home with my leg elevated. The plaster had to remain on for eight weeks. Dr Stephen had set the cast so that my foot was pointing downward, which allowed the tendons to heal properly without being used in any way. This meant I couldn't put any weight on my leg and would have to use the crutches the entire time.

There wasn't much I could do while my leg was in plaster. Flying was definitely out of the question, and I couldn't drive, so I spent most of the time at home reading, driving Mum mad and getting very, very bored. The worst part was after finally getting some independence back after my accident, I was relegated to the role of dependant once again, having to rely on family and friends to drive me around and fetch things for me.

This nearly drove me crazy. I was too stubborn to ask for help most of the time and wanted to do things for myself. Finally, at my wits' end and bored out of my brain, I took matters into my own hands. I decided to get into my car and try to drive, even with my plaster on. It was probably a stupid thing to do, but I went ahead and did it, anyway.

It was even more difficult than the first time, as the plaster was set in such a fashion that I couldn't reach the pedals comfortably. But I managed to slide my foot down so that I was using the heel, the way I did to fly. I could only use this foot to accelerate, I had to work the brake with my left foot, which I also used on the clutch. It was not the most conventional way to drive, but neither was the way I flew. But it worked and I was able to control the car with safety, which was the most important thing.

Mum was flabbergasted when I told her, and scolded me for being impatient again. But then I was born impatient. Now that I could drive again, I informed her, I would head back to the airport and start flying again.

Mum conceded defeat and reluctantly agreed to swap cars with me, as she had an automatic which would make it a lot easier. I made my way out to the airport with two things on my mind. Firstly I had to complete the rest of the flying hours I needed for my commercial licence, and secondly I wanted to inquire about doing an instrument flying rating (IFR) course. So far I had only been flying visually, and the next step was to learn to navigate relying solely on instruments, so that I could fly in any conditions and at any time, not just in fine weather, during daylight.

It was almost two months since I had flown and I wanted to arrange some refresher flights, as I knew I would be pretty rusty when I got back in the cockpit. I spoke to Neville at the flying school and booked in a couple of flights. I also asked him about getting my Night VMC rating, a requirement for the CPL which demanded special navigational skills as flying at night, of course, depends largely on using instruments. He told me that after a few catch-up flights I could sit for the night test and then if all went well for the commercial test a week later.

Next I went over to a school which specialised in instrument flying on the other side of the airport, to inquire about doing my instrument rating. Bill, the chief instructor, gave me the syllabus for the course and booked me in for some lessons. He did his instrument flying in a twin-engine plane called the Duchess, so I could get my endorsement for twin-engined aircraft at the same time.

As it happened, one of his instructors, named Peter, wasn't doing any flying for the morning and offered to take me up in one of the twin-engined planes that was on line at the school. I hadn't been up in a twin before and jumped at the opportunity.

We were going up in an aircraft called an Aztec, which looked a bit bigger and heavier than the Duchess that was parked next to it. Peter had to help me into the aircraft, as the crutches made it difficult for me on my own. The plan, he told me, was to head over to Camden aerodrome, to the south of Bankstown, and shoot some circuits. In the process, he'd also show me some of the idiosyncrasies of flying a twin, such as asymmetric aircraft control in the event of engine failure.

In the aircraft I had been flying up to this point, there was of course only one engine, so if it failed there was only one place to go—down! But in a twin, if one engine failed, there was still another one running and under optimum conditions it was possible to maintain flight and reach the destination in one piece. However, having two engines didn't guarantee success all the time. If you didn't know how to fly them correctly, it meant you could be in twice as much trouble.

We took off and made our way to Camden. The biggest difference between this plane and the ones I had been flying was that there were basically two of everything—two throttle controls, two mixture controls and two pitch levers. The take off and climbing speed were a lot higher and we cruised a lot faster. We seemed to zip past all the other aircraft in the training area and before I knew it we were at Camden.

Peter flew a few circuits, then asked if I'd like to have a go.

'Of course, I'd love to, but you'll have to take the pedals,' I said, patting the plaster cast on my leg.

I took the controls and followed Peter's instructions regarding power control and speeds around the circuit. We turned base and then final, and everything looked good. I kept my eye on the airspeed, making sure not to go below the approach speed that Peter had given me. Everything seemed to be in fast motion.

The runway came up to meet us and I began my flare. Without any effort the aircraft just settled down on the tarmac in a near-perfect landing.

'Ah, that's a greaser!' Peter exclaimed. 'Power on. Let's go around again.'

I moved the controls forward and we took off for another circuit. I was pleasantly surprised. It was a very easy aircraft to land. It had a heavy feel to it and tended to settle on the runway on its own. After a few more circuits Peter took over again and said he would show me some asymmetric controls, simulating an engine failure by bringing one of the throttle control levers back to idle, leaving power in only one engine, just as would happen in the real thing.

Waiting until we had some height, he brought the lever back. The engine hummed and the aircraft began to yaw, or turn, to one side. Peter quickly stamped on the left rudder, which brought the nose back around. He then began to go through a series of drills, saying them out loud for my benefit.

'Mixture, pitch, throttle ... full forward. Landing gear up, flaps up. Identify ... dead leg, dead engine, confirm ... close throttle.'

He simulated shutting down the dead or failed engine, but of course the throttle was already closed. Then he demonstrated how to use the rudder to control the engine. It needed a full bootload on it! How would I ever be able to do that? My legs weren't strong enough.

He then showed me how to trim the rudder once the aircraft was under control. This relieved the pilot of some of the pressure that had to be exerted and relaxed the rudder. He completed the circuit and brought us down to a smooth landing. I was impressed by the way he handled the aircraft well, which wasn't so surprising as he had had a lot of experience and had spent several years in the air force.

We flew a few more asymmetrics and then headed back to Bankstown. On the way Peter asked if I would like to try a simulated failure of the right engine, which meant I would only have to use my good leg. I thought I might as well, as it would give me some idea of what I was getting myself into as far as leg strength was concerned. I cut out the engine and booted in as much rudder as I could. I couldn't get it all the way in, but it was enough to control the aircraft.

Back on the ground, I thanked Peter for taking me up and letting me have a fly. At least now I knew I would be able to handle the Duchess. As soon as the plaster was off, all I wanted was to come back and start my instrument rating.

Chapter 20

THE TIME FINALLY arrived to have the plaster removed. I was raring to jump back into a plane as soon as my leg was out of the cast, but Dr Stephen told me that I had to take it easy for at least a few weeks to allow the tendons to heal completely. I'd thought I would immediately be able to put my leg down and walk around, but that wasn't to be the case.

I propped myself up on the table and Dr Stephen took to the plaster with the old familiar saw. When he finally made it through the last layer and peeled it off I was surprised to see the number of incisions he had made to my leg. It was covered in stitches. No wonder it had been so sore!

He showed me how he had transferred the tendons by cutting right down the front of my leg and inserting them in the ankle and the inside of my foot. He said they had healed well, but it looked like a real mess to me.

I swung my leg over the side of the bed to see if I could walk. The moment my foot touched the floor I recoiled in excruciating pain. I realised I had better keep my crutches at hand for a while.

It was more than two weeks before I could put my foot down again. Even then it was so sore that I was limping around on it for quite some time. And it was several more weeks until I was able to get myself out to the airport and start flying again, during which I went swimming and did stretching exercises to try to get some mobility back in my leg and ankle.

Once I was back at the airport I had a lot of catching up to do. It was over three months since I had flown and I was sure there would be a lot of things I had forgotten. I started by doing some refresher flights and was relieved to find that it all came back to me in no time. When I thought I was pretty well up to scratch I booked in for my Night VMC test and my commercial licence test.

The day before I was due to sit for my night test, I booked a plane to take Dad flying for the day. I still had some hours to complete before my CPL test, which was scheduled for a week's time. I always preferred to take a passenger along, it was good to have some company and Dad was always keen to come. Mum, on the other hand, wasn't so easy to convince. It wasn't anything to do with my flying, of course—she just hated the thought of going up in a 'little' aircraft.

She was going to come along that day but once we got out to the airport she saw that the wind had picked up and she became a bit nervous.

'Isn't that wind too strong to fly in?' she asked. I think she believed the plane would fall out of the sky. I tried to convince her it would be perfectly safe but she had already made up her mind—she wasn't going.

That didn't stop Dad and me having a great day. We took off and headed across the Blue Mountains to Oberon and Orange and then landed in Wagga. Dad had always been interested in planes so it was a bonus for him to find that there were some air force Machi jets going through their paces at the airfield.

I let Dad take over the controls for a while on the way home, which he really enjoyed. It was the first time he had flown so far in a light aircraft and the fact that I was the pilot made it all the more special for him. He had seen the effort I had put into learning to fly and it was satisfying to be able to show off my 'new' skill and the results of all the time I had devoted to acquiring it.

As we approached Bankstown I tuned into the ATIS and was surprised to hear what the weather conditions were. The wind had picked up even more while we were away and the controllers had changed the active runway. Instead of the tarred runway, 11/29, which was the only one that I had used to this date, they were now using the grass runway, 18/36, which ran across the main one. There was a wind warning of severe turbulence in the area with expected gusts of up to 30 knots on approach to landing. There were no other aircraft in the area, as no-one would have been stupid enough to venture out in such conditions. It was just us and the tower.

I had been briefed on the grass runways in the course of my training, but I had never landed on them. Nor had I ever landed in such windy conditions. I was getting a bit apprehensive, and didn't quite know what to expect. But I didn't want to worry Dad. There was no need for both of us to panic!

I quickly went through all the details on the runway in my head, and then called up the tower and gave my inbound call. I made my approach to the airport, but it was strange to be flying a different pattern from the one I normally flew. Don't blow this one, Janine, I kept saying to myself, not with Dad on board!

I looked down at the runway and saw that my touchdown point was tarred, but then ran out onto grass. As I started to turn onto final I decided to keep my speed up to compensate for the gusts and turbulence that had been predicted. I also decided not to use full flap on approach, as I wanted to keep the speed up and this also gave me more control over the aircraft.

I aimed for the threshold and set the aircraft up, then glanced at the windsock. It was straight out to the side and we were bouncing all over the place. My poor little plane was really being shaken about. I kept my eye on the airspeed, but just when things seemed to settle, a gust of wind would pick us up and throw us about. I really had to battle to maintain my approach.

Nearing the threshold, I put the aircraft down as soon as I could manage it. I didn't want to take any chances of holding off for too long and run the risk of a gust picking us up again. We rolled down the runway, off the tarred surface. I could feel the rough ground underneath as we went over the grass.

We had made it. Then I remembered Dad. I was concentrating so hard I had no idea how he was taking it. I looked around to see him smiling broadly.

'That was good fun!' he said.

'Good fun!' I said. 'Are you kidding? That was hell.'

'Oh, I wasn't worried at all,' he replied. 'You handled it well.'

What a surprise, I thought. Dad actually thought it was exciting. It was just as well Mum hadn't come along, though. She wouldn't have handled it at all! But the flight really did a lot for my confidence. If I could land in those conditions I could land anywhere, any time, I thought.

I passed my night test and then a week later went out with Neville to sit for my commercial test. It took over four hours and by the time we got back to Bankstown I was absolutely exhausted. Neville had really put me through the hoops, and I was pleased that I had handled the pressure without any problems, I was even more elated when Neville told me I had passed. I was now officially a commercial pilot.

There wasn't any time to waste, however. In a week's time I was due to begin my instructor's rating course. The sooner I completed this, the sooner I could start working at the school teaching other people how to fly. While I was waiting, I booked in with Bill to start my twin-engine endorsement. The flying bug had well and truly bitten me. I wasn't happy unless I was out at the airport and up in a plane.

Flying the Duchess wasn't difficult, but the challenge came when I had to control the aircraft during engine failures with my dicey right leg. I didn't want Bill to give me any special treatment—I had to be able to handle whatever he gave me just like everyone else—but when he failed the right engine and I had to boot in with the same rudder, the pain was agonising. After a while Bill caught on.

'Ah ... is that hurting your leg, Janine?' he asked.

'Oh, a bit, but it's OK Bill, it's not that bad,' I lied.

After that Bill made a point of failing the left engine instead of the right. 'Ah, we'll do the other one when your leg gets better,' he said. Actually it was quite a relief, as my leg was starting to swell badly and I really needed to rest it. Besides, there would be plenty of time to practise engine failures during my IFR flights.

I started my instructor rating course with four male aspirants. Jeremy was a geology graduate from the same university that I had attended, while Peter was a graduate in business studies. But both had decided to follow in the footsteps of their respective fathers, who were professional pilots. Then there were Herc and Rocky, both of Greek background and both with degrees in aeronautical engineering. They had started flying when they were at university and had decided to take it up full-time.

I had already met Jeremy as we had begun flying at the same time. He was a keen skier and had been a member of the ski club while at uni, though we didn't know each other at the time. He lived near Daven and knew of him and his brothers and we had a lot of mutual friends.

I had got to know his parents while we were learning and one day his father very kindly took Jeremy and me to the Qantas jet base to fly the 767 simulator. It was all very impressive inside the cockpit with its bewildering array of gauges and instruments. I was pleased to say that all my passengers would have survived, although they would have found the landing a bit rough!

Neville was taking us through the course and with this and my IFR course I knew I would have my work cut out. Neville would give us all a briefing on the ground on the exercise we would be doing, then he would take us up separately in the aircraft to complete it. We would then have to fly what was called 'dual', which meant that two of us flew with each other to repeat the exercise that we had just done with Neville.

It was a bit of a laugh at times, as one would have to play the role of instructor and the other that of the student. We were all meant to be deadly serious, but I'm sure there wouldn't have been a student anywhere who could possibly fly as ineptly as some of us 'students' flew!

I continued my instrument rating course with Bill at the same time as the instructor's program and I enjoyed the contrast in the flying. The IFR required a great amount of discipline, which I enjoyed, and it gave me a lot of confidence. It really sharpened up my flying skills. It took some time, but eventually I handled the rudder with my right foot without too much discomfort. I zipped through the lessons and passed my IFR test four weeks after I had started.

After almost three months on the instructor's course, we were all starting to feel like instructors. The only thing left before we sat for our flight test was to get some instructional navigation time under our belts, so we decided to take a trip away together to clock up the hours. As the plane was a four-seater, only three of us could go, as one seat had to be taken by Neville. Jeremy, Herc and I were the lucky trio. We made plans to fly north to Coolangatta, where we would spend the night, and return next day to Bankstown.

We all took turns in flying, relaxing in the back and enjoying the scenery when someone else took over. At Coolangatta we went out for dinner and some dancing before retiring for an early night, as we had a long day ahead of us.

On the way back to Bankstown next day it was my turn at the controls, and the weather was absolutely foul. With my newly acquired rating under my belt, I grabbed the opportunity to log some instrument time. We were in cloud almost all the way and when we arrived back in Sydney airspace Neville said it would be all right if I shot an ILS into Sydney.

An ILS, or instrument landing system, is a special procedure which can be used to land at certain aerodromes which are equipped with the particular type of instrument. You fly solely by referencing the instruments inside the cockpit, which take you down to only a couple of hundred metres above the ground until suddenly, hopefully, you break free of cloud and voilà!—there is the runway right below you. If the weather is really bad, you may not break into visibility at the designated height, in which case you have to apply power and go around for another try. I enjoyed flying the ILS, and always found it satisfying to come out spot-on for the runway when I finally broke clear.

This was the first time I had flown in instrument conditions since I passed my test with Bill, and it was a relief to find that it actually worked in real conditions. A lot of the time I trained for my instrument rating the weather was fine, so I had to fly literally with a hood over my head to simulate not being able to see outside. I didn't need a hood this day and it was an exciting way to end the excursion.

It seemed like forever, but the day finally arrived for me to do my instructor's test. Until now I had gone through all my tests with Neville, but I had to do this one under a Civil Aviation Authority examiner. I was the first in the course to finish the flying program, so I was the first in line for the test.

John, my examiner, was a serious-looking, short man with slightly receding hair who had been an air force pilot. He told me the lessons that he wanted me to demonstrate to him and then left me in the classroom to prepare them. He made me feel nervous from the start, as he didn't speak much and gave me only the barest outline of what he wanted.

I finished the classroom lesson, having no idea how I had gone, and he followed me out to the tarmac where he watched me like a hawk while I did my pre-flight on the plane, quizzing me on everything and anything about it.

I had decided beforehand that I was going to treat my examiner just as if he was a real student—I didn't know him from a bar of soap so it shouldn't be too hard. And it might help me feel less nervous. We took off and I started to go through the lesson, just as I had practised it so many times before. John was pretty convincing as a student, questioning me on every aspect of the procedures as if he had no idea what they were about. He made me go through almost every lesson in the private pilot syllabus, after which we headed over to Camden aerodrome to shoot some circuits.

I felt good and knew I was flying well. Everything just seemed to fall into place. John finally told me to fly back to Bankstown, but not before failing the engine a few more times to check out my forced landing procedures over a densely populated area. I think I had God on my side, however, as each time I looked down to find a suitable place to put the aircraft down, there it was staring me in the face—the perfect spot to land!

We landed and headed back to the flying school. The test had taken over two hours, and I was really anxious to get my results. However, John wasn't exactly the expansive type. He said absolutely nothing as we walked across the tarmac, not even a pleasantry about the weather. I was on tenterhooks. I must have messed it up, I thought. I just wished he'd tell me.

Inside the school and still no word.

'Er, John, would you like a cup of coffee?' I asked.

'Yes, OK,' he said curtly.

I made him a coffee and then we headed out the back for the debrief. I was really worried by now. We sat down and he looked at me.

'How do you think you went?' he asked.

'Well, I was pleased with the way I flew,' I said cautiously. He just stared at me.

Come on, can't you see I'm suffering? Just spit it out, for goodness sake!

'Ok, well ... I'm going to pass you,' he said. He finished his coffee, wished me luck, filled out the paperwork and went on his way.

I felt like jumping for joy. I'd done it!

And so, on the ninth of June 1988, just two years and nine days after my accident, I became a flying Instructor.

I started work almost immediately after passing my test,

setting up a desk in the instructors' room at the back of the flying school. The walls were covered with posters, mostly of 747s, as they were what all the other instructors aspired to fly one day. All they wanted to do was to log as many hours as quickly as possible so they could quit instructing and join an airline. The same was true of my fellow-students on the course—it was just a means to an end. But for me it was different. I was happy just to be able to be given the chance to work and use my new skills to help others achieve their dream of flying.

Getting my instructor's rating had been a huge accomplishment for me. My injuries still left me feeling tired most of the time and I constantly had to endure a certain level of pain, especially in my legs and feet. But the struggle had given me a sense of achievement, a feeling that nothing could hold me down. I had no idea of where this job would take me, but to be honest I didn't really care. It was enough just to be there.

My first lesson was exhilarating. It was so satisfying to go out with a student and actually teach them something and to be able to 'see' what they had learnt. It was great to see their faces light up when they took control of the aeroplane. I remembered how much I loved it when I had first gone up.

One of my early students was a young man of Chinese descent named Matthew. He was probably sixteen or seventeen years of age and still at school. He told me he didn't like school and had always wanted to fly, so he thought he'd do a few lessons to see if he really liked it. He was very keen and whereas at school he found it difficult to concentrate, when it came to discussing the aeroplane he was all ears.

One day I drove him over to the airport shop to get some lunch.

'So, Matthew, do you think you'll continue with your

flying?' I asked as we turned into the driveway of the school on the way back.

'Oh yeah, I don't want to finish school. This is what I want to do,' he replied.

'But don't you think you should finish school first and then get your licence?'

'Well, that's what Dad wants me to do.'

'Is your dad a pilot too?' I asked. This was common among boys who were learning to fly.

'No, he's a heart surgeon,' he answered.

A heart surgeon. That was a bit out of the ordinary, I thought. It didn't take me long to put two-and-two together Matthew's surname was Chang.

'Your dad wouldn't be *the* Dr Chang, would he?'

'Yes, that's him.'

I don't think Matthew did finish school, as his father wished. I saw him some time later around the airport—he had gone on to get his commercial licence and was training to be an instructor. It was great to see that he had come so far and it was satisfying to know that I had given him his first few flights. I was absolutely shocked a few years later when his father, the famous heart specialist Dr Victor Chang, was tragically murdered, and I really grieved for Matthew and his family.

All of my students were extremely enthusiastic. Most of them had saved like mad to be able to come out to the airport on weekends to fulfil their ambition. Flying was like a drug. Once it got hold of you it was impossible to break the addiction and you would do anything to satisfy it.

One day I had a student who came out for a trial instructional flight. He had always been keen to fly but thought he would never be able to, as he feared he wouldn't pass the medical examination. He told me that he had broken his back some time ago, though without suffering any spinal damage. He had always thought this would preclude him from holding a licence. Well, he had come to the right place. I sat him down and told him that if I could pass a medical, anyone could. When I told him my story, his eyes lit up and he said he would see a doctor as soon as possible to have it done.

My students came in all shapes and sizes, and of course ability. Some of them came along partly because they wanted to learn to fly and partly because they wanted to overcome an inner fear of flying in a light aircraft. I became quite adept at picking the ones who would be a bit tense when they were up in the air, as they were always tense in the classroom. When they took hold of the control column, their grip was so tight I almost had to prise their hands off to get them to relax. But they were all keen and good fun.

Someone gave me some advice once on instructing potential pilots—treat each student as if they were trying to kill you. That way you would stay on the ball and be certain to make it back in one piece! I'm sure they didn't mean it, but I did have my doubts on a few occasions!

I was standing out on the tarmac one day when a little black plane sped past the taxiway towards the run-up bay. It was one of the fleet of Robin aircraft from the aerobatic school which operated on the aerodrome. It looked a sleek little model, smaller than the type I flew, having only two seats, and with a bubble canopy overhead.

I noticed that the instructor, who was sitting in the right-hand seat, wasn't wearing the standard white shirt which all the other instructors on the aerodrome wore—in fact he wasn't in anything like a uniform. The common opinion around Bankstown was that the instructors at Sydney Aerobatic School, or SAS, were a bunch of louts. They taxied too fast, they flew like maniacs, they were undisciplined and they thought they were better than everyone else. The school itself was considered a hotbed of anarchism which did pretty well as it liked and I was warned to stay away from the little black Robins in the training area. They were a real nuisance.

However, the thought of doing aerobatics fascinated me. I remembered that when I was doing my instructor's course, Peter had told me of the few lessons that he had had in aerobatics. He said that it was great fun and that it really helped to improve your flying skills. The thought of flying upside down appealed to me and secretly I had always intended to venture over to the aerobatic school when I had the chance and inquire about lessons.

The only thing stopping me at the time was the big green factor—money! It was something that I really couldn't afford right now and I would just have to save up until I could. However, there was no harm in going over to the school to see what it was all about—which I did.

The school wasn't situated in the airport itself, but in a small and rather nondescript fibro house not far away. Some of the inside walls had been knocked out to make an office. It was decorated with all sorts of pictures of aerobatic aircraft in all sorts of attitudes. In short, it looked like fun and I couldn't wait to give it a try.

I was greeted at the front desk by a friendly-looking woman.

'Hi, I'm Virginia, can I help you?' she asked.

'Yes, I would like some information on learning aerobatics,' I said.

'Right. What flying experience do you have?'

'Well, I'm an instructor at AFTS.'

'Oh, I see,' she said, a little pointedly. 'Have you done any aerobatics before?'

'No, I haven't,' I said.

'Right, well, what you would be looking at is the phase-one aerobatics. I'll give you some information which will explain what that covers and an idea of the cost.'

She handed me some pamphlets and told me there were four instructors at the school, including her husband Noel, an ex-air force pilot and owner of the school, who mainly supervised the pilots and taught advanced aerobatics. The other three instructors were Steve, Tim and Rob, and it was mainly they who taught the phase-one syllabus.

I thanked her for the information and made my way back to work. I didn't know how long it would be till I could afford to learn aerobatics, but I knew it was something that I would get around to some day.

Sometime earlier, I had spent a holiday at the home of a girlfriend of mine on the north coast, during which I met a retired RAAF pilot who told me about some of the aircraft he had flown. The thought of flying a supersonic jet really fascinated me. Imagine travelling at Mach 1, faster than the speed of sound—that would really be a buzz!

So I got the idea of writing to the air force to ask if they would let me go up in one of their aircraft. Everyone at the airport said I'd have no chance of getting a flight, as the air force would get literally hundreds of similar requests which they invariably refused. Why on earth would they give one to me? It would never happen, but there was no harm in trying.

I addressed my letter to the RAAF base at Williamtown, near Newcastle, where one of their FA-18 Hornet fighter squadrons was stationed.

Before long I received a reply from the group captain in charge of fighter operations at Williamtown, saying that it was against RAAF policy to let civilians ride in an FA-18, but that he was touched by my story and would be more than happy to let me fly the Hornet simulator. He advised me to contact a flying officer at the base named Jenny Howell to make arrangements.

Though it wasn't the real thing, the simulator would still be a great experience. I immediately rang Jenny Howell to say that I wished to accept the group captain's kind offer, and she suggested a day on which I might come up. I asked if I could possibly fly myself up to the base, as it would save me a three-hour car trip, and after checking with the group captain, she rang back to say it would be OK. She added that I was welcome to stay for lunch at the officers' mess and also invited me to spend the night at her place, and fly back the following morning. 'That'd be great,' I said enthusiastically.

I booked in to take JTY up to Williamtown and Neville made sure that it was clean and sparkling for the big event—after all, I couldn't fly into an air force base in a shabby-looking aircraft, could I?

Although the airstrip at Williamtown was used by both military and civilian planes, the RAAF area was off limits to all civilian aircraft. When I arrived and landed I was given permission to taxi over to the air force side, where I was given directions on where to park my plane overnight.

A signalman flagged me to stop where I was so I ran through my shut-down procedures until the engine fanned out. Then I looked out to see a blonde-haired woman running over and waving at me.

'Hi, I'm Jenny Howell, welcome to Williamtown,' she called as she reached the aircraft. She had a pretty face and bright blue eyes and I liked her immediately.

'Hello, Jenny, it's nice to finally meet you in person,' I said as I climbed out onto the wing and then down on the tarmac.

We made our way back to her office to meet her boss, Group Captain Dunn. After that, Jenny said, she would take

Janine Shepherd

me down to the simulator where I would be shown around before having a turn myself. Then after lunch she would take me around the base and when I'd seen as much as possible we'd go back to her place for dinner.

Jenny introduced me to Group Captain Dunn and we sat down for a cup of coffee and a chat. He was a lovely man and interested in knowing how I had come to take up flying after all that I had been through. Then we talked about the Hornet and he described what they were like to fly. I listened intently, as I wanted to learn as much about it as possible before actually flying one myself—even if it was only the simulator.

Finally it was time to make our way to the simulator. It was very different from the one I had flown at the Qantas base. It was a shell, quite small in size really, placed in the middle of a room. The operating crew showed me over it and then I climbed into the seat and was strapped in. I even had to put a helmet on.

Once inside I was impressed at how real the simulator was. Through the helmet I could hear instructors speaking to me from the control room, which was located behind me. They closed the canopy and then talked me through the directions to get the aircraft off the ground. Instead of the control column that I was used to, the Hornet had a control stick with buttons on it which fired the missiles and cannon with which it was equipped.

They got me to fly around to get used to the handling of the aircraft, then told me to try a roll. It was so responsive it took me by surprise. With just the slightest movement it rolled rapidly to either side. It was fantastic. I 'flew' around doing all sorts of things, rolling, diving, climbing, dropping bombs and shooting at enemy aircraft. They even had me fly through Centrepoint Tower!

After the session was over we had lunch in the officers'

252

mess. I felt a little out of place, being the only one not in uniform. Jenny and I sat at a table with Group Captain Dunn and a few other VIPs and we chatted about the simulator ride. After lunch, my host said, he had arranged for me to be shown over a 'real' FA-18.

Jenny took me over to where the Hornets were parked and I climbed up and had a look inside one of them. I wasn't allowed to get in the cockpit, as this was against regulations, but I was happy just to see it close-up. It was very impressive. Then we went on a tour of the base, including a display by the guard dogs' unit, which convinced me that it would be a very dangerous place for an intruder to try to enter. We then went back to Jenny's house, where she cooked dinner and we chatted late into the night.

The day began early on the base, so the following morning I made an early start back to Bankstown. Before I left, I called in to say goodbye to Group Captain Dunn and thank him for making my stay so enjoyable. He said that I was welcome to come up to the base any time and fly the simulator again. I thanked Jenny for her hospitality and making me so welcome during my short stay.

When I lined up on the holding point that morning, waiting for an FA-18 to land ahead of me, I knew it wasn't going to be the last I saw of Williamtown.

*C*hapter 21

EVEN THOUGH I HAD finally found a new direction in my life, it was still impossible to put the past completely to rest because I still had the court case to contend with.

When I first had the idea of learning to fly, I was told by many people that I could be jeopardising my action for damages. It was really an open-and-shut case, it seemed to me, as the man who hit me had been charged with negligent driving and was clearly at fault. However, the defence were out to ensure that I received as little as possible in the way of damages, and to do this they had to prove that my injuries and the trauma I suffered as a result were minimal.

It is an indictment of the insurance system that anyone who attempts to get on with their life, irrespective of their physical condition, is actually penalised. I could have sat around, collecting sickness benefits at the taxpayers' expense, like the man I had met at the swimming pool, and I would have received a lot more in compensation than if I tried to resume a normal life. But I didn't care. My future was far too important to throw away for the sake of a bit more money.

The court case was a great interruption to my life. It seemed as if every week I was out seeing doctors, reliving that awful day and the trauma I had been through, all for the sake of trivial legalities. I constantly had to leave work early or come in late because of appointments with doctors or lawyers. Somehow I managed to fit in time for work between them.

When I wasn't teaching I was usually at the front desk answering the phone or giving people who came in information about lessons. On one particular day it had been very quiet all morning and I thought I would give the aerobatic school a ring to discuss booking in for a course. I now had enough money saved up at least to start.

I recognised the voice on the other end as Virginia, the woman I had spoken to almost five months ago. We chatted for a while and she asked me how my work was going at the school, to which I replied that it had been rather quiet lately. I said that I would drop over some time in the next few weeks to organise a flight with one of her instructors.

When I arrived home that afternoon, to my surprise there was a message on the answering machine from Virginia.

' ... Hello, Janine, this is Virginia from SAS here. I was wondering if you would drop over to the school tomorrow? I have something I would like to discuss with you. Hope to see you then. Bye.'

I played the message again. What could that be about? Why would she go out of her way to ring me when I had just spoken to her a few hours ago? I'd just have to pop over tomorrow and find out!

Next day I arrived at work as usual at eight o'clock. It was a little early to go over to the aerobatic school so I thought I would wait until my lunch hour. However, my curiosity was getting the better of me and the first break I had from teaching, I drove across the airport to see what it was all about.

When I arrived Virginia and her husband Noel were in the office alone. After getting myself a cup of tea—'help yourself' seemed the order of the day—we got down to business.

'Janine, you're probably wondering what this is all about,' Virginia said. That was an understatement. 'Noel and I would like to offer you a job. We've been thinking of putting on another instructor for a while, and we think you'd be just right for it.'

I was more than a little surprised. Why me?

'You need an aerobatics endorsement before you can teach,' she continued. 'Then we would have to teach you how to perform aerobatics from a teaching point of view. This is what we have to offer . . . '

She went on to say that at first I'd be mainly working behind the desk. But whenever Noel had some spare time, he would take me through a course to get an aerobatics endorsement and then one to teach aerobatics. After that I would be on line as one of their instructors. That sounded great to me.

After we discussed a few more details, they asked me when I would be able to start. Realistically I thought I would have to give AFTS two weeks' notice, but I would discuss it with Neville and see what he said.

I was flattered that they had gone out of their way to offer me a job, but I was still a bit suspicious. After all, they didn't know anything about me, or even if I could fly well, which seemed a bit of a gamble. It was only later that Virginia told me how it came about. Apparently it had all been her idea. Knowing that I was an instructor and so keen to take up aerobatics, she had suggested hiring me to Noel. They then did a bit of snooping around. Noel rang one of his old air force buddies who happened to be an aviation examiner to see if had heard of me, as they wanted to make sure I could fly well before they approached me.

As it turned out the old buddy was none other than John, the examiner that had tested me for my instructor's rating. He gave me rave reviews and said I would be great for the job. That cemented the position for me.

I accepted the offer without a second thought. However, at the back of my mind I knew it would be quite a challenge. To fly aerobatics I knew that you needed to use the rudder extensively to be able to execute the manoeuvres, and that wasn't exactly my strong point. My little wasted legs got me through straight and level all right, but I would have to be really competent in aerobatics if I was going to teach it to students. But there was no use worrying about it now. I would cross that bridge when I came to it. I had to give it a go, no matter what.

As I was about to leave and go back to work, one of their instructors returned from a flight with a student. He walked in behind me and went to a filing cabinet on my left.

'Tim, this is Janine, she's going to be joining our team,' Virginia introduced us.

Tim looked around in surprise. Evidently it was the first he'd heard of it. He looked familiar, and I realised I'd often seen him taxiing past me in a little black Robin while I was waiting to take off myself. He was quite short, not much taller than me actually, and he had blond hair. Dressed in jeans, T-shirt and heavy boots, he didn't look like the average instructor.

He gave me a wry smile, made some comment that went completely over my head and then went into the kitchen for a cup of coffee and a debriefing with his student. He looked like a bit of a character, fun to work with. I guessed I would be seeing a lot more of him when I started working at the school.

I drove home that day excited at the prospect of my new job. Teaching aeros, I couldn't believe my luck. Wait till I tell

Mum, I thought ... On the other hand, maybe I shouldn't tell her!

I finished up at AFTS after only a week and turned up at SAS for my first day of work. Right from the start I realised it was going to be different from what I was used to. Thinking that it was what was expected of me, I wore my pilot's uniform of blue pants and white pilot's shirt. Virginia was at the front desk and Noel and Tim were in the kitchen.

'What's that you're wearing?' Tim laughed when he saw me. 'You look like an instructor.'

'Um, I thought this is what I was meant to wear,' I said nervously.

'Well, that's not allowed here,' Tim declared. 'Strictly jeans and T-shirts.'

'Oh, well, I'll remember that tomorrow,' I said.

'Yeah, that's right, we want people who can fly, not ones who just look as if they can,' Noel laughed.

There was more to it than just image. It was actually a very practical attitude. When you flew aerobatics you had to be as comfortable as possible. Loose-fitting clothes and big boots were best, especially when you had to stamp on the rudder consistently. And ties were definitely out of the question, unless you fancied a face full of one when you turned the aircraft upside down!

Virginia showed me where everything was and then gave me a copy of the syllabus to read through. It was different from anything that I had seen before, and completely different from my instructor's notes. The reason for this was that Noel had developed his syllabus around the RAAF flying syllabus and therefore offered his clients an air force style of training.

I spent the morning familiarising myself with the paperwork and getting to know the students who came in. It was a very relaxed atmosphere, quite unlike the typical flying school environment. It was like being at home, which was what gave it its distinctive character.

Behind the office was a lounge room where students could watch TV or take their pick of the dozens of videos on hand, mostly on flying, of course, and in between lessons everyone would just sit around and talk flying. I listened to their stories of flying aerobatics and longed to get out and have a go.

During my first week I met one of the regulars at the school, named Allan Hannah. Everyone called him Boggie, which turned out to be short for 'bograt', hardly the most endearing nickname in the world, I thought. This was because Allan was in the air force, and apparently 'Boggie' was the tag given to the most junior officer in the ranks. Allan was a fanatic when it came to planes—he lived and breathed them and spent every spare moment he had hanging around the airport. I'm sure he got high on the smell of av-gas.

A few years before I arrived at SAS he had been an instructor there himself. Whenever he had leave from the air force he would drive the three hours from his base at Williamtown and sleep in his car outside SAS so that he could get up early and cram in some extra flying. But the RAAF didn't take too kindly to this and forced him to give up his weekend 'job'.

Boggie was an FA-18 pilot—in fact he was the youngest pilot ever to be selected to go on the Hornet course after finishing his RAAF training. I was told he was a bit of a top gun in the air. But Boggie looked more like a jockey than your typical Hornet pilot. Thin as a weed and dressed in daggy jeans and old sandshoes with the odd hole in them, he seemed barely old enough to be out of school, let alone fly an aeroplane.

But it didn't take long for me to find out that the stories I had heard about him were spot-on. He dropped in during my first week at SAS, just to sit around and talk flying.

'So how do you like aerobatics, Ma'am?' he asked. He always used air force slang when addressing women. Every female was called 'Ma'am'.

'Well, I don't know. I haven't done any yet.'

'What? You're kidding! We'd better fix that,' he said. 'Let's go out and turn an aeroplane upside down.'

'That would be great,' I said.

He looked at the booking sheet to see which aircraft was available.

'We'll take Sexy. No-one's flying it at the moment.' This was the name they gave to the aircraft SXY, and she did it justice, black and sleek-looking all around.

We walked down to the parking area where Sexy was standing. We did our pre-flight and hopped into the cockpit. Boggie had to show me how to fit the seatbelts, which were a bit more complicated than those in the aircraft that I had flown. They had a five-point harness to keep you in your seat when the aircraft inverted.

The first thing that struck me was the fantastic visibility in the cockpit. Not only could I see in front of me, but above and behind. This was so you could see all around you when the aircraft turned upside down, and where the ground was.

We took off for the training area and once clear of the Bankstown zone it was time to try some tricks.

'Are you ready?' Boggie asked, as he finished his pre-aerobatic checks on the aeroplane.

'You bet,' I answered. I had no idea what to expect.

'I'll show you a barrel roll first. It's nice and gentle, all positive "G".' This was a flight manoeuvre in which the aircraft rolls while following a spiral course in line with the direction of flight.

'Sounds fine to me.'

He put in full power and then pulled the nose high up above

the horizon. All I could see was sky as the aircraft pulled through the horizon. Then I could feel the 'G' forces starting to weigh my body down as he rolled us around to the left. The ground appeared underneath us as we continued to roll until we were upright again.

'Wow, that's fantastic!' I said. 'Let's do some more.'

I loved it. It was the most amazing sensation to be upside down, but surprisingly not the least bit unnerving.

We did some more rolls and then Boggie showed me how to do a loop. I followed him through before attempting one myself. It was amazingly simple.

'Are you ready to do a spin?' he asked.

'Yeah, let's do it!'

This wasn't like the spin I had done in my instructor's course, which was actually just a wing drop at the stall. This was a fully developed spin, perhaps ten revolutions in all. I had heard so many stories about spinning—people killing themselves getting into spins and not being able to get themselves out—but this was absolutely fantastic. It wasn't the big, frightening manoeuvre that many of the instructors around the airport believed it to be. Perhaps it was just that Boggie made it look so simple and routine.

He went through the spin as if he was on automatic pilot. Seventy knots, sixty knots, approaching the stall—then back stick and rudder *now!* The aircraft rotated rapidly, first turning upside down then settling into a constant rotation which saw us hurtling downwards.

Boggie was calling the airspeed, telling me to look inside, not outside as that might make me sick. Time to recover. Hands off the stick, he applied full opposite rudder. After a few more spins the aircraft stopped abruptly and was pointing straight down to the ground. For a moment I noticed an almost eerie silence. The engine had stopped, the propeller was no longer turning. I was looking down at a paddock underneath me with a few cows scattered among the trees. I grabbed onto the instrument combing in front of me.

I had been told this was meant to happen as the engine actually flooded during the spin, and the airflow wasn't sufficient to keep the propeller spinning, but when you experienced it for the first time it was a bit daunting.

He held SXY in a steep dive to air start the engine. It spluttered and made a few crude noises, then finally, much to my relief, it cranked over—and not a moment too soon! What an experience!

I noticed that Boggie had to use a full boot of rudder in the recovery and hoped when it came to my turn I would be able to do it, otherwise I might not be able to recover at all. That would be something I would have to deal with later.

We did some more aeros, and I think Boggie threw everything he could think of at me. We flew around the clouds, dodging under them and over them, perhaps a bit too close but it was fun anyway. I just sat back and enjoyed the ride, better than a fun park!

We finally headed back to the flying school. I was on a real high and couldn't wait to start my endorsement. My first test was over. I had been through the hoops with Boggie and I hadn't been sick, although I'm sure this had more to do with his skilful flying than the strength of my constitution.

During my second week at SAS, Noel must have wondered what he had got himself into. I had gone into the main bathroom in the house, which was the one designated for women to use. While I was standing there at the sink I reached for something and lost my balance.

I could feel myself falling, as if in slow motion, but there was nothing I could do to stop myself. Down I went, straight into the bath behind me and hit my head on the tiled wall with a thud that sent my brain spinning.

I don't know how long I had to sit in the bath until I could actually see straight, but when I eventually managed to get myself out I had to sit on the toilet lid in case I collapsed again. My head was pounding and I felt extremely faint. I put my hand up to my head and felt something wet. I pulled it away and saw that it was coated in blood.

I stood up and looked in the mirror and saw that my shirt was covered in blood too. Oh boy, I thought, what will everyone say? What a great initiation to my new job.

I gingerly walked out to the office where Virginia and Tim were talking.

'Um, I've had a little accident,' I said rather sheepishly. I pulled my hand away to reveal the blood running down my shirt.

'Oh Janine, what have you done?' Virginia exclaimed. I explained as best I could and Tim volunteered to drive me to the local doctor, who had to put a few stitches in the back of my head.

This unfortunate incident earned me the nickname 'OJ', which stood for 'Oh, Janine!' How could I tell them the reason I fell was because my balance was bad, one of the consequences of my accident. I was sure it wouldn't be a very good recommendation for a future aerobatics instructor.

As the weeks turned into months, I eventually got my aerobatics rating and started to take up my own students. The school had a unique atmosphere about it, mainly due to the fact that it was small and personal. We all liked working there so much that we would even come in on our days off, just to have a fly and talk flying.

As well as the instructors, there was another man on staff, named Paul, whose job was to look after the planes, refuel them after each flight, keep them clean and ensure that their maintenance was up to date. He was also a keen pilot who worked in order to finance his flying. Sometimes his brother Dan would come and help him out.

We were later joined by one of Noel's air force buddies, Louie, who had worked there previously. Often only Paul, Louie and I would be at work and if we had no students to teach we would take a plane out to the training area and just have some fun. We would then come back, have some lunch and watch a video. I'm not sure how many times I have watched *High Road to China*, but it was a lot, and we all knew the flying scenes and the dialogue off by heart.

I loved my work and I loved my flying. I had learnt so much since I had been at SAS it was as if a whole new world of aviation had opened up to me. In aerobatics I had acquired a wonderful skill which had improved my flying one hundred per cent and given me a confidence I hadn't had previously. With it came a sense of power over the aircraft, and even though I still had the utmost respect for what it was capable of, I now had a feeling of being totally in control and that, in aviation, is invaluable.

I took up the air force offer to go back to Williamtown for a second ride on the simulator. Jenny said I was always welcome to stay at her house, so I coordinated my trips with her days off and I would extend my visit to a few days. Although I was grateful for the chance to fly the simulator, I still hadn't abandoned the idea of actually flying in an FA-18. I talked to a few of the pilots on the base and they told me that I basically had two chances, Buckley's and none. No outsider could get a ride in one, and that was it. It would never happen. There was that word again, never. I was really starting to dislike it by now!

So I did what I normally did in these situations. I decided to give it a go, anyway, and go right to the top. I drafted a letter to the Minister for Defence, in Canberra, requesting special permission to fly the FA-18. As a matter of courtesy after all he had done for me, I thought I would first write to Group Captain Dunn to inform him of my intentions. If he particularly asked me not to pursue the matter further, I would give up the idea. I didn't want to tread on anyone's toes, least of all his.

I received a reply from him without delay.

Dear Janine,

... As for your advice on writing to the Minister to seek his assistance in helping you to attain your desire for a Hornet flight, you are an Australian citizen and have every right to ask the question. The chances of Air Force Office acceding to the request are extremely slim. You will understand from my first letter to you and through subsequent visits to Williamtown, we are a fighting Service and simply cannot afford the 'luxury' of sparing scarce flying hours on tasks that have no training benefit. The short answer is that you have two chances—none and Buckley's; but have a go anyway!

Having said all that, you remain most welcome to continue to visit Williamtown. Wishing you all the very best as a 'Total Aviation Person' in Flight's Roger Bacon's terms,

Yours sincerely,
Group Captain Dunn.

Well, now I had nothing to lose. He said I should have a go anyway, so that was exactly what I would do.

I sent my letter off to the Minister for Defence—and then forgot all about it.

Seeing the air force in operation and what it was all about made me decide to join the Air Force Reserve. I realised that it was probably a foolish idea, knowing the stringent medical requirements, and that with my list of injuries I had not much chance of being accepted. But I went ahead and applied anyway.

I wrote away for an application form for the position of Operations Officer, or 'Ops O', as they were called for short. This mainly entailed relieving regular air force operations officers at requested times, if they were on leave or for similar reasons. It was a job that appealed to me, being responsible for coordinating flight operations in the Hornet squadrons so that the flying schedule ran smoothly.

After some time I received a letter asking me to present myself for interviews at the recruiting office in Sydney. I would be required to undergo an aptitude test, a medical examination, and an interview with a recruiting officer. If I was successful I would then be required to come in again for a board interview, to answer questions from a panel of six to eight senior air force officers.

I reported as requested with the documents I was required to produce—my birth certificate, education records, passport, and a dressing gown and slippers. The slippers and dressing gown were a strange request. I wondered what they had in mind when I got there!

By the time I arrived the room was already filled with other applicants, most of them men. My biggest worry was the medical, the mere mention of which was enough to give me butterflies. I could predict the doctors' reaction when I told them my history.

'Shepherd ... Janine,' a male voice called from the other side of the room. I stood up and was told to report to a room a few floors below for an aptitude test with all the rest of the applicants. It turned out to be a three-hour examination in two parts, just like being back at university or sitting for the HSC. When everyone was ready an officer at the front told us to turn our papers over and commence work.

I worked steadily away, and when the officer announced that time was up, I was surprised to see that it was almost midday. We were told to have a break for lunch, after which we were called in for an interview with a psychologist to discuss the results of the tests. Then we went back to the room to which we had reported in the morning for a medical examination. This was what I had been dreading.

After taking down some personal particulars and giving me the usual once-over, the doctor proceeded to ask me about my injuries. Once again I had to go through the whole scenario, from go to woah, detailing the accident, my operations and my present condition.

Next came the most bizarre part. The position I was applying for was an office job, but the doctor asked me to hold onto one leg and hop across the room! What on earth did that have to do with it, I thought? There was no way I could hop, let alone balance on one leg with the other in a firm grasp. But I had to give it a try.

I grabbed my leg as best I could and stumbled across the room. The doctor took one look at me and scribbled something down. To say I didn't go too well on that test would have been an understatement. Then she put me through a series of similarly ridiculous tests. Apart from these, I was obviously fit and well, but I could tell she wasn't very impressed. When it was over, she sat down, pen in hand, and looked me sternly in the eye.

'I'm afraid I won't be able to recommend you, Janine,' she said.

'Why not, doctor?' I asked.

'Well, unfortunately it's against air force policy to accept anyone who has suffered a spinal injury as you have.'

'So even though I passed everything else it doesn't matter?'

'Unfortunately, no.'

'But I've passed the requirements for a commercial pilot's licence. Doesn't that count towards anything?'

'I'm sorry, it's really out of my hands. I just can't pass you.'

I thanked her and went outside. I couldn't believe I was being rejected just because I had been a victim of an accident, when I was only applying for an office job, not to go off fighting in the bush! I walked over to hand in my papers to a sergeant on duty behind a desk in the foyer.

'Well, how'd it go?' he asked.

'No good. She said she couldn't pass me,' I said despondently.

'That's bad luck. What was the problem?'

'Oh, it's a long story,' I replied. 'I was in an accident a few years ago and broke my neck and back. She said she couldn't recommend someone with a history of spinal injury, even though I passed the rest of the medical.'

'You know you have the right to appeal against the decision,' he said. 'It's called redress of grievance.'

I pricked up my ears. 'Really? Who do I write to to do that?'

'Let's see. In your case you'd write to the chief medical officer.'

'Could you write down his name and address for me?' I asked. 'I'll write straightaway.'

'You're not going to believe this, but I think it's a Dr Death,' he said.

'No way, are you serious?' I laughed.

'Yes I am,' he replied. 'But I think you pronounce it

"Deeth".' 'Oh well, let's hope he's having a good day when he receives my letter!'

He gave me the address to write to and wished me luck. I left the building determined to do everything I could to get my application accepted.

I drafted my letter to the air force outlining the reasons why I believed my application should be reconsidered. I believed that despite my injuries, I would be most able to fulfil the requirements of the job for which I was applying. It was some time before I received a reply, but it was definitely well worth waiting for. The air force had accepted my appeal and my application was back in the system! I was on my way again!

The next step was to present myself for interview with the chief recruiting officer in a few weeks' time. This was the one that I had missed earlier when I had failed my medical. If I was successful then I would be recommended to the board.

The interview went as well as I could have expected, and when it was over the recruiting officer told me he was going to recommend me to the board. This meant another, more gruelling interview in about six weeks' time.

I had heard some disquieting reports about the board interview and having got this far, I didn't want to blow it. I had to make sure I knew everything about the air force so I could answer any questions they threw at me. So I sent away for a copy of a government White Paper on defence force policy, which I went through with the proverbial tooth comb.

Armed with everything I thought might be of assistance to me, including my education qualifications, references, and even my log book from flying, I duly presented myself for the interview, to find myself confronted by a panel of six people, ranging from air force officers to psychologists, sitting behind a long desk. I was directed to a chair in the middle of the room facing them, with nothing to hide behind.

The questions covered everything in my personal and professional life, including inevitably my accident and how I would cope with it in the air force. When it was over, I had no idea which way the decision would go. But I felt happy with my performance. I had answered honestly and to the best of my ability.

Six weeks later I finally received a reply. To my amazement and delight, they had offered me a place in the reserves as an operations officer for a period of five years, starting at the rank of pilot officer.

I had really surprised myself, after everyone had told me I didn't have much chance of getting in, and it gave me a great deal of satisfaction to know I had succeeded, despite my injuries, and hadn't given up when my application was first refused. Even more satisfying was the thought that I had perhaps broken down some barriers that had existed for so long, and that it might be easier now for others in my situation to be accepted.

A few weeks later I received another official letter, this time from the federal Minister for Defence, Science and Personnel. At first I thought it must have had something to do with my post in the reserves, but then I realised it was in reply to another application I had made, and which I had forgotten all about. It read:

Dear Ms Shepherd,
Your letter concerning your request for a ride in a Hornet F/A 18 was passed on to me recently ...
I passed your letter together with the papers which

accompanied it, to the Chief of the Air Staff, Air Marshal R. G. Funnell, for his consideration. Both he and myself are indeed impressed with your amazing spirit and determination in the light of your most unfortunate and untimely accident.

Given the injuries you suffered in your accident Air Marshal Funnell is more than a little concerned about the implications of your flying in an ejection seat aircraft. These concerns relate to your possible reduced ability to withstand the high 'G' forces involved in Hornet flying, and also to whether you might be predisposed to aggravated spinal injuries in the unlikely but nevertheless possible event that you may have to eject.

I have considered these factors and am happy to agree to your request for a ride in an F/A 18 subject to satisfactory RAAF aviation medical advice of your ability to withstand the effects of G and of an ejection . . .

I almost dropped the letter. I had to read it again—yes that's what it said. I had the ride!

After I calmed down, I finally managed to read the rest of the letter. It said that I was required to attend an examination by the medical officer at Williamtown to make sure that I would be able to cope with the stress factors involved in such a flight.

Another medical, but so what! This was one I was absolutely sure I was going to pass. There was no doubt about it.

Chapter 22

AFTER RINGING THE offices of the Minister for Defence, Science and Personnel and the Chief of the Air Staff to thank them for their kind offer, I was invited to their rooms to meet them personally. First stop was Parliament House, to the office of the minister at the time, Mrs Ros Kelly. After some routine procedures getting into the building her secretary led me in to meet her.

I was immediately struck by her charm and warmth and she made me feel very welcome. She arranged for morning tea to be brought in while we chatted about my situation and how I first became interested in flying. She was a very down-to-earth person, despite her high profile, and I was impressed by her.

As I was leaving her office I was intercepted by a newspaper reporter who had heard of my getting permission for the flight. He wanted to get my story and asked if I could attend an air show that was to be held soon at Richmond air force base, so that they could take some photos of me there with Mrs Kelly. I already had tickets for the air show, so I arranged to meet up with him there.

Next stop was the Defence Force building to the office of the Chief of the Air Staff, Air Marshal Funnell. It seemed to take forever to pass through security just to get to the right office, but once there they were expecting me and I was quickly ushered in to see him.

I was a bit nervous, as I had never met such a senior military person before. I didn't know how to address him or if I should salute him. I wasn't too sure of protocol and I didn't want to offend him.

I went in and a very trim good-looking man walked towards me.

'Hello, Janine, I'm Ray Funnell, pleasure to meet you,' he said.

'Hello, sir, thank you for inviting me,' I responded. It was a nice surprise. He didn't look anything like I had expected. Although he introduced himself as Ray Funnell, I just couldn't call him anything but 'sir'. It wouldn't have been right.

We had a very pleasant chat over a cup of tea. He told me about his experience flying the Hornet, which made me very excited thinking about my own forthcoming flight. He said he had to keep his passion for flying on the backburner these days as he was too busy in the office. I didn't want to take much more of his time, knowing his schedule must have been very full, and after finishing my tea I rose and thanked him for seeing me and especially for approving the flight in the Hornet. He wished me luck and assured me that I would enjoy the ride—he could definitely vouch for that!

As planned, I went to the air show a few weeks later with a friend of mine named Jo. Mrs Kelly's office had sent me tickets to attend a special morning tea in a marquee which was being held for her.

When I arrived at the marquee, I was surrounded by

reporters from all the major Sydney papers wanting to interview me. They followed my every step, not letting me out of their sight for a minute.

I was ushered into a bus with Mrs Kelly and down to a display of Hornet aircraft, where the press photographers took shot after shot of me, in every conceivable pose and position—under the wing, leaning on the wing, on a ladder leading up to the cockpit, under the rear of the aeroplane, with Mrs Kelly, without Mrs Kelly, in fact just about everywhere with just about everyone.

I had to look tough, determined, happy—in fact I think I covered every human emotion possible! It took forever; there were photographers everywhere snapping madly away. The attention was a bit daunting, not to mention tiring as I had to do a lot of standing around in the heat of the day.

After the photo session was over, I spent the rest of the day enjoying the air show with Jo and watching the air displays. As it drew to a close, I was trudging wearily along a dirt road, with my shoes in my hand and my feet covered in blisters, when I became aware of someone coming up behind me.

'Hello Janine, how are you?' he said as he drew level.

I looked around to see that it was Air Marshal Funnell.

'Oh, hello, sir,' I said in surprise.

We chatted for a minute or two about the show and he strode off down the road. It had been quite a day and I was really exhausted. It was time to face the traffic and head home.

The following day after the air show the papers were filled with my picture and the story of the FA-18 flight. The attention I received made me take the flight very seriously. I decided that I was going to be the most informed passenger who had ever been given a ride in the jet fighter. I knew that it was an expensive exercise for the air force and I wasn't going to waste their money, so I read everything I could lay my hands on about the Hornet beforehand. Then I travelled up to Williamtown to undergo a medical and was duly passed as fit to fly, then arranged a firm date for the big event.

I arrived at the base the day before and went down to '3' Squadron headquarters to meet the pilot who was taking me up. I was surprised and not a little flattered to find it was a very senior officer, Squadron Leader John O'Halloran, or 'J.O.H.' as he was known to his fellow-crew. He gave me the Hornet flight manual so that I could make myself familiar with the aircraft, and then we had a briefing on its safety aspects which J.O.H. said he would test me on next morning as he wanted to be sure I was *au fait* with everything in case we had an emergency or had to eject.

We then went down to the safety equipment room where I was fitted with a flight suit and boots. The boots were so heavy and stiff that I could hardly walk in them. Shoes were a real problem for me since the accident, as my feet were now so abnormally formed, but the boots were a necessary piece of protection for the feet and I had to wear them. I was to be fitted out with my 'G' suit and other equipment in the morning.

I took the flight manual and some other reading material back to my room and stayed up late studying them furiously to make sure I could answer all J.O.H.'s questions in the morning. When I woke I was disappointed to find that the weather was a bit inclement. I knew this meant that the low-flying area would be closed, which was something I really wanted to do.

I got dressed in the flight suit and sandshoes, leaving the boots for the last minute as they were too cumbersome to wear until I actually had to, then I packed the camera I had brought to capture this once-in-a-lifetime experience, and headed over to squadron headquarters.

J.O.H. was there waiting for me to go through the sortie and what I could expect for the day. He gave me the weather details and as I expected told me that the low-flying area was closed. He asked me if there was anything in particular I wanted to do in the aircraft and I had my list all ready to give him. Obviously I wanted to go Mach 1, or faster than the speed of sound, and to experience some high 'G' turning, slow-speed flight, high angle of attack manoeuvring and, of course, some aerobatics.

J.O.H. then tested me on the emergency drills, and I answered every question perfectly, as well as others on the cockpit layout which, after studying the manuals, was starting to become familiar to me.

J.O.H. was more than happy with the effort I had put in and we headed back to the safety equipment room to get the rest of the gear I needed. Over my flight suit I was fitted with a 'G' suit, which was designed to be very snug to ensure that the blood didn't rush from your head when you were pulling excessive 'G' loads. I was given some gloves and then fitted for a helmet and oxygen mask. The guys in charge of fitting me up had printed my name on a tab, which they stuck on the front of the helmet so that I could have a picture taken of myself in the cockpit with the helmet on to prove it was really me. It was a nice gesture on their part.

Finally I was given an LP (life-preserver) unit, which was to be used by the pilot in the event of an emergency, such as having to eject, so that he could be found easily or survive under any conditions. It contained a radio and flares and an inflation device for a stole, an air bladder shaped like a horseshoe, which was worn around the neck and acted as a buoyancy device in the event of the pilot having to eject over water. It was designed to inflate on impact with water and, in the event of this failing to happen, I was briefed on the tab which could be pulled which would act as a secondary inflator.

Finally I was ready for action. I followed J.O.H. down to the aircraft, wishing he'd walk a bit slower as the boots were killing me.

Out on the tarmac, I was confronted by a bunch of photographers, some of them from the daily papers and others from RAAF public relations. J.O.H. and I stood around while they got a few shots and then we climbed into the aircraft for the sortie.

It was a training model with two seats, one behind the other, for the instructor and his student. I climbed into the rear seat and looked around the cockpit. I was surrounded by all sorts of sophisticated equipment designed with one purpose in mind—combat. Like the simulator I had been in previously, there was a control column in the middle with buttons on it which the pilot pressed to release bombs or shoot down enemy fighters. This was no toy!

One of the crew helped strap me in, which was quite a complicated process. The harness was a single-point unit with six straps—two around the shoulders, two around the lap and two for the parachute webbing that came up from the crutch, which all went to a single point forming a 'T' handle. Then the aircrew checked the harness and the 'bowyangs', as they were called—straps attached to both legs which pulled them firmly against the seat to stop them from flailing if and when you had to eject. Without them your legs would be broken in a flash.

I had already been briefed on the HUD, or head-up display, and the DDI, the digital display indicator, which allowed vital information from the instruments to be displayed in front of the pilot so he—or she—didn't have to look down. The throttle was on my left and it was designed in two parts, one for each engine. On the right of the cockpit were the controls for the internal lights and on the left was the intercom panel, which I would use to talk to J.O.H.

There was a control at the front which was used for the radio volume and to dial up the aids used for instrument approaches. On my right was the ejection seat safe arm handle with sequence knob controls. This was the device that was used to eject out of the aircraft and it was imperative that it was set in the correct position. In the normal position it meant the pilot in the front seat had control, while in the aft-initiate position the pilot in the rear would have had control—who in this case was me, and I don't think J.O.H. would have liked that!

After being strapped in, I was shown how to operate the oxygen mask. It was hooked into a chest regulator which converted one hundred per cent oxygen to an air-oxygen mixture. It was checked to see if it was functioning properly. It felt almost suffocating to have it around my mouth, but it was a necessity. The pilots normally flew with a diluted oxygen mixture.

'All set?' J.O.H. asked, as he climbed into his seat and strapped in. He was naturally a lot quicker at it than I was.

'Yes, I'm all ready,' I answered, trying to suppress my excitement.

'I just want to go through a few of the things that I briefed you on,' he said. 'If I say "Eject, eject, eject", I want you to grab the handle between your legs with your right hand, then grasp your right wrist with your left hand and pull up. Can you see the handle?'

'Yes, the one with the black and yellow loop?'

'That's correct.'

All I could see ahead was the back of J.O.H.'s seat. When they closed the canopy, the vision was fantastic. I could see clearly all around me.

J.O.H. briefed me through the start-up, and then we taxied

off to the runway. I looked down to the people still on the ground, photographers and air force personnel, now standing at a distance. The noise must have been intense. I gave them a wave as we started to roll.

I could hear J.O.H. talking on the radio getting our clearances. He kept talking to me, letting me know what he was doing and asking if I had any questions. We approached the threshold, and onto the runway.

He moved the throttle forward and I could feel the power surge through my body as it forced me back in the seat. The pick-up was awesome. One minute we seemed to be standing still and the next we were shooting down the runway like a rocket.

The nose went up and we were in a vertical climb. With amazing speed we had broken the bonds of earth and were now shooting skywards. I grabbed my camera and took a few quick shots outside. I wanted to remember what this was like.

'How was that?' J.O.H. asked.

'Amazing, just amazing. How high are we now?'

'Thirty-five thousand feet. Not bad, eh?'

Thirty-five thousand feet! Wow! We had only been in the air for less than a minute. That was power.

'OK, you ready to have a fly?' he asked.

'Oh boy, I sure am,' I said.

I took the control column in my hand. Slowly at first, I moved it from side to side.

'All right, now let's have a look at the throttle and the afterburner,' J.O.H. said. 'I want you to put your hand on the throttle and smoothly move it fully forward. You'll feel a little resistance when you get to the first detent.'

I advanced the throttle forward past normal military power to max afterburners, to supersonic flight to 1.3 Mach, which in everyday terms was about 1400 kilometres an hour. We did this a couple of times, then we moved on to do some high angle of attack flying.

From supersonic to 130 kilometres an hour is pretty spectacular. The aircraft felt as if it was just hanging in the air, J.O.H. pointed out the contrails on the wing. I looked out to see wisps of condensed air drifting from the wings, caused by the low pressure over them making the air freeze.

Now it was time to try some high 'G' turns. J.O.H. took the controls and hooked it into a tight turn of about 5 to 6 'G' or about five to six times my body weight. I hadn't put my head back on the seat before he started the turn, but once we were established in the turn it was too late—my head was stuck and I couldn't move it. I had pulled 'G' many times before doing aerobatics in my little Robin, but I would only do it for an instant and then it was off. But the feeling of pulling sustained 'G' was incredible. We stopped the turn and resumed normal flight.

'Ready for another one?' J.O.H. asked.

'Sure, ready when you are,' I replied. This time I made sure I sat straight with my head hard back on the head-rest.

He hooked it into the turn, this time even harder. I could feel myself starting to 'grey out'—a sensation when the field of vision starts to narrow down and everything starts to get hazy. It was no wonder. J.O.H. later told me that we were pulling 7.5 'G'.

'OK, all yours,' J.O.H. said. 'Why don't you fly some aeros?'

I took the controls again and tried a loop. It took 10 000 feet to complete, unlike the Robin which took only one thousand feet! I threw it around, did some barrel rolls and aileron rolls, and dodged in and out of the clouds. There wasn't anyone to worry about up here—we were all alone.

Unfortunately, the time came to head back to the base. J.O.H. let me do all the flying, which was great fun because we came back on a Tacan, a military version of an instrument approach. He did all the talking and told me what heading to follow, so that I just had to fly. I kept the airspeed to 350 knots and as we got lower slowed down to 300 knots. At 250 knots J.O.H. put down the undercarriage and it wasn't till we had the runway in close sight that he finally took over to land.

My flight in aircraft A21-108 was over, but my memories of that day would stay with me forever. It was one hell of a ride!

Chapter 23

HAVING FINALLY ACCEPTED the fact that my sporting life was over for good, and having established myself in the world of aviation, I felt my life had some clear direction. If someone had told me before the accident that I would have to live the rest of my life without my sport, and be happy with my lot, I would have thought it impossible. But I was truly happy.

I wanted to try my hand at things I had missed out on before, because I was too busy with my sport. I took up new interests, like learning to play the flute. I vowed to return to my studies at university and began to study part-time to finish off my degree.

It was a sign of how I was managing to come to terms with things that I joined the Disabled Ski Federation and ventured back to my old ski lodge for the first time. Even though my injuries prevented me from skiing as I had before, I was still determined that one day I would at least be able to stay up on my feet well enough to go touring from time to time. After one holiday in the snow I came home with a black eye and swollen lip, the result of a nasty fall. This didn't worry me, though, as I had proved something to myself in the process. I had promised myself that by the end of the season, I would make it around the ten-kilometre track that we used for racing and, after much practice, I had finally done it.

I had received quite a lot of publicity over the years since the accident, and as a result I was often asked to speak publicly about my experiences.

The first occasion was to a group of around 300 people. I had never actually confronted the situation publicly before, but only on a personal basis. I was standing on the stage describing my life as an athlete, when I started to talk about the accident. When I began telling them of my injuries, I was suddenly overcome with emotion and before I knew it I was standing in front of the crowd afraid that if I continued I would burst into tears. The room was silent.

I tried to continue, but I was unable to speak. It had been so long ago, but at that moment I realised that the pain and hurt of what I had been through were still with me deep inside. Having to confront it in the presence of so many others was overwhelming. In a flash the memories started to flood through my head: the physical agony, ICU, the spinal ward, the nightmares, the operations.

I looked at the sea of faces, tears in my eyes. I realised that everyone was staring at me, waiting for me to continue, but I couldn't. Then a voice called out from in the room, 'You'll be all right love,' and with that people started to clap. The silence was broken.

I was then able to continue. Once I was over the accident and talking about flying I was OK. When I finished, I spent some time talking to people in the audience, who offered words of thanks and encouragement to me. Many of them shared their own private stories of tragedy and thanked me for sharing mine with them. Although it had been a painful experience to talk of my accident, I knew that in so doing I had helped others come to terms with the pain that still lingered in their own lives. That made it all worthwhile.

I received a letter from the Surf Life Saving Association of Australia inviting me to attend a function on their behalf. They were to receive a sponsorship cheque from Westpac Bank and they wanted me to accept it on behalf of their National Helicopter Association. As a former helicopter patient I was delighted to be asked.

I turned up on the day expecting to be presented with the enlarged cheque from the bank, and ready to say a few short words on behalf of the helicopter association. However, I wasn't expecting to be presented with a basket filled with all sorts of goodies and a flying jacket embroidered with the emblems of the Westpac helicopter crew. It was a very touching gesture, and I knew I would get a lot of use from it when I went flying.

It was only a matter of time, however, until my life underwent another interruption in the form of another operation.

Because of the way I walked, with certain muscles having to compensate for those I could no longer use, my feet had developed in a way that was anatomically damaging. My toes had to claw the ground just so that I could stay upright. It was almost impossible for me to wear shoes, as the toes had curled up so much and the bones had become calcified and very swollen.

The answer, of course, was more surgery. Dr Stephen said he would be able to cut the tendons that were causing the toes to pull up, and hopefully that would rectify the situation. After the operation, I would be back in plaster and off my feet for at least six weeks. This meant another break in my flying and back to dependence, but I really didn't have a choice. I just had to have it done.

I was booked into the Mosman hospital again, in a large ward next to the room I had been in the last time I was there. I was the only patient in the ward at first, so I was able to pick my bed. I chose one in the corner, near the window, so that I could see out to the trees and garden below. It was a light, bright room that seemed to be filled with sunshine for the most part of the day.

No sooner had I arrived and the nurse had done her routine examination, than another patient was admitted and took the bed next to mine. She was a painfully thin young girl, no more than twelve or thirteen years of age. Her mother had brought her in and after they had settled in and unpacked her bag, I thought I would introduce myself.

The girl's name was Cecile and her mother was Rita. They had come all the way down from Inverell in northern NSW for Cecile to have her feet operated on. She had bunions which needed removal and a few other problems that needed fixing up. Dr Stephen was her doctor as well.

We were both scheduled to be operated upon the next day. This was Cecile's first operation, and she was a little nervous. I was getting pretty used to it by now, and assured her that she had nothing to worry about. She was in good hands with Dr Stephen. The nurse came around and gave Cecile her pre-med, which helped to calm her down, and then an orderly came and wheeled her away for her operation.

Soon after the nurse returned. 'Janine, Dr Stephen wants to know if he can borrow your radio for the operation. He hasn't got any music in the theatre.'

'Oh sure,' I said, and handed it to her. 'Just tell him he'd better concentrate on what he's doing though,' I laughed. Nothing surprised me with Dr Stephen. I knew they always had music playing when they operated, as I had heard it before when I was being wheeled into the theatre.

Soon it was my turn. I had my pre-med and then Cecile was

returned to her bed, fast asleep. By the time I was taken down to the theatre, I was feeling absolutely sick. No matter how many times I had been through this before, I still felt anxious about being cut open. Dr Stephen met me at the door of the theatre.

'Janine, so we meet again,' he said.

'Dr Stephen,' I said groggily. 'It's my feet today, not my leg, remember? Make sure you get it right.'

'I thought it was your arm. Nurse what are we doing today?' he said in his cheeky manner.

The anaesthaetist put the needle in my hand. I could feel myself quickly losing consciousness. I hated that feeling.

'Come on, Janine, see if you can fight it,' Dr Stephen said. He always made a joke of things. The coldness swept through my veins in an instant. I could feel it rushing towards my head . . .

When I awoke I was overwhelmed by the pain. I looked down to see that my feet were both elevated on pillows. They were throbbing. I called the nurse over and she informed me that I had pins in my big toes where Dr Stephen had fused the bones together. He hadn't told me that he was going to put pins in, but he always had something in his bag to surprise me.

He soon came around to check on Cecile and myself. He told us he was going to wait a few days before he plastered our feet, to give them time for the swelling to go down. I was half-relieved that he said it would only be a small cast, covering our feet and leaving a gap around the heel. This way we would be able to walk when the feet healed sufficiently.

Cecile and I stayed in hospital for a week and we both managed to procure our own wheelchairs to get around in. Everyone at the flying school kept in touch while I was there, ringing me each day to see how I was going, and Tim and Rob came in to visit most days.

Cecile loved having them around. I think she actually had a crush on my older men friends! She didn't have many visits, as Inverell was too far away for her friends to come down, and she enjoyed the company. We gave the staff a bit of a headache, though, having wheelchair races up and down the hallway. We weren't actually sick, just temporarily out of action, so it gave us something to do.

Tim loved stirring Cecile up—she was easy bait at her age! When she wasn't looking he greased her wheels with vaseline and then challenged her to a race down the hall. She thought she would teach him a lesson, but much to her disgust she couldn't get going and had no idea why!

It was pretty clear to me that Tim and Rob were both vying for my attention, and it became slightly uncomfortable. We all worked together and had become good friends and the last thing I wanted was to hurt anyone's feelings. I didn't want to choose between either of them. Besides, I really liked the friendship I had with them both and still didn't feel able to commit myself to a relationship of any sort other than friendship.

They were both very different. Tim was the typical Irishman, full of Celtic wit that more often than not passed over the heads of the uninitiated. He was always making us laugh with his antics and wisecracks and had a keen sense of the absurd that was most appealing. Rob, on the other hand, was more the serious type. He was a bit of a romantic, always going out of his way to help others, and nothing was ever too much trouble for him. But they were both good fun.

After a week in hospital, both Cecile and I had mastered the use of crutches. With plaster on our feet, they weren't the easiest things to master but it was either that or stay in a wheelchair, which wasn't much of a choice!

Rita and Cecile had a few days in Sydney before they were to head back to Inverell, so I arranged for them to come over for lunch one day. Afterwards we went to the Powerhouse Museum. Tim came along with us and we managed to procure a couple of wheelchairs to get around the museum, as it was a lot faster than crutches. We must have looked quite a pair, with our feet encased in identical plaster. When someone commented on the plaster and inquired as to what had happened, we told them about the tandem parachute jump that had gone terribly wrong ... it was a lot simpler than the real story!

After I had been home for a few days, the pain in my feet became almost unbearable. Tim had come by to visit one day and I could hardly talk to him, the pain was so intense. Both Mum and he were convinced that it was normal for my feet to hurt and that the pain would eventually subside. However, I knew there was more to it than that.

I finally persuaded Mum to take me to see Dr Stephen. I was right. The problem was that my feet were unable to breathe under all the plaster and the stitches were beginning to weep with pus. Dr Stephen arranged for me to go straight to his physio to have the plaster removed and replaced with bandages. A few days later, the pain was even worse, and I begged Mum to take me to the casualty ward of the nearest hospital. She realised at last that it must be bad.

At the hospital they removed the bandages to reveal badly infected feet. The stitches were all red and swollen and oozing with pus. The doctor on duty did the old plunge-and-stab routine trying to get a drip into my arm to pump antibiotics into me, which he managed to do just as I was about to faint. I had to stay there for another few days until my feet started to heal and I could go home.

It was another six weeks until I was to get the pins out and could wear shoes again.

Seeing so much of each other on the job, Tim and I started to spend a lot more time together. We both had a few days off from work and as the weather was perfect and looked like staying that way, we decided to go and visit some friends of mine in Cooma. Tim often flew a friend's plane that was hangared at the airfield in Mittagong, which was where he had learnt to fly. Tim had been a member of Berrima district aero club since he was a teenager. They used to operate from a small dirt strip just near the Bong Bong racecourse, called the Old Bowral Airfield, but since relocated to a decent-size strip at Mittagong. He worked as the duty pilot while he was at school, which involved spending every weekend washing planes, mowing lawns and refuelling. In return he would get half an hour of flying for each day he worked. That was how he paid for his flying lessons.

He rang the owner to check if the aeroplane was free and it was, so it was all ours.

We drove down to Tim's mother's farm, near the airfield. This was the first time I would see Tim where he was most comfortable—out of the city and on the land. It was also the first time that I met his mother.

I think she saw me straightaway as a potential daughter-in-law, as the whole time I was there she did nothing but talk about Tim, how wonderful he was and how he could do absolutely anything. Well, I didn't believe her for a minute. How could anyone do absolutely anything! I wasn't about to be matched up by anyone. Besides, although I enjoyed Tim's company, we were just too different to be anything more than friends.

The people we were going to visit were the Wilkenson family, whom I knew from skiing. They lived on a large farm just out of Cooma and when I rang them to ask if we could stay, they said they would be happy to have us.

The aircraft we were taking was called a Skybolt. When

Tim pulled her out of the hangar, I thought it was just beautiful. Painted green and white and in pristine condition, it looked like a lot of fun to fly. It was a biplane, with an open cockpit and no canopy above it. I had never flown in an open cockpit before, or a biplane for that matter, so I was really looking forward to it.

After our pre-flight, I climbed into the front cockpit and Tim showed me how the seatbelts worked. There were two sets of them for each passenger as an added precaution. I made sure they were done up very tight, as I didn't want to fall out if we were upside down! I had to wear one of those old-fashioned caps, the type I imagined the Red Baron used to wear, with headsets over it. When I was firmly fixed, Tim strapped himself in and we were ready for action.

We did our run-ups and wasted no time getting airborne. The open cockpit made it pretty noisy and very windy, but it was an absolutely perfect day, with not a cloud in the sky.

We set a heading for Cooma and Tim took me through some of the Skybolt's idiosyncrasies. The only problem I had was that the rudder pedals were such a long way from my feet that I couldn't reach them. There was a stick in the centre and a few basic instruments, but other than that there was nothing. This aircraft was meant for aerobatics and not much else.

I could see for miles. This is what flying is all about, I thought. We winged our way wherever we wanted. We had a compass to tell us roughly what direction to head but otherwise we went where our fancies took us. This was real freedom.

We were having a ball. We flew up the valleys at low level then over the mountain ridges to the next valley on the other side. As we saw Cooma airport in the distance, Tim began to set the aircraft up for our approach to land. It was my first time in a biplane and I was unaware of what the view would be like on our final approach, or should I say lack of view. The nose of the plane was so high as we came in that we couldn't see a thing ahead of us, and had to sideslip all the way down to the runway to guide ourselves in. Just before touching down Tim kicked it straight with the rudder and set us down on the tarmac for a wonderfully smooth landing. I was impressed!

June Wilkenson and one of her sons, Sinclair, were at the airport to meet us. I could see that Sinc was just itching to have a fly. Tim offered to take him up and he jumped at the opportunity. In the meantime June headed off for the farm so that she could watch them as they flew over the property.

I helped Sinc get into the aircraft and put on his seatbelts and they took off. He had a grin on his face so large I could see it even when they were rolling down the runway. When they arrived over the property, only a few minutes away, June was waiting for them with a big sheet in her hands she was waving madly. In response Tim swooped so low he covered her in dust!

Tim told us later that he decided to show Sinc a few tricks, and yelled out to him to hold on. But Sinc wasn't sure what was about to happen and grabbed the crossbars of the plane just in front of him. Tim put the aircraft in a dive and then pulled up into a stall turn. All he could hear, he said, was Sinc screaming as the aircraft went through to the vertical then flicked around and headed back down to earth. Tim threw it around for a while, showing Sinc what aerobatics was about, then they headed back to the strip. It was an experience Sinc wasn't likely to forget.

Out at the farm we had some lunch and then Tim went off with June's husband Bob to help him fix some fences. I stayed behind with June. There was a lot of catching up to do.

June knew Daven well, and asked how we were going. I

told her that our relationship was over long ago, and that we were just friends. That was what I wanted.

'Well, what about Tim then?' she asked. 'He seems like a really nice boy.'

'Oh no, June, it's purely platonic, although I think he would like it to be something else. Besides, we're just too different.'

'Believe me, Janine, sometimes that's the best way. Opposites do attract, you know,' June said in her soft voice.

The thought of getting into a serious relationship with Tim hadn't even entered my mind. We did get on well together and enjoyed each other's company. He made me laugh, which was pretty important to me. But I really didn't feel I could cope with a relationship, or at least a serious one. Besides, being on my own meant that I was protecting myself and made me feel in control. I had been through so much I didn't need any more hassles in my life. Tim had been very patient with me, which I really appreciated. He was willing to accept whatever form of relationship I wanted, and for now it was his friendship and nothing more that I was after.

June and I talked at length about the situation and I don't think I convinced her that it could never be any more than friendship. I knew she was partial to country men—she had married one, after all—and she took an immediate liking to Tim.

After dinner Tim and I sat down with our maps to plot our route home the next day. We would head back a different way from the one we had come, going over the mountains to Moruya on the coast, and then flying back to Mittagong. Once that was settled, we sat around the fire chatting with the family before retiring for the night. As I lay in bed, I thought about what June and I had talked about—the possibility of entering a relationship with Tim. No, it just didn't seem to fit. I wasn't ready for that sort of commitment.

The next day we said our goodbyes to Bob and the boys and June drove us out to the airport. We gave her enough time to get back to the house before taking off and flying over it on the way home. This time she left the sheet inside!

The weather was starting to close in, unlike the fine, clear day that we had had coming down, but it was still glorious to be up in the sky. We headed over the mountains separating Cooma from the coast, having to fly around the clouds scattered over the top of the range.

Up in the open cockpit I could feel rain starting to fall. Around me was the most breathtaking sight I had ever seen. We were in the middle of what seemed a vast expanse of untouched land as far as the eye could see. I didn't have my camera handy, but it didn't matter. I knew I could never capture the beauty below me on a roll of film. This was a sight I would just have to store in my mind.

It didn't take us long to reach the coast and arrive at Moruya. I was struck anew by what a beautiful country we lived in. One moment we were in the magnificent, rugged country of the Snowy Mountains, and just half an hour away by air we found ourselves on the most breathtaking piece of coastline one could imagine. The airstrip was situated right on the coast, only a short walk from the beach, and what a sight it was when coming in to land.

We parked the plane, then walked over to the beach and sat on the sand, enjoying the view for a while before going back to get some gas for the last leg of our journey. After taking off we flew back along the coast, so low we must have given a few sailboarders a bit of a fright, not to mention the fishermen on the rock cliffs. They almost had to wave down to us as we scooted past.

We were cleared through Nowra military zone to continue along the coast, before turning inland to head back to Mittagong. When we finally got there we still had one more thing to complete before landing—some aerobatics! We had been too heavy with fuel to do any earlier, but now that we had burnt off some of the weight it would be OK. Tim handed over to me and I put it through some loops and rolls, then into a spin. It was very different from the Robin that I had been flying especially when we flew inverted. I was just hanging upside down in the seatbelt, which was the only thing between me and the ground. I hoped it had been checked out recently—I didn't fancy it failing right now!

The trip was over and we had had a great time. We really did have fun together. Maybe we had more in common than I thought. After all, we had our flying and that was something. Maybe June was right. Maybe being so different wasn't such a bad thing. Who knows? Anyway, our friendship was deepening and we began to see even more of each other after our trip away.

'Hey, would you like to go out to dinner tonight?' Tim asked as we walked out of the flying school after work one day.

'Sure, that would be great. Where do you want to go?' I said.

'Well what about Bobby McGee's?'

'That's fine with me.'

'OK, I'll pick you up at seven.'

I jumped in my car and headed home. A group of us had been to this restaurant before and I was looking forward to returning. At home, I showered and put on my dressing gown. I knew I had a bit of time before Tim was to pick me up so I went and ironed my clothes and sat around chatting to Mum and Dad.

I heard the doorbell ring, and much to my surprise, it was Tim. I looked at my watch—maybe I had the time wrong. No, it was only six o'clock.

'Tim, what are you doing here now?' I asked.

'Don't you remember? We're going out for dinner.'

'Well, I know that, but you're an hour early. It's only six o'clock.'

He checked his watch, looking very embarrassed, and more than a little stupid. He apologised and said he would come back in an hour.

'Don't be silly, come on in. You can wait here. I'm not ready but you can sit with Mum and Dad until I get dressed.' With that I ushered him inside to the kitchen.

When I was ready we said goodbye to mum and dad and made our way to the restaurant. There were quite a few stairs to negotiate once we had parked our car, and I needed a hand to negotiate my way up them. Tim stood behind me and gave me a bit of a push to help me up, which I'm sure must have looked a bit strange to the passers-by. I'm sure they must have thought I was just lazy! We placed our orders and after we'd eaten stayed on talking until we were just about the last people left in the restaurant.

I was fiddling with a heart-shaped ring on a finger of my right hand. A friend had made it for me for my birthday years earlier.

Tim noticed it and commented, 'That's a nice ring,' then took my hand to have a better look.

'Mm,' I nodded. 'It was a present for my birthday.'

'I think we should do something about getting one for the other hand,' he said.

The remark went right over my head.

'What was that again?' I asked.

'I said, what do you think about getting one for your left hand?'

I was a bit slow. I still didn't get it.

'Why?'

He took both my hands in his and looked at me, a little nervously.

'Janine, don't make this any harder for me than it is. I'm asking you to marry me.'

My stomach churned. Marry! ... Maybe I hadn't heard him right. We hadn't known each other for that long—surely he couldn't be serious?

'What did you say?' I asked.

'Will ... you ... marry ... me?'

Now I was sure what he was saying, but I just had to hear it again. After all, it's not everyday that someone asks you to marry them. 'Could you just ask me one more time?'

'This is killing me! For the third and final time, please Janine, will you marry me?'

His hands were shaking. I had never seen him so emotional. This was obviously a very difficult thing for him to do. I was overwhelmed and moved that he had the courage to ask me to spend the rest of my life with him. He knew all my problems, my injuries, the care and physical assistance I required. I was sort of high-maintenance when it came to being looked after. Yet he still wanted me to be with him— and I realised that I felt the same. The differences weren't so important. This was what I wanted. I had made him sit in agony long enough.

I looked into his eyes. 'Yes. I will marry you.'

His relief was obvious. He leant over to kiss me. I saw there were tears in his eyes.

What a twist of fate, I thought. Not long ago I would never have imagined this to be possible. But now it all seemed so right.

The wedding was planned for eight months' time. Plenty of time, I thought. However there was so much to organise I was kept busy until the final day. We decided to get married in the southern highlands, where Tim had grown up.

The ideal place for the reception was a grand old guest house in Robertson, high up on the coastal escarpment, called Ranelagh House. When Tim left school and was saving for his flying lessons, he had worked there for a year as a general rouseabout. Kay, the owner, was like a second mum to him, and when she heard we were getting married she wouldn't hear of us having the reception anywhere but there. I couldn't think of a better setting.

Ranelagh was an imposing building, originally built in 1924 as a hotel for well-to-do patrons, but later converted to accommodate nurses and doctors during the Second World War. It had had quite a few transformations since and at one stage it was even a friary. It was set in several hectares of beautiful lush grounds which were home to a proliferation of wildlife. It was full of character and charm, not to mention a cute little wombat which used to greet the guests as they arrived for their stay.

Normally, it wasn't available for hire, but this was an exception. Not only were we going to have the reception there, but Kay booked the entire house out for the weekend so that our guests could stay on afterwards.

We planned to have the wedding ceremony in a church in Bowral and then go on to Ranelagh for the reception. The minister of the church kindly allowed us to be married by another minister and dear friend of ours, Les Nixon. I had got to know Les and his wife Martha when they read about my story and sent me a card and letter while I was in hospital for one of my operations.

As it happened, he lived quite near the airport and I dropped around to see him and thank him for the letter. It was the beginning of a great friendship. Les was a very keen pilot, so we had a lot in common. He and Martha ran a ministerial organisation called 'Outback Patrol'. They flew around the country with their many volunteers, offering fellowship to people in outback towns which were too small to support a church.

Les and Martha spent much time helping us to select a ceremony which meant something to us and would incorporate some of our own personal touches. Martha had a beautiful voice and we were delighted that she agreed to sing at the service. I asked my good friend Pab to play the trumpet at the wedding, and Steve, another friend, who was a professional musician and also a dear friend of Les and Martha's, agreed to play the organ.

I had four bridesmaids—my two sisters Kim and Kelley, and two of my friends, both named Jo. It was a nightmare trying to get them organised for dress fittings, as they all seemed to be in different parts of the country at the same time, but we managed somehow. Then of course there were the invitations, the cars, the cakes, the photography and goodness knows what else.

In the end it all seemed to come together with perfect precision, and before I knew it there I was walking down the aisle on my father's arm with Pab's 'Trumpet Voluntary' resounding throughout the church.

I had gone through this moment in my imagination so many times, walking down the aisle. But when the time finally arrived I was unprepared for the nervousness, let alone the emotion, that would touch me. I could feel tears starting to well up inside, and no matter how much I tried to hold them back, I couldn't.

The service was wonderful and Martha charmed everyone with her singing. There were a few tears shed all around during the service, though I think Mum took the cake. She was pretty emotional at the best of times, but I knew this would be one day she wouldn't forget, a day she once thought would never have been possible. Once outside the church we chatted to our guests for a few minutes before driving to Ranelagh for the reception.

We were greeted by the most glorious of sights. The day had so far been perfect, dazzlingly blue with not a cloud to spoil it. But now the mist had begun to roll in over the escarpment to create an almost magical, mystical backdrop. The fog twisted its way through the trees and over the lawns, and as the bridesmaids wandered through the mist in their full-length gowns, it created a fairyland setting. With the champagne flowing, it was the perfect atmosphere for our wedding photos.

The wedding breakfast was all that anyone could ask for. Kay and her partner Jo had made sure that nothing was missed and we enjoyed an exquisite dinner followed by pastries and a beautiful French wedding cake.

My old friend Hap, renowned for his gift of the gab, was our MC for the night and had everyone in stitches during the speeches. He made sure he gave me a good ribbing, but I seized the chance when responding to the traditional toast to the bride to give him a good taste of his own medicine!

After the speeches, there was dancing in the ballroom to the tune of a brass band. As nobody had to drive home that night, our guests well and truly let their hair down. The band was also staying the night, and the festivities continued long after Tim and I retired for the night. There were quite a few sore heads next day.

Our honeymoon was one of those once-in-a-lifetime trips— two weeks soaking up the sun in the Maldive Islands followed by a week in Bangkok and Singapore for some duty-free shopping.

The Maldives are a long chain of islands in the Indian Ocean south-west of Sri Lanka, consisting entirely of coral deposited over thousands of years to eventually form an atoll surrounded by a glorious reef of coral. As soon as we arrived on our island we got ourselves a set of snorkels and flippers and headed out to explore the glorious reef surrounding it. The coral was beautiful but it was the fish we found most fascinating, as they swam around us in swarms of exotic colour pecking inquisitively at our masks and even nibbling our arms and legs.

Both Tim and I had always wanted to scuba dive, so we took a course in the fortnight we were there, which was long enough to get our certification and also be able to enjoy some free diving afterwards. The snorkelling was great, but it was the scuba diving that was the highlight of the holiday.

The only problem I faced was that with the tank on my back, it was almost impossible for me to walk. With my weak legs and lack of balance, I couldn't manage to get out of the water. Tim had to carry my tank for me down to the water, as well as having his own tank on his back. Once I was fully submerged and the water supported my weight, he would help me put my tank on. Then I was fine, and we enjoyed some absolutely spectacular dives. We explored a shipwreck, saw some sharks and other weird and wonderful fish and rubbed noses with the occasional eel.

On one of our dives we headed off by boat to an atoll called Banana Reef with our instructor, Henrik, and the other half-dozen people in our class. The day was unusually bleak, with thick clouds warning of an impending storm. The reef was quite a way from our island so we had to make an early start. When we arrived, there wasn't a soul to be seen.

With our tanks securely on our backs, and all our checks done, we plunged into the water. It was an unusually cold day but I was pleasantly surprised to find the water was still warm. We dived beneath the surface, staying in our group, and following the other divers. Below the surface the rip was quite strong and we had to hold on to the coral to stop ourselves floating away. The coral reef seemed to go forever, and was absolutely beautiful with its myriad colours.

We gave the thumbs up to Henrik, meaning that we were all OK and ready to go exploring. We were in the water for about fifteen minutes, looking in all the nooks and crannies as Henrik pointed out various pieces of sealife to us. It was so tranquil, just us and the ocean. Then suddenly, out of nowhere came a huge group of Japanese divers. All armed with underwater cameras, they were clicking away furiously at everything they saw, even us!

I couldn't believe this was happening, out in the middle of nowhere. I looked over at Tim to see him almost choking on his regulator, laughing so much he had trouble keeping it in his mouth. I knew the Japanese were great travellers, but this was really taking it a bit far. It would have been a great ad for Nikon, though!

We returned from our honeymoon, relaxed and reinvigorated but a few kilos heavier than when we left. It was the end of one adventure and the beginning of a whole new one—as husband and wife.

Chapter 24

ONE OF THE questions that was left unanswered about my physical condition was whether or not I would be able to have children. My doctors couldn't confirm that it would be possible considering the extent of the internal injuries and bleeding I had sustained. This was the last thing on my mind at the time of the accident, it was actually Dad who had asked the doctors about it.

It was odd that when someone says that something isn't possible any more, the desire to do it or have it becomes even greater. That is what happened with me. To be really certain of the chances of my becoming pregnant the doctors suggested that I undergo a series of tests, though even then the result wouldn't be absolutely certain. Tim and I discussed the problem. He thought I had been through enough and didn't want me to expose myself to any more strain than I had to. But we finally decided that if I did become pregnant some time in the future, so be it. If not, then we would perhaps think about adoption or some other course.

As it turned out I didn't have to wait very long. Soon after we were married I discovered that I was pregnant. We were both very excited.

I knew from the beginning that this pregnancy would be no run-of-the-mill affair. I expected, as did the doctors, that I would have my share of problems. There was the probability that I would have to wear a brace throughout the pregnancy as my back might not be able to withstand the extra pressures on it. There was the added risk of urinary tract infections, and of course no one had any idea how my body would stand up to labour when the baby actually arrived.

For one thing, I didn't have normal pelvic tone, which is needed to push the baby out in the final stages, and there was the likelihood that I would need a Caesarean section. Then there was the fused vertebral column in my spine which had no flexion and could prove a problem for the baby, not to mention myself. Epidurals were out of the question, so the options for pain relief were limited.

Preferring women doctors, I found myself a female obstetrician. I had always believed that the best person to deliver a baby was someone who had had one herself, because she knew exactly what it was all about. That was just common-sense, as far as I was concerned.

My obstetrician's name was Sue. She had two children herself, so that put me at ease straightaway. She was an impeccably dressed woman, entirely professional yet able to maintain the right degree of intimacy to win the patient's confidence. She always went out of her way to explain what was happening, which I appreciated greatly as a first-time mother.

I had booked in to have my baby at King George V Hospital in Camperdown, which was only a short drive from our home, at its new birthing centre. Sue was a bit hesitant at first, doubting whether they would take me, as the centre was for low-risk pregnancies and with the uncertainties of how my pregnancy would proceed, it didn't sound like a wise option.

When I first visited the centre I was even more keen to have the baby there. It was just like being at home. The rooms were furnished in country style, with a large bed, a wooden cradle and tasteful decorations, and of course a telephone. There was even a spa bath to luxuriate in. It was very comfortable and cosy and looked more like a guesthouse than a maternity hospital. It offered prospective mothers the opportunity of a more natural birth experience, with the aid of compassionate midwives and minimal medical intervention, without resort to drugs. Instead they used alternative methods of pain relief, like heat, water and massage.

The staff at the centre were prepared to accept me and Sue finally agreed to let me go there, with the proviso that if anything went wrong I would be transferred to the labour ward. That was fine by me. I was determined to make sure the baby had the best possible start in life. I knew I had to keep myself healthy too, not only for the baby but so my body would hold up to what it had to go through.

I finished up at work when I was three months pregnant. Flying aerobatics wasn't the ideal occupation for an expectant mother. My injuries always made me very tired and being pregnant exacerbated my fatigue. So I hung up my headsets until after I had given birth.

I wanted to keep my weight down as much as possible so my back would withstand the stress and exercised whenever I could. I was fortunate to have the support of the Hyde Park gymnasium in the city, which had sponsored me when I was still training. They allowed me full use of their facilities, which included a pool and first-class gym equipment. I spent at least three days a week doing weights and swimming. I rode my exercise bike and did sit-ups every day and spent lots of time stretching, as well as just preparing myself mentally for the big day.

By the time the big day approached, I had put on only ten kilos, which was at the lowest acceptable level. My back was starting to play up, which really didn't surprise me. I had difficulty getting around as my poor legs were struggling to cope with the extra burden. I couldn't wait to offload it and I convinced myself that the baby was going to come on the expected day. By the time it came around I couldn't wait any longer, I waited, and waited and ... you guessed it, I waited. Nothing happened!

Day two was the same, and day three. By day ten I was getting a bit fed up. More annoying was everyone ringing up and saying. 'Oh you're still at home.' At last, when Tim and I were watching television one night, I felt a twinge of pain. I immediately thought it was just another false alarm. I had had a few of them over the past few weeks and didn't want to get too excited. I started to time the contractions, to make sure it was the real thing before I told Tim. After a few regular contractions I was sure this was it. Life was on its way.

Being the laid-back type, Tim's reaction was predictable. 'Oh well, if it's going to be a long night, I might as well get some sleep,' he said, and went to bed. It was probably the most rational thing to do under the circumstances. But then again, who wants rationality when you're about to give birth!

Not knowing what else to do, I ran the bath and got in. Just as I was about to lie back and enjoy it, the contractions came on with a vengeance and I had to get out again. I started to pace up and down the lounge room telling myself to relax, but each time the contraction hit, the pain was maddening. I had been to a 'natural' birth class and right now the most natural thing seemed to be to make as much noise as possible. I stumbled around the room doubled over and clutching my stomach, groaning at the top of my voice. I must have looked as though I was performing some sort of primitive war dance!

After what seemed like hours, though it was most likely

only minutes, the contractions were coming with such intensity and regularity that it was impossible to think straight. Tim had slept long enough, I decided. He was getting up whether he liked it or not! It was time to make the trip to the hospital. When I woke him, he convinced me we should wait a bit longer. In the meantime he would make us something to eat.

Food was the last thing on my mind and when he returned with some tea and toast I had to run to the bathroom where I began vomiting uncontrollably. I felt absolutely awful. I emerged determined that we had to go *right now* and Tim packed me and my bag into the car.

At the birth centre I was met by the midwife on duty, Kim. She was already expecting me as I had rung her earlier to tell her I was in labour. She gave me an examination and then we had to go to the front desk to register. I decided to go along for the walk as moving around seemed to be the best thing for the pain.

Once in the comparative comfort of my room, I tried everything possible with Kim's help to alleviate the pain. Along with the contractions, I was vomiting at regular intervals, so I rotated for some time between the bathroom and the bedroom. Then Kim suggested that it might be a good idea to get into the spa. I was willing to try anything. She put on some classical music and dimmed the lights, but unfortunately she couldn't dim the pain. The contractions had become almost unbearable, lasting two-and-a-half minutes with only twenty seconds between each one.

The pain in my back was now so intense that I thought my back wouldn't be able to stand up to the stress. The baby had now moved down and was pushing on the area of my back where I had the fusion. There was no way it was going to give, the pain now intolerable.

What could I do? An epidural anaesthetic into the spinal

area was out of the question, and I was already nauseous so gas would only make it worse.

There wasn't much alternative. In between each contraction I didn't have time to relax. All I could think of was the next one that was about to strike with as much ferocity as the last.

'I can't take another one,' I would gasp.

'Just one more,' Tim kept saying, over and over.

I was now past the transition stage and we moved back into the bedroom. Tim pulled up the blinds and said, 'It's a lovely day.'

Daylight! I couldn't believe it. I had been going at this all night. When was it ever going to end?

The staff had changed shifts and a midwife named Geraldine was now by my side. The usual pushing urge never happened, and I was left to whatever inner resources I could still call on. I was sitting on a birthing stool when the obstetrician came into the room. It was Ann. She was filling in for Sue, who was away on a conference. I already knew her from the gynaecological testing she had done for my court case.

'Please, get the baby out. My back can't take any more,' I pleaded.

'Janine, I can get the forceps if you really want, but ...' she started to say.

I didn't want to listen. I just had to get it out. It had to stop.

'Get them, please, just get it out!' I screamed.

Ann left to fetch the forceps.

Geraldine looked at me. 'Janine, you know if she gets the forceps you'll have to get up and walk to the bed. You'll have to lie on your back. The pain will be even worse.'

How could it be worse? My back felt as if it was breaking. I couldn't take any more. I looked at the bed. The thought of getting up and walking there was too much. But my back couldn't take any more. I had to do something. I mustered all the strength I had inside of me. *Please baby, come out ... please ...*

I gritted my teeth, using all my strength. I had to push this baby out.

'Janine, that's great, almost ... just one more,' I heard Geraldine say.

One more, come on ... you're almost there. I closed my eyes, I gave one last effort. This had to be it. In one momentous heave, I could feel the pain draining from my body.

'That's it, you've done it!' Geraldine exclaimed. 'It's a girl, Janine. You have a beautiful baby girl!'

I looked down to see Geraldine nursing a child—my child. It was over. I had a baby girl.

A new life ... not just for this babe but for me as well. I had a daughter, and she had a mother. Nothing would ever be the same again.

I held out my arms and she passed her to me. She was a wet, slimy, bawling bundle of joy, more beautiful than I could ever have imagined. I hugged her closely. Even my tears couldn't hide her from me. She was extraordinary.

She filled me with more joy and love than I could ever have hoped for.

Thank you, God, for my special gift.

She was my miracle.

Chapter 25

ANNABEL IS ALMOST three years of age now. She continues to delight and enthrall me with her enthusiasm for life, her spirited innocence, her humour. I have watched her grow from a tiny, totally dependent babe into an independent toddler, defiant at the best of times. She possesses a boldness and stubbornness that is at times frustrating, but she tackles life's challenges head-on—some would say recklessly—preferring to do things her way, in her time. I know in the end, she will be the stronger for it.

I have watched her crawl, watched as she struggled with the daunting task of standing on her own two feet and finally when she took her first steps. I remember thinking, *I know exactly how you feel!* She fell many times in the learning process, but she always got up and tried again. Such a simple skill, or so we may think, which most of us take for granted. I wondered how many adults would in fact have given up in such trying circumstances, but a baby doesn't yet know the meaning of giving up. It just keeps trying. There really is a lesson to be learnt in that.

I have loved my time at home with Annabel. It has given me a respect for motherhood that I once sadly lacked. I wouldn't swap these early years for anything in the world. They can never be replaced. I remember Mum telling me when I was young that the love a mother has for her children was something very special and unique, and that one day when I had children I would understand. I didn't understand then, but how could I?

Having Annabel has changed my life and yes, Mum, I do understand now.

I was over at Mum's place not long ago when she got out one of my old toys that she keeps for Annabel to play with when she is baby-sitting. It was my favourite teddy. I looked at it and my mind filled with thoughts of my own childhood. My teddy went everywhere with me; it was my best friend. I remember how fondly I would snuggle up to it at night to go to sleep, feeling safe in the knowledge that nothing could harm me as long as teddy was with me.

To me it was the most beautiful bear in the world, and I was never aware of how tattered it really was. Its fur was almost completely worn off from the years of cuddling it had been subjected to, its eyes were missing, and its legs and arms were so loose that had it not been for some mending on Mum's part, they would have fallen off. But it didn't matter, because I loved that teddy so much I was blinded by such things.

It reminded me of my favourite children's story, *The Velveteen Rabbit*. It is about a stuffed rabbit who from his arrival in a Christmas stocking quickly becomes the favourite toy of a little boy. The rabbit is surrounded by lots of other toys in the nursery, which have been there much longer than he has, and have survived the succession of mechanical toys that have passed through the nursery over the years. One of them is the Skin Horse, who has lived longer than any other toy in the nursery and is very wise indeed.

'What is Real?' asks the rabbit one day, when they are lying side by side near the nursery fender, before Nana came to tidy the room. 'Does it mean having things that buzz inside you and a stick-out handle?'

'Real isn't how you are made,' says the Skin Horse. 'It's a thing that happens to you. When a child loves you for a long, long time, not just to play with but *really* loves you, then you become Real.'

'Does it hurt?' asks the Rabbit.

'Sometimes,' replies the Skin Horse, for he is always truthful. 'But when you are Real you don't mind being hurt.'

'Does it happen all at once, like being wound up,' the Rabbit asks, 'or bit by bit?'

'It doesn't happen all at once,' says the Skin Horse. 'You *become*. It takes a long time. That's why it doesn't happen to toys who break easily, or have sharp edges, or who have to be carefully kept. Generally, by the time you are Real, most of your hair has been loved off, and your eyes drop out and you get loose in the joints and very shabby. But these things don't matter at all, because once you are Real you can't be ugly, except to people who don't understand.'

'I suppose *you* are Real?' the Rabbit says. And then he wishes he hadn't said it, for he thinks the Skin Horse might be sensitive. But the Skin Horse only smiles.

'The boy's uncle made me Real,' he says. 'That was a great many years ago; but once you are Real you can't become unreal again. It lasts for always.'

As the story continues the Velveteen Rabbit learns a very important lesson—that it is through the magic of love and friendship that *you* can become Real. And so we finally see the magical transformation of the rabbit when he becomes Real—and his life begins anew.

It really is an enchanting story, and it has a special significance for me because I too have become part of the magic of the nursery, the magic of a child's love. It took a long time, and a lot of pain, and sometimes I feel like my old teddy, like the toys in the nursery and the Velveteen Rabbit, all tattered and falling apart at the seams. I certainly have the scars to prove it!

The emotional pain I suffered as a result of my accident has never really left me. The disappointment of missing out on the Olympics, of never having the chance to truly develop my potential at a time when I had the world at my feet—that is all still with me. I don't think it will ever go away completely, but just fade with time. For an athlete there can be no greater loss than what I have been through, and learning to live with it and make the most of it, has been the greatest challenge of my life.

However, I'm not about to let that disappointment, nor my accident, stand in the way of all the things I want to achieve in my life time. I look forward to living the rest of my life with as much determination and vigour as I have in the past.

And besides, Annabel has given me something more precious than I ever could have imagined—and I wouldn't swap that for all the gold medals in the world.

$P_{ostscript}$

THE BODY'S ABILITY to cope with pain never ceases to amaze me. Six years after my accident I was finding it increasingly difficult to use my right arm. After seeking medical attention it was revealed, much to my amazement, that my arm was broken, and had been so since the accident. I had to go back into hospital to have a plate inserted in my arm. I was later told that it had been overlooked at the time as it was of such low priority compared to my other injuries.

And talking about pain . . . since I wrote the last words to this book, I have given birth for a second time to a beautiful little girl whom we have named Charlotte Rose. She is an absolute treasure.

I love my family, I love my life. It really is a wonderful time to be alive.

What if you slept? And what if, in your sleep you dreamed?
And what if, in your dream, you went to heaven and there
plucked a strange and beautiful flower? And what if, when
you awoke, you had the flower in your hand?

SAMUEL TAYLOR COLERIDGE